Liberating Sex

Also by Adrian Thatcher and published by SPCK:
Truly a Person, Truly God (1990)

Liberating Sex

A Christian Sexual Theology

Adrian Thatcher

First published in Great Britain 1993
Society for Promoting Christian Knowledge
Holy Trinity Church
Marylebone Road
London NW1 4DU

British Library Cataloguing-in-Publication Data

A catalogue record for this book is available from the British Library

ISBN 0-281-04699-9

Typeset by Datix International Limited, Bungay, Suffolk
Printed in Great Britain by
Biddles Ltd, Guildford and King's Lynn

Contents

Acknowledgements

Liberating Sex has been greatly enriched because friends have generously given their time and wisdom.

I thank Philip Law of SPCK for kindly suggesting that I send him the initial proposal for 'Guidelines in Christian Sexual Ethics', as it was originally called, and for commenting helpfully on the different drafts and stages that led to the present work. John Matthews, John Henson, Elizabeth Stuart and Roger Perkins read the manuscript as it became available and provided me with a wealth of insights, suggestions, criticisms and comments. Frank Gillies and Meic Phillips also made full comments on the text, and Jim Little and Ruth Matthews provided helpful early feedback. Peter Selby, one of the publisher's readers, made many astute and witty observations. I thank them all for bringing more clarity, sympathy and understanding to the text than would otherwise have been there.

This book was conceived, if that is the right term, during the teaching of the Church Colleges' Certificate course called 'Faith, Sex and Gender' at the College of St Mark and St John, Plymouth. I thank the course team, Elizabeth Stuart, Paul Grosch and Gaynor Pollard, for hours of fruitful discussion and the students whose good-humoured curiosity convinced me that this book should be written. I thank Frank Clements and the staff of the College library for helping me with searches and obtaining invaluable photocopies of articles and inter-library loans.

I also thank Grace and John for their cheerful tolerance of my preoccupation with the writing of this book.

CHAPTER 1

Sex after Patriarchy

Liberating Sex is about a *remaking*, an *unmaking* and a *merrymaking*.

Remaking

Christian faith is about the *remaking* of all women and men in the image and likeness of God in Jesus Christ. The full embodiment of the divine nature of God in a human being is at the centre of Christian faith. The followers of Jesus believe that all humankind is invited to rejoice and share in that mutual love which is both the meaning of 'God' and which was shared between the Father and the Son in the Son's incarnate life (John 15.7–17).[1] The incarnation or 'enfleshment' of divine being in a human being is a marvellous affirmation of the human body. Human flesh and blood becomes the living expression of deity. Here is an understanding of God which is unrivalled in the religious literature of the world. Because of Jesus all men and women can know and experience themselves to be recipients of life-affirming, life-enhancing divine love.

Christian faith acknowledges relationships as belonging to the very heart of God. God's nature is love, and this nature has become known to Christians in what became called 'Persons' – Father, Son and Spirit. These Persons[2] are so closely related to each other and inseparable from each other that each is constituted only by the others and its relationship to them. In short, these Persons are co-equal, and exist 'through' each other, 'for' each other, 'from' each other and 'in' each other. The importance for our *human personal relationships* of those divine Personal relationships within the very

I

Being of God cannot be over-estimated. In loving, embodied relationships we discover the nature of God. The incarnation of God is not confined to Jesus, but is re-enacted to different degrees and in different ways in all human bodily life.[3] In Christian faith sexual relationships are rooted in the incarnated holiness of human bodies and the divinity of loving relationships.

Human sexuality is about how men and women respond to themselves as sexual beings, and how sexually they relate to each other. Sexuality 'is the mode or manner by which humans experience and express both the incompleteness of their individualities as well as their relatedness to each other as male and female'.[4] In remaking us as sexual beings, God, through the Holy Spirit, gives us the power and the vision to make relationships which resemble those relationships existing eternally within God. They will be mutual, reciprocal, equal, open, intimate and partner-affirming. The trinitarian vision for human personal relationships is, by God's grace, slowly dawning upon the Church. Why has it been so long delayed?

Unmaking

Unfortunately throughout most of Christian history (and of course beyond) there has been, and there remains, an entrenched set of attitudes which has systematically discriminated against women, and infected relationships both between men and women, and between men and men. The name of this complex amalgam of attitudes is 'patriarchy'. *Liberating Sex* is a deliberate *unmaking* of patriarchy. Patriarchy is an ideology which brings about 'the systematic social closure of women from the public sphere by legal, political and economic arrangements which operate in favour of men'.[5] It is an 'ideology' in the precise sense that it deceptively describes women and women's experience in ways which further male interests. Patriarchy is 'that social order in which women were declared to be the possessions of first, fathers, and later, husbands – the aim of which was to produce children who would "belong to" the father and take his name. . . '.[6]

A recent study from the Presbyterian Church of the USA has argued that a 'clearly patriarchal structure of sex and sexuality' is said to be revealed by:

> a) a mystification of sex based on ignorance of human sexuality; b) the association of sex with sin and evil; c) the use of sex as an instrument of power; d) economic discrimination against

women; e) the acceptance of violence as natural and inevitable; f) the commercialization of human needs; g) widespread addiction to obsessive–compulsive behavior; and h) unequal responsibility for human relationship.[7]

Another list of symptoms includes 'love of hierarchical structure and competition', 'alienation from nature', 'suppression of empathy' and 'haunting insecurity'.[8]

Merrymaking

Involvement with patriarchy then is inevitable, for all of these patriarchal symptoms provide a 'structuring of sexual relations'[9] which influence us all, whether male or female, whether Christian or not, whether consciously, or not. Since this structure announces itself as 'given', one's entanglement within it may pass by unnoticed. Sexual relations are part of that remaking which in Christian faith constitutes redemption and salvation. An attempt will be made to 'unmake' entrenched patriarchal assumptions in theology and sexual ethics and rethink sexual relationships in the light of that divine love which has been shown to us in the self-giving of God in Christ and reflected in the unity of the equal Persons within the Trinity. That is why the book is also about *merrymaking*. To be merry is to be joyful, festive, slightly drunk. Merriment is an antidote to the deadening seriousness that has attached itself to sexual activity in much of Christian history. Unless sex is playful it is intolerable. *Liberating Sex* is an intended reversal of patriarchal treatment of sex which makes it a burden, an embarrassment, a constant source of guilt, a male-defined obsession to be overcome by the iron discipline of the will, or best avoided altogether. Merriment is about pleasure,[10] and deep pleasure in our bodies is a precondition of that deep gratitude to God for our sexuality which is itself the key to responsible and passionate loving.

Patriarchy and credibility

Patriarchy is older than the Judaeo-Christian tradition and found 'in every known society'.[11] The contemporary dilemma for thoughtful contemporary Christians is whether the Christian churches, having been 'the willing tool of patriarchy, the instrument of oppression and the sustainer of exploitation on a vast scale',[12] have any remaining credibility in the sphere of sexual relations. Feminist theologians are deeply divided over whether a post-patriarchal Christianity is possible at all. For some, the possibility of a Christianity free of patriarchy is the supreme act of faith and the expression of an ultimate hope. Is Christianity so deeply implicated in the manufacture and maintenance of patriarchy that it is inevitably and unalterably an oppressor of women? Or is there within the Christian gospel and the Christian understanding of the embodied, relational, divine reality, freely available to us through grace, an emerging vision of non-patriarchal, non-oppressive, fully mutual ways of living and relating which could lead us to discover afresh the claim that in Christ there is 'no such thing as . . . male and female' (Galatians 3.28)? Must there be a post-Christian spirituality and theology as women 'revolutionists' want?[13] Or, following the 'reformers', can there be a 're-visioning' of the tradition 'in ways that honor the feminine element, as well as women, in other than compensatory fashion'?[14]

The origin of patriarchy in western civilization is almost impossible to trace. One authoritative account places it in the inter-tribal trading of women's 'sexual and reproductive capacities and services',[15] but other accounts of its origin abound. Men may have dominated women because, it is said, the male hormone testosterone makes men restless, 'aching for a fight', or because tribes displaying most aggression survived, and more peaceful, less militaristic ones did not.[16] Because women produce children, they have been 'associated with nature rather than culture', and in the eyes of men never made 'the transition from animality to culture'. The reproductive powers of women are thus sufficient to explain 'the universality of women's subordinate status in society'.[17] Men wishing to hand down property to their sons exercised very strict control over their wives for fear of bequeathing their estates to illegitimate heirs.[18]

The anxiety of heterosexual men about their possible sexual impotence when face to face with women sexual partners, their envy of women's greater capacity for 'sustained sexual activity' when compared with their own post-orgasmic flaccidity, and their fear of the sheer power of women's sexuality experienced in finding women permanently and irresistibly desirable, may have led the male to transform anxiety into aggression toward the female. It is a common complaint of heterosexual women that, when making love, the man climaxes too quickly just when the woman is becoming fully aroused and wants to continue. There is no reason to think these problems are new.[19] Male fear and insecurity are readily translatable into aggression, and once the male becomes sexually aggressive, 'he can perform, he can dominate, and he can penetrate'.[20] Equipped with a primitive biological theory about semen providing all the means for conception and a male god who legitimates male power, an all-pervasive mind-set with sociological, psychological, physiological and theological roots becomes understandable, even though we may never have a clear view of its causes.

Our question is: is the Judaeo-Christian tradition so contaminated by patriarchy that no credible sexual teaching can emerge from it?

Patriarchy and the Bible

From cover to cover the Bible contains patriarchal assumptions. The task of defusing these is made more difficult because side by side with them stands a minority strand which is critical of patriarchy and to some extent subverts it. A well-known example of this duality is found in the creation accounts of Genesis 1–2. In one account the woman is made, almost as an afterthought, from the man and for him, since her role is solely to keep the man company (Genesis 2.25). Yet in the later account (which comes first in the biblical text), both women and men are said to share in God's image. 'God created human beings in his own image; in the image of God he created them; male and female he created them' (Genesis 1.27). They are simultaneously and equally created, blessed and charged with responsibility for the world. Yet by chapter 3, the woman is blamed for causing the man to disobey God (Genesis 3.12), and patriarchy predominates thereafter.

The New Testament is quick to use these narratives to reinforce women's subordination to men (1 Corinthians 11.7–12), to silence them in church and suggest they can collectively absolve the guilt of their entire sex for causing men to sin, by bearing men children (1 Timothy 2.12–15). In almost the last chapter a woman is used as a symbol for the evil city of Babylon and heavenly worship offered to God who has 'condemned the great whore who corrupted the earth with her fornication; he has taken vengeance on her for the blood of his servants' (Revelation 19.2). If Christians cannot find a way of dissociating themselves from scores of biblical passages which demean and insult women, there can be no progress in the conquest of patriarchy. Yet that minority strand continues in the New Testament also and flowers in the teaching of Jesus. A method for the interpretation of Scripture which honours Christ and copes with scriptural patriarchy is proposed in chapter 2.

Androcentrism

Feminist theology has made abundantly clear that much biblical thought, and almost all subsequent historical theological thought is *androcentric* (male-centred), and *sexist* (discriminatory, on the irrelevant ground of gender). Our task is to identify how such attitudes may continue to govern sexual relationships. Is it still true that discussion of traditional moral questions continues to be 'largely founded upon male perceptions and reflecting male interests'?[21] Recent descriptions of male attempts within the Christian tradition to subjugate women and deny the sexuality of women and men make terrifying reading.[22] The sheer unquestioning depth of androcentricity can be illustrated by a remark of Thomas Aquinas. It is one of thousands that might have been chosen from male writers of the Christian past. Thomas is discussing why some sex acts are morally wrong. Any sexual act at all which does not aim at procreation, he says, is wrong. He then gives a further reason why sexual intercourse involving seduction and rape are wrong. 'Sometimes', he says, 'the object of the act is unsuited because of relationships with other human beings. To have sex with this particular woman may dishonour a blood or kin relationship, as in incest; or do injustice to her guardian – her husband in adultery, her father in seduction and rape.'[23] He adds parenthetically, 'We differentiate with respect to the woman rather than the man since in sex acts she is acted on, and he the agent.'

This passage, like so many others, speaks most through what it does not say. It is true that Aquinas does not intend to give in this passage an exhaustive list of reasons why seduction and rape are wrong, but it must come as a shock to contemporary Christian wives and daughters that their legal and moral status consists in their being the property of men. They have no value apart from being owned. That was a fact of thirteenth-century life, and remained so in western societies until the present century. Rape and seduction are not wrong in themselves; it takes a further reason to spell out their wrongness. They are wrong because they are unjust acts against their owners. And this shows how terrifying androcentric thinking can be. Any consideration by men of women themselves, a female perspective about being seduced and raped, is foreclosed. It does not enter the great saint's head. It is irrelevant. A highly rational male discussion of sexual intercourse betrays a chilling unawareness that anything important has been omitted, like injustice to women themselves.

Patriarchy and the churches

Our interest in patriarchy is confined to its influence on sexual relations. That influence is profound and enduring. But is there not some plea of mitigation that can be entered when accusing the churches of continuing patriarchal attitudes? It has been powerfully suggested that in modern western societies a transition from 'patriarchy' to 'patrism' has taken place. Patriarchy is the organized 'social closure of women from the public sphere',[24] while 'patrism' involves 'prejudicial beliefs and practices of men towards women without the systematic backing of law and politics'.[25] This distinction relies on an accurate parallel between sexual and racial discrimination. In race relations theory the distinction exists between racism as a social system which excludes racial minorities from power and racism as a 'collection of prejudicial attitudes'. One is, we might say, objective, the other subjective. Progress has been made in dismantling objective constraints against people on grounds of race and sex. It is sometimes suggested that the churches too are moving, albeit at different paces, in the same direction. What remains to be removed is psychological or subjective patriarchy (i.e. patrism), and for this the best means is individual persuasion.

This suggestion is misleading, not to say mischievous. The decision of the General Synod of the Church of England in November 1992 to open up the priesthood to women is a most welcome step towards the dismantling of patriarchal power. Yet the public attitudes of Roman Catholic, Orthodox and some other churches to this issue are a painfully obvious example of the 'systematic social closure of women'. Sexism in liturgies and the identification of the sacrament of Holy Communion with conspicuous male clerical dominance have led to the claim that women in most churches 'are suffering from linguistic deprivation and eucharistic famine'.[26] The continued exclusion of women from the priestly role in most of Christendom maintains patriarchal power very effectively, and undoubtedly reflects the Church's historical attitude to women, whatever other compensatory gestures and soothing remarks may be made (generally by men). Indeed the situation may well become worse. It is likely that where there is actual dismantling of the *social* structure of patriarchy, there will be a corresponding increase in its *psychological* structure (i.e., in patrism). Where patriarchy has crumbled, 'The patristic attitude of men towards women becomes more prejudicial and defensive precisely because women are now often equipped with a powerful ideological critique of traditional patriarchy.'[27] It is important to take sides over this issue. It is just as important to think beyond it and attempt to envisage a non-patriarchal faith which, simply by being what it is, will draw women and men to it in increasing numbers, and be pleasing to God.

Five reforming arguments

Within feminist theology there is disagreement between those who, because of patriarchy in the churches, the Bible and the traditions of Christianity, can no longer profess the faith, and those who, while acutely conscious of these difficulties, remain inside the churches and seek reform from within. This is a problem for many people, and is not confined to readers of theology. Those who remain are generally called 'the reformers' and in support of them I offer the following arguments.

1. Men are victims too
Patriarchy is not simply the oppressor of women. Most men, historically, have been oppressed by patriarchy and those who have not have been damaged by it. Patriarchal societies are dominated by a class structure in which 'men were primarily exploited as workers; women were always exploited as workers, as providers of sexual services, and as reproducers'.[28] Men too have suffered untold pain in being unwilling recruits for pointless wars and unrewarded labourers for indifferent masters.

2. The past must be fairly judged
How do we contemporary people make moral judgements about the moral judgements of the past? Critics of Christian traditions, judging harshly the abundance of inequality and androcentrism, should resist the temptation to judge past beliefs and attitudes from a perspective which holders of those attitudes could not have had. We are certain to be criticized by future generations for failings which are as hidden to us as they will be obvious to them. It may, for example, seem outrageous to us that Aquinas thought the wrongness of rape consisted in the violation of the property of the victim's guardian. Yet he said this on the basis of presumptions which had existed for centuries and which he saw no good reason to question. However dismayed we may rightly be by these presumptions, we have the benefit of hindsight. It is important to reserve moral judgement for *contemporary* patriarchal practice, using the legacy of dismay as a powerful argument for reform.

In order to avoid misrepresentation of the beliefs of former generations it might be helpful to compare the history of Christianity with,
say, the history of medicine. A sick person considering a visit to a
doctor is unlikely to want to consider the former practices of that
profession, like the treatment of wounds with boiling oil, or illnesses
with emetics, purgatives and leeches, etc. While these and countless
other similar practices belong indelibly to the history of medicine,
they do not constitute a good reason for shunning that whole
tradition of medicine which once regarded these practices as therapeutic.

The parallel between developments in medical and theological
thought is a useful one, since theology too has shown itself capable of
divesting itself of harmful legitimations of harmful practices, like the
persecution of Jews and witches and the widespread use of slaves. Of
course religion is slower to change and is burdened by conservative
forces. Some sexual teaching is still governed by pre-Christian purity
laws, patriarchal fears about women's bodies, medieval biology, pre-
critical attitudes to the Bible, and what might be called 'wilful
ignorance' about the role of sexual expressiveness in human fulfilment.

3. Reform is at the heart of Christian faith

Christian doctrine has become more morally acceptable as a result of
the efforts of its doctrinal reformers. Within the last 150 years
millions of Christians have changed their minds about for example,
whether unbaptized babies are condemned to hell; whether hell is a
place of unending torment and all 'infidels' and 'pagans' pre-destined
for it; whether Jews are murderers of God; whether humanity is
depraved; whether the Son of God was really punished by the Father
in order to reconcile us. The resulting changes represent a moral and
theological gain, since in their unrevised form they were hopeless
compromises of God's unbounded love, and were responsible for
much loss of faith in a previous age. Through the Spirit, and
doubtless for more pragmatic reasons as well, Christians are now
being required to rethink the arrogant exclusivism which has marred
inter-faith communication. Perhaps a similar prompting of the Spirit
can be discerned in unmaking patriarchy and remaking sexuality.

Christians have to face the difficult issue about what is changeable
in Christian teaching, and what is not. This is a fraught question since
even our understanding of what looks to be unchanging (e.g., God or
Christ) has changed profoundly in the last century. It is commonplace
nowadays to hear that God suffers or that the human Jesus was, in
some respects, ignorant. Such emphases were unthinkable a century

ago. What does not change is that God has been graciously disclosed as unbounded, healing love, and that this love, revealed in the life, teaching and self-giving of Christ, and in the relations between the Persons of the Trinity which God is, is available to us to share in through the Spirit. There are problems, of course, with this position, not least the different and shifting understandings of 'love' through the centuries, and the state of neglect of the doctrine of Trinity.[29]

4. Repentance is an expectation of Christians

The Church is the community which exists to proclaim the necessity of repentance, forgiveness and reconciliation in human personal and social relationships, and to announce the good news that God has provided the means of achieving this through Jesus. It is therefore doubly sad that the community which exists to proclaim reconciliation should maintain discriminatory attitudes towards large sections of society and towards many of its own members. A 'public act of reparation to women for the way their Christian brothers have treated them down the ages'[30] is needed, and we should add, to gay, non-white, Jewish and other people. This inconsistency within the Church is precisely what leads an increasing number of feminists to leave it. Here the arguments for reform admittedly falter.

The Roman Catholic Church is especially culpable in resisting the case for sexual justice. While the Second Vatican Council (1962–65) made a public apology to the Jews for the disgraceful treatment they had received at the hands of Christians down the ages, 'there was not a single layman nor one woman deciding on a single issue in the nave of St. Peter's'.[31] Why? Because patriarchy and clericalism rule in the Roman Church, and since the Council they have tightened their grip. The sincere apology offered to Jews has been compared with the 'ostrich-like reticence' of the hierarchy to modify its sexual teaching. It did not because it could not. In this church, women were not recognized as part of the laity until the new code of Canon Law was published in 1983. Ever since the Council of Elvira in 309 the church has exercised strong control over the sexual behaviour of its members: 'To change the sexual teaching of the church, still sustained by an ideal of an unmarried clerical élite and by a dominant–dependent order in human relationships, would mean to shake the very power structure of that church.'[32]

But Catholic Christianity is not solely Roman. The decision which some have made to quit the Church (not just the Roman Catholic) because of its entrenched patriarchal attitudes is understandable. Those who remain will realize that all human organizations are imperfect and flawed, whether churches, political parties, universities or companies. They will refuse to bequeath the ownership of the means of grace for posterity to a male élite. They will look away from the broken symbols of institutional religion, as women and men have had to do in every generation, to that divine love which transcends every symbol and judges every human power.

5. The example of Jesus

Lastly, Christians these days are likely to take comfort from the fact that the Jesus of the Gospels was resolutely opposed to clericalism in all its forms and that there is little trace in his teaching of the fear of women and misogyny that is found in later Catholic thought. They are likely to be more interested in the Kingdom or loving reign of God in the world than in maintaining ecclesiastical organizations which are currently somewhat impervious to ecumenical and anti-sexist progress. While it may be true that equality between men and women is a thought that simply could not have occurred to Jesus, 'given the society in which he lived',[33] it is also true that within the limitations of first-century Palestinian Judaism a new beginning for all oppressed people takes root (Luke 1.51–5). That is what God's rule means. In Christ's relations with women, the woman with the haemorrhages (Mark 5.25–34), the Samaritan woman (John 4.8–30), the prostitute in the Pharisee's house (Luke 7.36–50), and so on, there is a remarkable lack of condescension or discrimination in his words and actions.

Faith without patriarchy

For these five reasons, I believe it is unnecessary to conclude that Christian faith is irredeemably sexist, even though some of its oppressive institutional forms are an invitation to despair. There are elements in Scripture and tradition which empower the struggle against patriarchal forms of religion. There may not be a tradition in the world even half as old as biblical faith (whether of religion, of philosophy, of nation, or professional practice) which does not at times fill its contemporary adherents (at least those prepared to be critical) with shame at obvious inadequacies or shortcomings. But we are not yet enlightened ourselves. And present readers of the past must be wary of accusing previous generations of culpable failure, just for seeing things differently.

Daphne Hampson, the post-Christian feminist theologian, comes to the opposite conclusion. For her, 'feminism represents the death-knell of Christianity as a viable religious option'.[34] The formidable array of arguments she deployed (in 1990) are likely to set the agenda between Christian and post-Christian feminists for the rest of this decade, and there is no space to contribute to it here. My stance is that of a 'reformer' and I hope to show through this book that the path of reform is both a possible and a necessary one to take. Of course, the possibility of a non-patriarchal faith is no guarantee at all that one will arrive.

Sexual Theology

Liberating Sex is about sexual theology. Some clarification of this term may be helpful. According to James Nelson the difference between 'theologies of sexuality' and 'sexual theologies' is that theologies of sexuality have begun with the Bible and the tradition, and then moved, in a 'one-directional' manner, to discuss sexual experience. Sexual theologies, on the other hand, also ask how our sexual experience influences our understanding of the Bible and the tradition, resulting in a 'dialogical, two-directional inquiry'.[35] The identification of patriarchy as an *oppressive* influence on sexual experience makes possible a fruitful comparison between sexual theology, and liberation or feminist theology.

But the distinction Nelson makes may not be widely known outside the USA. If the distinction is accepted, then this book is clearly a work of sexual theology. The dialogical approach to sexual experience is essential. Yet even where the validity of this distinction is more likely to be queried, there are other reasons for preferring 'sexual theology' to 'theologies of sexuality', or to other possible sub-titles, e.g. 'sexual ethics'. The most important one has to do with the sheer quantity of theological considerations relevant to thinking about sexual behaviour and to expressing our sexualities. The great themes of the Christian faith, incarnation and trinity, atonement and redemption, sin and salvation, covenant and eucharist, all contribute to sexual theology, and how they do so will be unfolded in later chapters. The term 'sexual theology' is therefore preferable to 'sexual ethics' on the grounds that it describes the content of the book in a way 'ethics' does not. A further preference for 'sexual theology' has to do with the word 'sexuality'. Word histories often show an escalating tendency towards vagueness. The abstract term 'sexuality' has already been elongated twice (sex, sexual, sexuality) and lost its adjectival form on the way. It is given a particular (yet standard) use in this work, as a God-given dimension of human being and relating, which itself raises many theological questions. For these additional reasons, 'sexual theology' has been adopted as a primary term.

Notes

1. All biblical quotations are from the Revised English Bible, unless otherwise stated. In order to reduce footnotes, biblical references are normally left in the text.
2. Upper case is used for the divine Persons; lower case for human persons.
3. See James B. Nelson, *The Intimate Connection: Male Sexuality, Masculine Spirituality* (London: SPCK, 1991), p. 8, and below, ch. 4.
4. A. Kosnik, et al. (eds), *Human Sexuality: New Directions in Catholic Thought* (London: Search Press, 1977), p. 82. The Sacred Congregation for the Doctrine of the Faith was sufficiently worried about this book to issue a statement about its alleged errors. See 'Human Sexuality', in Austin Flannery, OP (ed.), *Vatican Council II: More Post Conciliar Documents* (Leominster, Hereford: Fowler Wright, 1982), pp. 505–9.
5. Bryan S. Turner, *The Body and Society* (Oxford: Blackwell, 1984), p. 119.
6. Shere Hite, *The Hite Report: Women and Love* (London: Penguin/Viking, 1988), p. 532.
7. *Keeping Body and Soul Together: Sexuality, Spirituality, and Social Justice* (Presbyterian Church, USA, 1991), p. 6. This conclusion was based on an earlier report of the same church, *Far From the Song of Songs* (1988), p. 178.
8. J. Berry, C. Spratnek, quoted in Hite, p. 745 n.
9. *Keeping Body and Soul Together*, p. 6.
10. For a positive analysis of pleasure, leading to a 'Litany of Pleasure', see David M. Paton, 'Paltry Pleasures', *Theology*, 80 (March 1977), pp. 116–20.
11. Gerda Lerner, *The Creation of Patriarchy* (Oxford: Oxford University Press, 1987), p. 213.
12. Paul Avis, *Eros and the Sacred* (London: SPCK, 1989), p. 12.
13. This position is well described by Sallie McFague, *Metaphorical Theology: Models of God in Religious Language* (London: SCM Press, 1983), ch. 5. Daphne Hampson advocates a post-Christian reconstruction of God in *Theology and Feminism* (Oxford: Blackwell, 1990), ch. 5.
14. Morny Joy, 'Equality or divinity: A False Dichotomy?', *Journal of Feminist Studies in Religion*, 6 (1990), p. 16.
15. Lerner, p. 212.
16. Hite, p. 704.
17. Turner, p. 115.
18. ibid. p. 117.
19. Annette Lawson, *Adultery: An Analysis of Love and Betrayal* (Oxford: Blackwell, 1989), pp. 49–50.
20. James B. Nelson, *Embodiment: An Approach to Sexuality and Christian Theology* (Minneapolis, MN: Augsburg, 1978), p. 62.
21. Susan Dowell, *They Two Shall be One: Monogamy in History and Religion* (London: Collins/Flame, 1990), p. 150.
22. E.g., Karen Armstrong, *The Gospel According to Woman: Christianity's Creation of the Sex War in the West* (London: Pan Books, 1986); Uta Ranke-Heinemann, *Eunuchs for Heaven: The Catholic Church and Sexuality* (London: Deutsch 1990).

23. Thomas Aquinas, *Summa Theologiae*, II. 11. 154.1. Quoted from: A concise translation edited by Timothy McDermott (London: Eyre & Spottiswoode), p. 431.
24. See above, p. 2.
25. Turner, p. 155.
26. Rosemary Radford Ruether, *Women-Church: Theology and Practice of Feminist Liturgical Communities* (San Francisco: Harper & Row, 1985), p. 4.
27. Turner, p. 155.
28. Lerder, p. 214.
29. See below, chapter 4.
30. The words of Bishop Holloway to describe the book he edited, *Who Needs Feminism? Men Respond to Sexism in the Church*, (London: SPCK, 1991).
31. Samuel Laeuchli, *Power and Sexuality: The Emergence of Canon Law at the Synod of Elvira* (Philadelphia: Temple University Press, 1972), p. 122.
32. ibid. p. 123.
33. Hampson, p. 87.
34. Hampson, p. 1.
35. Nelson, pp. 115–6.

CHAPTER 2

The Place of the Bible in Christian Sexual Theology

The argument of this chapter is that a distinction must be made between a *biblical* sexual theology and a *Christian* sexual theology. First, four examples of biblical teaching about sex, all from the New Testament, indicate that the Bible, without explicit principles for its interpretation, cannot be our guide in sexual, or other moral issues. This presents an acute problem for Christians, especially those who identify the text of the Bible with 'the Word of God'. Second, the treatment of Scripture in two recent reports on sexuality published by British churches is criticized because it does not take the patriarchal character of much of the biblical teaching about sex seriously enough. Third, a different method of interpreting the Bible is offered which places Christ before the Bible, retains the essential place which the Bible has in Christian thought, while also attempting to overcome biblical sexism and prejudice against women. Then, fourth, a further interpretative framework is introduced and commended for reading the Bible, which is both applicable for *any* reading of Scripture, and which will regulate how Scripture is used in the rest of the book.

Four examples of New Testament teaching about sex

1. The subordination of wives to husbands
According to the New Testament, wives 'must be subject to your husbands; that is your Christian duty' (Colossians 3.18). 'You women must submit to your husbands' (I Peter 3.1). 'Wives, be subject to

your husbands as though to the Lord' (Ephesians 5.22). These are imperatives, not options. They assume and reinforce a relation of domination and submission between the sexes. Equality between wives and husbands in biblical thought is unimaginable. Husbands have responsibilities to their wives which are generated by their wives' dependence on them. 'Husbands, love your wives, as Christ loved the church and gave himself up for it' (Ephesians 5.25). 'Husbands, love your wives and do not be harsh with them' (Colossians 3.19). This is no basis for love. Within this entire way of thinking about marriage 'love is characterized as a constituent element of a relationship of domination. The dominant reciprocates the submissiveness of the dominated with love.'[1] This kind of relationship is sometimes called 'love-patriarchalism'.[2]

This biblical teaching about marriage is locked into a wider set of assumptions which the biblical writers do not question. The texts show there is a hierarchical order of slave-owners, their wives, their children and their slaves. The head of the household owns the bodies of all the members of it, and rules the household, rather as the emperor rules the empire. God is even depicted as the heavenly slave master (Colossians 4.1). This social system of hierarchical relations provides the material for theological reflection: 'The man is the head of the woman, just as Christ is the head of the church' (Ephesians 5.23). 'Slaves, give single-minded obedience to your earthly masters with fear and trembling, as if to Christ' (Ephesians 6.5). 'Fear and trembling' was a grimly appropriate phrase, given the widespread abuse, including sexual abuse, to which slaves were subjected.[3] Biblical advice to slaves who are abused is 'submit to your masters with all due respect', since Christ suffered for them (1 Peter 2.18, 21).

This advice shows clearly that the institution of slavery with its attendant violence and injustice is accepted as part of the general world-view of the New Testament. The point to carry forward is that the theology of marriage is so integrated into the institution of slavery and the hierarchical order of social relations which slavery services that, once slavery has been repudiated by Christianity (after nineteen centuries), the theology of marriage based upon it must also be repudiated. At least it must be revised. This is an impossible bind for so-called 'biblical theology' or 'biblical ethics'. If the teaching on marriage in the New Testament letters is accepted, women are forever to be submissive to men and the same teaching justifies owning slaves. It is inadmissible to appeal to biblical teaching on marriage while at the same time rejecting slavery since marriage and slavery are as indissolubly linked as a man and a woman are linked in marriage. What is needed is a fresh approach to marriage and human relations generally which is not based on domination at all, but on equality.

2. Celibacy and the world's end

The church at Corinth contained an extreme party which, in anticipation of the imminent return of Jesus in the sky, had decided to renounce marriage altogether, to abstain from sex within marriage, and to separate from pagan partners. Unmarried adults and children would remain perpetual virgins.[4] Paul took care to renounce the extremism of this group, and what he said to them about sex, marriage and divorce is contained in 1 Corinthians 6.12 – 7.40. He says marriage is permitted (7.2); refraining from sexual relations is recommended for short periods only, since the sexual frustration (presumably male) that results may lead to alternative methods of sexual satisfaction being sought, that is, being 'tempted by Satan'(7.5). Other instructions follow. The obvious point here is simply that the text is an attempt to reply to particular and peculiar circumstances (which had already been raised in correspondence with the apostle (7.1)). Paul shared with this group the belief in the return of Christ within his lifetime (15.51), and he thinks that during this brief period 'married men should be as if they had no wives' (7.29), since husbands and wives inevitably experience a clash between 'pleasing the Lord' and pleasing each other (7.32–34). Nonetheless marriage is permitted, especially if a man's 'passions are strong', even though it is very much second best (7.36).

This argument for the priority of celibacy over marriage, justified by belief in the imminent return of Christ, quickly became an argument for celibacy throughout the Church, and its influence remained long after the expectation of Christ's return within the generation of the apostles had been revised or abandoned. Paul was plainly wrong about that, and since his sexual teachings are based on specific replies to a specific extremist group, and a false belief about the imminent return of Christ, the teachings themselves are inherently unstable. Of course, if his teachings had been understood contextually, and belief in Christ's immediate return understood as one regulative though mistaken feature of the context, the harmful influence of this part of the letter could have been prevented. Unfortunately, the text quickly became established as authoritative teaching for the view that celibacy is *always* better than marriage. According to Peter Brown, 'by this essentially negative, even alarmist strategy, Paul left a fatal legacy to future ages.'[5] The reluctant concession to marry,

. . . slid imperceptibly into an attitude that viewed marriage itself as no more than a defense against desire. In the future, a sense of the presence of 'Satan', in the form of a constant and ill-defined risk of lust, lay like a heavy shadow in the corner of every Christian church.

3. The perversion of homosexuality

The Gospels are entirely silent about homosexuality. St Paul, however, in a long condemnation of the sins of Gentiles, notes: 'Men too, giving up natural relations with women, burn with lust for one another; males behave indecently with males, and are paid in their own persons the fitting wage of such perversion' (Romans 1.27). The general condition of Gentiles is said to be one of culpable idolatry, culpable because God has disclosed the truth to them (1.18, 25), and idolatry because they have exchanged 'the glory of the immortal God for an image shaped like mortal man . . .' (1.23, 25).

The rejection of God is said to lead to moral depravity, a symptom of which is the unrestrained expression of sexual desire (1.24–7), leading to a further catalogue of some twenty different vices (1.29–31). Within this framework, homosexual acts are the expression of 'vile desires' and 'shameful passions' which are themselves general effects of the yet more general cause of idolatry (1.24,26). Under the influence of such passions, women and men alike give up 'natural' intercourse (1.26–7) and reap self-destructive consequences (1.27). This passage, together with the references to 'perverts' in 1 Corinthians 6.9 and 1 Timothy 1.10, has been thought to legitimize the exclusion from the Christian community of all male homosexual relationships. But, as brief attention to i) Paul's overall *argument*; ii) the *meaning* of the terms he uses; and iii) the *types of behaviour* he most probably had in mind, it is clear they provide nothing of the kind.

(i) The argument

The argument is addressed to both the Jewish and non-Jewish sections of the Roman church. Paul might have expected the support of his Jewish readers in this denunciation of human life outside the Jewish Law. Since homosexuality was punishable by death under Jewish Law, yet condoned in Greek and Roman cultures, it functioned as a criterion of Jewish identity, much as angry denunciation of it has become a criterion of Christian identity among strict Christian groups today.[6] The argument however is a rhetorical one, for the Jewish readers are abruptly rounded on when they attempt to 'sit in judgement' on the Gentiles (2.1). Paul, the Apostle to the Gentiles, reiterates that 'there will be affliction and distress for every human being who is a wrongdoer, for the Jew first and for the Greek also' (2.9). This universal condemnation of Gentile culture in its entirety is the precondition for his presentation of Christ through whom alone there is 'no condemnation' for anyone, whether Gentile or Jew (8.1). Homosexual acts, then, are one of the many indices of the alienated condition of non-Jews, who, according to Paul, have consciously rejected the truth of God.

(ii) The meaning of terms

The language of social dishonour ('shameful passions') should be understood in the ancient context where 'The most important social imperative was to maintain or improve the standing of one's family, whether positively by increasing its public honor or negatively by avoiding anything that might shame the family.'[7] The ever-present hierarchy of free men, their wives and slaves, which regulates the apostle's attitude to marriage, is implicitly challenged by sexual relations between men. Paul may well have drawn on two pagan arguments here. One was precisely: 'The pursuit of pleasure might lead some men to wish to play the female, by offering themselves to be penetrated by their lovers: such behavior was puzzling to the doctors and shocking to most people.'[8] The argument was based on social hierarchy, not on ritual impurity.

The second pagan argument against sex between men was the 'argument from desire'. It was accepted that men would desire men, but if the desire was so strong that it led to homosexual intercourse, then that desire was certain to conflict with the will and place the subject of that desire in personal difficulty.[9] What is meant by 'natural' is notoriously difficult to decide. What Paul meant by 'unnatural' sex in this passage probably follows from his belief that 'Gentiles experienced only heterosexual desire before God visited uncleanness on them and that therefore they have changed their "nature", that is, lost a certain continuity with their remotest past.'[10] The 'fitting wage of perversion' seems to mean the general cultural consequence of idolatry rather than some sexually transmitted disease.[11] The mention of 'perverts' may refer specifically to active and passive partners in homosexual intercourse.[12]

(iii) Homosexual behaviour

Paul's condemnation of male homosexual acts in Romans belongs to a wider judgement about Gentile culture with its surprising conclusion that no one can condemn anyone for anything, since all are equally guilty, and in Christ all are equally saved. The condemnation of homosexual acts belongs within a wider portrayal of life without God. Paul's choice of words in 1 Corinthians 6.9–10 'strongly suggests that he is warning the Corinthians against the institution of homosexual behaviour between mature men and youths, so commonly recorded in the secular literature of the time'.[13] Such a youth would have been called a 'catamite'. This practice is 'pederasty'. In Greek life, pederasty included 'a range of relationships from an honourable teaching and guardianship to wretched forms of depravity'.[14] Paul would also be aware, in writing to the church at Rome, of the widespread homosexual corruption in the capital city, as described in, for example, the *Satyricon*. The practice there included the violation of boys and slaves, and was cruel and exploitative.

There is, of course, no condemnation in these verses of homosexual *persons* at all, only of certain homosexual acts involving exploitation and violence which gay Christians today themselves unreservedly condemn. There is no sense in Paul of the homosexual person as a man or woman with a sexual *orientation* toward other people of the same sex.[15] He did not consider the possibility of loving committed relationships between gay men of the kind which contemporary gay Christians rightly wish to receive recognition and blessing from God. But he should not be condemned for this by Christians today. Indeed it has been suggested (by an evangelical Christian) that Paul 'might be more at home today in gay rather than non-gay society'.[16] Once again, the issue is not what the Bible *says*, but how the Bible is *read*.

4. *The unnatural intercourse of women*

Among the shameful passions which Gentiles are said to indulge, 'women have exchanged natural intercourse for unnatural' (Romans 1.26). It is uncertain whether anal intercourse with men is meant; more probably, lesbian sexual relationships are intended.[17] The horror expressed in the passage is, as with the pagan argument against anal intercourse between men, that 'such bonds between women subverted gender hierarchy'. Gender hierarchy requires sexual roles where men are active and women passive: 'Within the ancient understanding of sexuality one of the women in a lesbian relation must be usurping the active male role.'[18] The basic hierarchy, freemen–women–children–slaves underscores all four of our examples of problems for biblical sexual ethics. Within this hierarchy women must forever be subordinate to men. 'Honouring our body for a woman means subjecting it to the sexual control of a man.'[19] The hostility to lesbian relationships within a patriarchal view of women is obvious enough. Patriarchy itself is threatened, for men are unable to control lesbian women, and are patently unnecessary as providers of any sexual pleasure deriving from lesbian relationships. Viewed in this traditional, androcentric way, lesbian women are a problem for male control. Viewed from the point of view of lesbian women themselves, the Christian gospel is a liberation from that very apparatus of control that has oppressed them for so long.[20]

These four examples of biblical teaching about sex show that the application of the surface meaning of biblical texts to contemporary sexual problems is both naïve and dangerous. Biblicism, that rigid attitude of mind which lifts off literal meanings from biblical texts and superimposes them upon contemporary contexts, is fraught with disaster. It oppresses its victims, and it undermines the gospel. Scores of texts in the Gospels have been used in the same way to persecute Jews.[21] The distinction between Christian theology and biblical theology is introduced in this chapter in order to indicate that biblical theology, or biblical ethics, can be immoral and dangerous.

The Old Testament and sexuality

The recognition of patriarchal and hierarchical elements in the Bible is essential for arriving at a sense of the magnitude of the problem of the interpretation of Scripture that confronts Christians. But it would be misleading to say the New Testament as a whole discriminates against women. We have already noted the attitude of Jesus to women, and in opposition to the miserable subordinationism of some of the New Testament letters, the positive vision of Paul of a new community which shares in Christ's risen life must be firmly set. In this community historical barriers between people based on ethnic, hierarchical and gender characteristics are broken down: 'There is no such thing as Jew and Greek, slave and freeman, male and female; for you are all one person in Christ Jesus' (Galatians 3.28).

The same ambiguity may be found in the Old Testament. Patriarchal assumptions abound there. Yet there are 'liberating strands'[22] to be found there as well. The Song of Songs is a wonderful celebration of physical love, and the feelings of the woman are more prominent than those of the man. Women in the Old Testament are often seen to be acting in defiance of male control, and gaining the blessing of God thereby. The Hebrew midwives refuse Pharoah's order to let male children die (Exodus 1.15–22). His disobedient daughter secretly provides for the boy Moses and defiantly adopts him (Exodus 2.1–10). Lot's two daughters get their father hopelessly drunk in order to become pregnant by him (Genesis 19.30–8). They conspire together and act independently, in their own enterprising way, to 'preserve the family' (Genesis 19.32). Ruth and Naomi are prepared to contemplate life together without male protection. When Ruth makes herself sexually available to Boaz, it is as a result of the woman's choice, not the man's coercion (Ruth 3.1–15). Queen Vashti refuses to obey her drunken husband's command to flaunt herself before him and his entourage (Esther 1.10–12). His response (Esther 1.13–22) displays a whole range of patriarchal attitudes. Esther, his new Jewish queen, uses her sexuality and 'charm' (Esther 2.15) on behalf of her people.[23]

These examples of women's ingenuity, wisdom and defiance, however inspirational they may be, also draw attention to the discriminatory circumstances which call forth such courageous responses. There can be no question of regarding such historical circumstances as forever normative. It has been frequently pointed out that there are 'two views of womanhood' in the Bible, 'the subordinationist and the equalitarian',[24] and that a method of interpretation is required which can handle them both without compromising the gospel. Since there is no such thing as male and female in Christ Jesus, Christian men and women will look instead for ways of fostering non-oppressive relationships between each other. In this task they cannot and should not refrain from using the Bible, since it is the primary source of faith. What is required is a full, Christian sexual theology, as opposed to a mere biblical one, where that Love which God is and which is spread abroad in Christ is both our norm and gift. This will give us a point of reference in making ethical judgements, and a framework for interpreting biblical material.

A biblical basis for sexual theology?

Two recent Reports on human sexuality from British churches confirm the need for this framework. But both Reports may unwittingly indicate that the Bible can actually inhibit authentic Christian judgements being made. The members of the Commission responsible for the British Methodist Church Report on Human Sexuality (1990), found their differing attitudes to Scripture a constructive factor in their examination of 'the biblical material'. But they appear to agree both that there is a single, discernible 'mind of Scripture' behind the text,[25] and that whatever passage of Scripture is being examined, it is capable of becoming 'God's word for today'.[26] There are difficulties about each assumption.

The testimony of Scripture is diverse, and the search for a single 'mind' behind that diversity may actually impair the understanding necessary to grasp the Scriptures as in some sense a whole. This view of the interpretative task relies too much on the unstated comparison between the Bible and the human being. Once the comparison is granted, the mind of Scripture can be inferred from the text as a person's thoughts can be inferred from a person's behaviour. But the comparison is weak, and the harmonization of opposing strands in the Bible, such as the 'two views of womanhood' just discussed, cannot be easily achieved. The second difficulty may be raised by asking not *how* the text can become God's word for today, but *whether*, albeit in few cases, there are some passages in which God's word can scarcely be discerned at all.

One such passage (which the Report discusses) is the story of Sodom in Genesis 19, with its familiar themes of violence and xenophobia, and Lot's calm offer of his two virgin daughters to the entire male population of Sodom (Genesis 19.4) to 'do what you like with them' (19.8). It is difficult to see how this passage is capable of becoming 'God's word for today'. One wonders how it was ever God's word for yesterday. Time should now be called on earnest discussion of the details of such passages, such as whether or not the motives of the mob were homosexual. Heterosexual Christians provoke incredulity whenever, in discussing homosexuality, they show themselves to be still in the grip of such sources by referring to them. The contribution of the story to homophobic attitudes must be sadly acknowledged and more fruitful textual sources sought. The Report even avers that 'Scripture is in dialogue with contemporary society'.[27] This is surely an over-optimistic claim. The Church might be said to be engaging in a dialogue, yet one may wonder whether contemporary society will hear God's word through passages like Genesis 19.

The 1991 Statement from the House of Bishops of the Church of England, *Issues in Human Sexuality*, devotes a chapter to 'Scripture and Human Sexuality'.[28] This is a weak chapter in what is in some ways an encouraging and progressive report.[29] The proposals for interpreting Scripture, based on 'three distinct realities', that is the 'content of Scripture', 'salvation history' and 'our general view of the world and our experience of life'[30] are so vague that one wonders whether generalities are deliberately being used in order to mask the problems of interpretation instead of confronting them. The assumption is made that there is something singular called 'the scriptural view of human sexuality',[31] or 'the message of Scripture'.[32] But there is no single view of sexuality, nor a single message of Scripture, and to pretend otherwise requires passages like Genesis 19 to be given equal consideration along with, say, the teaching of Jesus on marriage. These problems constitute the catalyst for a more radical interpretation of Scripture than these Reports provide.[33]

The British sexuality Reports are far from being fundamentalist but they lack courage in dealing with sub-Christian assumptions in much biblical material. A decisive break with biblical patriarchy is a theological and pastoral necessity. One such break is suggested by a liturgy, one of a series for use by women who have formed 'an exodus community from patriarchy'.[34] The liturgy is about the 'Exorcism of Patriarchal Texts'.[35] As the liturgy is performed, a number of biblical texts deemed to be patriarchal, and so oppressive, are read out.[36] The congregation 'exorcises' their oppressive power by the shared public denial of their continued influence upon the community of worshippers. At the end of the service someone says, 'These texts and all oppressive texts have lost their power over our lives. We no longer need to apologize for them or try to interpret them as words of truth, but we cast out their oppressive message as expressions of evil and justifications of evil.'

Christian sexual theology: putting Christ first

The public acknowledgement of patriarchal influence within the Bible and its repudiation in the context of public worship is necessary. A radical proposal for interpreting patriarchal texts is needed which distinguishes between the gospel of Christ and the contexts in which that gospel and its pre-history is set. This is, of course, no new theme in theology.[37] The need for a radical approach is underlined by the failure of less radical proposals to overcome the difficulties just discussed.[38] The proposal commended here for using the Bible in sexual theology and ethics (and by implication in other areas too) is itself biblical. It puts God first. It assumes that God is fully revealed in Jesus Christ and made known to us through the Spirit. The starting point for the use of scriptures in the contemporary Church must be the words which John's Gospel attributes to Jesus – 'You study the scriptures diligently, supposing that in having them you have eternal life; their testimony points to me' (John 5.39).

Jesus exposes a characteristic religious attitude among his hearers towards sacred writings – the tendency to take them literally, and to use them as a basis for certainty and security when their purpose is to point away from themselves, and, in the case of the Christian Bible, to testify to the revelation of God in Christ. What we have seen in large sections of Protestantism is 'a kind of divinization of the Bible'[39] which results in the confusion of revelation and text. God's supreme revelation is a Person, the Son, not a book. The devotional Protestant habit of calling the Bible the 'word of God' fatally confuses the divine 'Word' which in Christ becomes flesh (John 1.9) with the words of Scripture. The text of Scripture is all too easily elevated to the status of the divine Word, the fallible human *oratio* with the very divine *verbum dei*.

The Bible should be interpreted rather as New Testament Christians interpreted the Old Testament. They interpreted it 'in the light of the revelation of the Christ event'.[40] The distinction between the revelation of God in the Person of Christ and the testimony of Scripture in anticipating and reflecting on that revelation, is paralleled by the distinction which Paul makes when describing the character of Christian ministry. He is the minister, he says, 'of a new covenant, not written but spiritual; for the written law condemns to death, but the Spirit gives life' (2 Corinthians 3.6). In the argument of the letter to the Romans, Christ died to exempt and liberate us from the bondage to law. 'In Christ Jesus the life-giving law of the Spirit has set you free from the law of sin and death' (Romans 8.2). The text of the Bible must never become another written law.

A framework of interpretation for a Christian sexual theology

The centrality of God's revelation in Christ allows the text of Scripture its indispensible place in tradition and devotion. It represents no attempt to bypass Scripture, or live without it, or rely on some direct link with God, perhaps 'through the Spirit'. The texts of Scripture, and the texts of subsequent generations of Christians record the testimonies which those generations made to Christ. In stating a procedure for handling Christian texts in the field of sexual theology I borrow Robert Carroll's schema of interpretation.[41] The reading of an historical text (it need not be biblical) requires consideration of six different factors.

The first is the *reader* herself. The reader brings his or her whole autobiography to the text. She will have a reason for reading, but the reading is likely to be fraught with difficulty because the text assumes, secondly, a *context* which is not the reader's own. The original language of the text, its idiomatic character and the pre-scientific, pre-critical thought-world it presupposes will strike the reader with its strangeness. So, thirdly, an *interpreter* is needed: indeed, several will already have been at work in providing a translation. The interpreter is likely to be someone who has studied the text and its context and may try to make connections (if any!)

between the text and the contemporary readership. The reader and the interpreter may share, fourthly, *the same social situation*. And this situation is likely to provide the reason for reading the text, and will certainly shape the questions that contemporary readers will want to put to it. It will also shape the interpretation which the interpreter will give to it.

Fifthly, the interpreter needs a *hermeneutical framework*, that is, some principles of interpretation which guide the questioning put to the text. Sixthly, there is *possibility*, the prospect of new understandings and practice arising from the process of bringing reader and text together, when the reader reflects upon the interpretation in the light of her situation, and appropriates the meaning. At this juncture it is necessary to mention the promise of Jesus that 'when the Spirit of truth comes, he will guide you into all the truth' (John 16.13). Sadly, countless people have claimed the prompting of the Spirit for all kinds of pious nonsense, and any Christian must be wary of claiming special revelation through the Spirit. Nonetheless, the bringing together of all six factors provides a kaleidoscopic opportunity for adventurous, imaginative insights to be generated, and it is in and through these that the Spirit may be found at work.

These six ingredients are particularly appropriate to the use of the Bible in sexual theology. A *reader* will bring her entire life story to the text of the Bible. Pressing sexual dilemmas may be the reason for turning to it. Since our appropriation of meaning in a text to some extent depends on our willingness to be open to what it has to say and this openness is an opening of ourselves, we cannot predict in advance how any text will impinge upon us, or indeed whether it will impinge upon us at all. If we are serious about letting the text speak, a knowledge of the *context* in which the text is set is indispensable. Our four case studies have shown how biblical sexual teaching is integrated into a context which takes for granted a hierarchical ordering of social and personal relations, and which (in the case of the Corinthian correspondence) is defensively and grudgingly shaped by a troublesome, extremist, anti-sexual minority and by the shared belief that Christians then living were the last generation before the end of the age. The condemnation of homosexual behaviour has also to be seen in a context where pederasty and sexual violence were practised and the natural hierarchy of men over women threatened. These are merely a few of the features of a context which is not our own, but a knowledge of which is necessary if the meaning of the text is to be illuminated.

An *interpreter* has an onerous responsibility of bringing together the reader, set in a contemporary *social situation*, and the text. He will know something about the text and the context. He will allow the work of interpretation to be influenced by questions drawn from the social situation. In the case of sexual decision-making, the questions may be influenced by, for example, the wide availability of reliable contraception, the different status of women, an earlier age of reaching puberty, a later age for becoming married, the commodification of sex in capitalist societies, and so on. Differences between the context of the text and the social situation of the reader must be honestly recognized for interpretation to succeed.

How is this work of interpretation done? An enormous theological literature exists on this problem. It is clear that interpretation cannot happen without a *hermeneutical framework*.[42] The Christian faith itself has existed continuously from the time of the text to the present social situation, and so is the historical link between them. The considerations governing the interpretation will be drawn from this tradition and concensus about what they are is difficult to achieve. I develop some clear theological and doctrinal principles in the next three chapters. But something must briefly be said now in order to complete the account of what a Christian, as opposed to a biblical, sexual theology looks like.

The doctrinal core of the enterprise is traditional. Christian faith provides the vision and experience of God as love. This love is identical with God's nature. It is manifest in the gift of Christ, the internal relations of the Trinity, and their external relations in creation, salvation and sanctification. It is mediated and fired by the Spirit and renewed in each new generation. The incarnation and trinity of God show both *that* God is love and *how* God is love. The failure to live in love is a perennial human tendency which is 'sin'. Christian faith is a sharing in divine love. Critical scholarship is one of the tools for identifying the patriarchy that mars this vision and experience of love. The interpretative task in relation to the Scriptures is to let their testimony point to Christ (John 5.39), the revelation of divine love in human, embodied, relational being. Some Scripture testifies to Christ by describing the need for redemption which he satisfies. This sharing in divine love is the basis for thinking about and having sex. The biblical themes of creation and re-creation, sin and redemption, brokenness and wholeness, estrangement and reconciliation, fill out the basic framework. Redemption is understood to be the release from lovelessness, from the inability to give or receive love. Belief in a God who becomes incarnate allows a celebration of embodiment, and of the potential sacramentality of human relationships.

Sexual theology: biblical AND Christian?

Christian sexual theology can and must be biblical. But if biblical theology is about discerning a single 'mind of Scripture', or wrenching from their contexts surface meanings of texts in order to apply them to contemporary social situations, it does a disservice to Christian faith. Sexual theology is Christian when it derives from a sharing in the vision and experience of God as love, made known in Jesus Christ. The role of the Bible in sexual theology must be that of testifying to that vision and experience.

Notes

1. Sheila Briggs, 'Sexual Justice and the "Righteousness of God"', in Linda Hurcombe, *Sex and God: Some Varieties of Women's Religious Experience* (London: Routledge & Kegan Paul, 1987), p. 255.
2. ibid. p. 257.
3. ibid. p. 254.
4. Peter Brown, *The Body and Society: Men, Women and Sexual Renunciation in Early Christianity* (London and Boston: Faber & Faber, 1990), p. 53.
5. ibid. p. 55.
6. See below, chapter 9.
7. William Countryman, *Dirt, Greed and Sex: Sexual Ethics in the New Testament and their Implications for Today* (London: SCM Press, 1989), p. 113.
8. Brown, p. 30.
9. Aline Rousselle, *Porneia* (Oxford: Blackwell, 1988), p. 3.
10. Countryman, p. 114.
11. ibid. pp. 115–6.
12. Peter Coleman, *Gay Christians: A Moral Dilemma* (London: SCM Press, 1989), p. 71. But see Countryman, p. 118 for some doubt about this.
13. ibid. pp. 81, 85.
14. ibid. p. 71.
15. See below, ch. 9.
16. Michael Vasey, *Evangelical Christians and Gay Rights,* Grove Ethical Studies No. 80 (Bramcote: Grove Books, 1991), p. 22.
17. Coleman, p. 77.
18. Briggs, p. 264. She draws from the important work of Bernadette Brooten; see p. 276, n. 11.
19. ibid.
20. See below, ch. 9.
21. Robert P. Carroll, *Wolf in the Sheepfold: The Bible as a Problem for Christianity* (London: SPCK, 1991), ch. 4.
22. Anne E. Carr, *Transforming Grace: Tradition and Women's Experience* (New York: Harper & Row, 1988),p. 207.
23. I am grateful to John Henson for pointing out the importance of this Old Testament strand for the present argument.

24. E.g. Mary Hayter, *The New Eve in Christ* (London: SPCK, 1987), p. 146.
25. The Methodist Church, *Report of Commission on Human Sexuality* (Peterborough: Methodist Publishing House, 1990), §§ 84, 88.
26. ibid. § 120.
27. ibid. § 126.
28. *Issues in Human Sexuality: A Statement by the House of Bishops* (London: Church House Publishing, 1991), pp. 5–18.
29. The Lesbian and Gay Christian Movement called it 'a positive breakthrough, with much to welcome, but with harmful inconsistencies and contradictions about clergy behaviour'. (Press release, 4.12.91.)
30. *Issues in Human Sexuality*, §§ 2.1–2.3.
31. ibid. § 2.12.
32. ibid. § 2.22.
33. These problems led Bishop John Spong to admit, 'sex drove me to the Bible' (see his *Rescuing the Bible from Fundamentalism: A Bishop Rethinks the Meaning of Scripture* (San Francisco: HarperCollins, 1991), p. 1.) The outpouring of 'proof texting and prejudice' which greeted the publication of his earlier book *Living in Sin? A Bishop Rethinks Human Sexuality* (San Francisco: Harper & Row, 1988) led him on to the further project of *Rescuing the Bible from Fundamentalism*.
34. Rosemary Radford Ruether, *Women-Church: Theology and Practice of Feminist Liturgical Communities* (San Francisco: Harper & Row, 1985), p. 122.
35. ibid. p. 137.
36. The passages listed are Leviticus 12.1–5, Exodus 19, Judges 19, Ephesians 5.21–3, 1 Timothy 2.11–15, 1 Peter 2.18–20, but they are only suggestions.
37. For a survey of the history of biblical interpretation and a much more detailed set of proposals for reading the Bible, see Anthony C. Thiselton, *New Horizons in Hermeneutics* (San Francisco: HarperCollins, 1992).
38. For the setting of sexual ethics in the context of contemporary hermeneutic thought, see Lisa Sowle Cahill, *Between the Sexes: Foundations for a Christian Ethics of Sexuality* (Philadelphia: Fortress Press, 1985), ch. 2, 'The Bible and Ethics: Hermeneutical Dilemmas'.
39. Carroll, p. 86.
40. James Dunn, *Unity and Diversity in the New Testament* (London: SCM Press, 1977), p. 369.
41. Carroll, p. 14.
42. This is also the conclusion of a lengthy study on biblical interpretation. 'Some theological perspective on God and the world, is the most far–reaching proposal to emerge from all that has preceded . . . The conclusion is that neither history nor literature without theory provides the kind of interpretations that believers need from their scriptures. The reasons for this lie in the nature of modernity.' See Robert Morgan with John Barton, *Biblical Interpretation* (Oxford: Oxford University Press, 1988), pp. 276–7.

CHAPTER 3

The Holiness of the Body

In this chapter, I outline and criticize a particular view of the human body, that it is something separate from and inferior to the human soul. I then argue that this view, *philosophical* dualism, has contributed greatly to *sexist* dualism, the view that women are inferior to men. An attempt is then made to sketch the damaging impact of both forms of dualism on male sexual consciousness. I contend that sexual theology must free itself from both forms of dualism and recover a sense of the human body as holy. In support of this position I draw on central Christian beliefs about creation, incarnation, eucharist and spirituality.

Dualism – the ideology of patriarchy

There is no agreement among human beings about what a human being is![1] This lack of agreement has allowed to flourish an argument, from Plato to the present day, about whether the souls and bodies of people are separate entities, as in 'dualism'; whether they are different aspects of the same entity, a person, as in 'double-aspect theories';[2] or whether the soul is reducible to bodily properties, as in materialism. The arguments continue to rage. A remarkable feature of the vast philosophical literature on the subject is an almost complete silence about the damaging and far-reaching consequences of the view that the body is inferior to the soul.

We must confront dualism in this chapter for two reasons. It is a way of thinking about human beings which has historically reinforced the subordination of women to men. It has caused the body, with its intrinsic senses and desires, to become alienated and devalued in relation to the soul. Sexuality under dualism ceases to be a celebration of God's grace and becomes instead the occasion of God's judgement. Through its negative valuation of the material world, Christian writers have held it also to be deeply implicated in the cluster of attitudes that cause and tolerate environmental pollution and even nuclear armament.[3]

Two kinds of dualism have become woven together in western thinking about human beings. Philosophical or anthropological dualism is that set of abstract theories which claims that the souls of people are immaterial, separate from bodies and eternal; and that bodies are material, separate from souls and perishable. Sexist dualism is that set of concrete assumptions which stipulate that men are superior to women.[4] Philosophical dualism is repeatedly used to maintain sexist dualism, and the submission of women to men. In accordance with the analysis of patriarchy in chapter 1, no consciously malicious and misogynistic motives are attributed to most of the male thinkers who succeeded so brilliantly in passing off the inferiority of women as beyond question. The legacy they leave us, however, may be compared with an abscess on the root of a tooth. An abscess is poisonous, hidden, and sometimes hard even to locate. But the pain is relentless and the treatment involves drilling, draining and filling. In order to assist the process of unmaking patriarchy and remaking our sexuality in the light of gospel expectation, dualism and its consequences need to be re-examined. Two sets of assumptions, one biological, the other sociological, have first to be exposed.

Failed males and weak seed

The inferiority of women in relation to men derived much support from ancient theories about the conception and ownership of human bodies. Hippocrates (fourth century BCE) and the Greek physician Galen (second century CE) both held that women produced what they called 'female seed'.[5] Doubtless they based their speculations on the fact of vaginal lubrication during the sexual arousal of women. Aristotle, however, had held that only males produce seed. The male seed provides the 'form' for the 'matter' provided by the woman, form being 'a determining principle which shapes matter, such that in human beings the form is the rational soul, the particular characteristic which makes us human'.[6] The etymological link remains between the Latin *mater* (mother) and *materia* (matter).[7]

Aquinas modified this theory by arguing that God gives the foetus its soul. The male seed, he thought, prepares the matter contributed by the female, so that it is ready to accept the soul.[8] Nothing is known by any of these writers of the ovum (which was not discovered until 1827), though women were thought to contribute seed or matter to the embryo. What is common to both accounts of conception, and remained unquestioned right through to the nineteenth century is that a woman is produced by defective seed, which was lacking in heat, strength or quantity. Women were 'failed males'. 'The precious vital heat had not come to them in sufficient quantities in the womb. Their lack of heat made them more soft, more liquid, more clammy-cold, altogether more formless than men.'[9] As Aquinas observed,

> Aristotle called the female a *male manque* ['something that might have been but is not, that has missed being']. The particular nature of the active male seed intends to produce a perfect likeness of itself, and when females are conceived this is due to weak seed, or unsuitable material, or external influences like the dampness of the south wind.[10]

Men are creative, active partners, women the passive, incubatory ones. Men provide the form. Women lack form, and are intrinsically weak and defective.

These biological beliefs were linked with a set of sociological beliefs about the male body. 'Body' is of course an elastic concept, as use of the terms 'corporate bodies', 'responsible bodies', implies today. But body has been an elastic, elusive concept at least since New Testament times. The consumption of the body of Christ in the Eucharist, and the identification of the Church with that body, is evidence enough of the inclusive, symbolic power of the term. However, there is another sense of 'body' which reinforces male domination, the sense in which the body of a man included not simply that physical anatomy to which as a rational soul he was linked and which he controlled, but everything else which he controlled as well, especially his 'household'. Christianity came to absorb that 'pagan notion of the person' according to which 'the soul had been thought of as ruling the body with the same alert, if occasionally tolerant, authority as the well-born male ruled those inferior and alien to himself - his wife, his slaves, and the populace of his city.'[11] His body, 'like his household, includes a wife as well as slaves'.[12] In other words, the bodies of wives, children and slaves were included in the body of the householder. They formed a unity with his body in belonging to that domain which his soul directly governed.

The forms of dualism

The complicity of philosophical dualism in reinforcing sexist dualism and therefore in the shaping of relationships between men and women may be illustrated by considering how it has become reproduced and embedded in common everyday notions associated with the human person. There are at least six pairs of terms which are carriers of philosophical dualism and contribute to sexist dualism. They have had great influence. Each will be briefly considered.

1. Body and soul

The basic version of philosophical dualism asserts that the human being consists of two entities or substances, body and soul, or matter and mind. It is a Greek doctrine, not a Jewish or biblical one. It influences Christian thought through Neoplatonism in the third century CE. It is rejected by Aquinas, but again becomes influential in European thought through Descartes. A dualist is likely to hold i) the mind or soul is a separate entity from the body; ii) the soul is immaterial while the body is material; and iii) the soul, being immaterial, is unaffected by bodily decay. While the body is perishable, the soul is imperishable. It is therefore as souls, according to this theory, that we survive our bodily deaths. The soul is the real 'me'. Catholics have been trained through the catechism to react to the question, 'Of which must I take more care, of my body or of my soul?' with the answer, 'I must take more care of my soul . . .'. As a consequence they have come to think of the body 'not only as something separate from their real self, but also as something inferior'.[13]

This view is widely held among Protestant and Catholic Christians alike, yet it is unbiblical, and, in a faith which teaches the goodness of the created world, the incarnation of God in flesh and the resurrection of human bodies at the end of the age, its survival is remarkable.[14] I agree with the verdict that 'dualism . . . is the enemy of women and of authentic Christianity'.[15] I think it remains, not because there are good theological or philosophical arguments for it, but because it effectively services the ideology of male domination. A view which regards people in a holistic way, as integrated unities of body-and-soul-together is greatly to be preferred.[16]

2. Reason and passion

Our concern is with how basic dualism reinforces sexism by reproducing itself through other pairs of opposites. This results in associating men with minds and souls, and women with bodies. It brings about the obvious ideological result that, in advance of argument or comment, men are assumed to be superior to women. Basic dualism is reflected in the further distinction between reason and passion, or intellect and emotion. This pair of opposites could be allowed to suggest different facets of the human being which are equally necessary for the achievement of wholeness, but in dualism, reason is separated from passion. 'Rationality constituted the essentially human' and became the means of identifying the human with the divine,[17] while passion remained sense-bound, unpredictable, ever a disruptive threat to the tranquillity of reason. In sexist dualism, men are rational, women are emotional. 'Women are defined as analogous to body in relation to the ruling mind; either obediently subjugated body (the wife), or sensual bodiliness, in revolt against the governance of reason (the harlot).'[18]

3. Will and desire

Will and desire constitute a further variation of anthropological dualism. Orgasm confronts reason and overcomes it. Reason cannot control orgasm, because there can be no orgasm without final loss of control. Augustine thought the inability of the will to control the sexual organs was a direct consequence of the sin of Adam and Eve.[19] The opposition between will and desire sometimes led to extreme measures, including mortification, starvation and castration. In sexist dualism women lack will and are creatures of desire. In seventeenth-century Anglican thought, more friendly to women than much earlier theological writing, the wife was subordinate to the husband so he might 'rule her lusts and wanton appetites'[20]. According to Richard Hooker and others,[21] women were 'alleged to be so constituted as to require guidance, control, and protection. They are intrinsically inferior in excellence, imbecile by sex and nature, weak in body, inconstant in mind, and imperfect and infirm in character.' Their weak nature, so one argument went, was the reason why they 'respond to solicitation or consent to brutality'.[22]

4. Spirit and flesh

Spirit and flesh restate basic dualism and reinforce sexist dualism. The historical exclusion of women from office in the Church has reinforced the assumption that men are the purveyors and mediators of spirit. Woman, through menstruation, procreation and lactation, have been more associated with flesh. Since it is impossible in some churches, even today, to receive Holy Communion from women, this dualism remains frighteningly alive. Women are more easily associated (by men) with uncleannness and temptation.

5. Culture and nature

This pair of opposites is the social extension of spirit and flesh. In the 'battle between the flesh and the spirit, the female sex was firmly placed on the side of the flesh'.[23] Because of their reproductive role, 'women are associated with nature rather than culture'. We have already noted how, according to Turner, 'The universality of women's subordinate status in society is thus explained by the universality of women's reproductive functions.'[24] The freedom of men from 'natural functions' has historically enabled them to 'occupy themselves with higher status activities', while 'women reproduce perishable bodies'.[25] Their lack of access to cultural opportunity merely confirmed their inferior status. As late as 1887, in Victorian England, women were still denied access to education on the grounds that 'heavy brain-work' was 'more exhausting than muscle work', and women were constitutionally capable of neither.[26] The strain of examinations on girls, claimed Samuel Smiles, would lead to 'a large crop of nervous and brain diseases, chorea, hysteria, and eventually the derangement of their vital functions, and an entire prostration of their bodily health'.[27] The culture-nature distinction explains this passage well. Smiles thinks that nature itself excludes women from culture.

6. Public and private

A further social dualism thus arises, between public and private. Men traditionally have inhabited the public world of professions, politics, finance, business and church; 'women occupy the domestic world of private emotions and affections'.[28] This arrangement, very convenient for men, is assumed in Victorian England with great confidence. John Ruskin asserts the 'office' and 'place' of a woman is in a man's home where it is her duty to offer him 'Praise'.[29]The man alone suffers the 'peril and trial' of the public world, but 'he guards the woman from all this; within his house, as ruled by her, unless she herself has sought it, need enter no danger, no temptation, no cause of error or offence'.[30] No arguments are offered in this mellifluous outpouring of ideological prejudice. The exclusion of women from the public world is assumed, and all the women who do not stray from their domestic 'queenly dominion' are even assured the adulation of angels.[31]

Conflicts in male consciousness

This is a formidable legacy to be unmade. Philosophical dualism lies behind the distinction, often used by the churches in current discussions about homosexuality, between *orientation* and *practice*.[32] It is often stated that a person is not culpable with regard to a same-sex orientation, but *is* culpable if the orientation leads to any same-sex practices. But the very idea that a person can have a disposition or state (an orientation) which is somehow separable from the body and its expression is possible only on the prior basis of a philosophical dualism. Dualism gives a spurious credibility to the notion of an orientation that can be uncoupled from bodily expression. Once this dualism is accepted, it is taken for granted that people with a homosexual orientation can and must refrain from same-sex practices. Philosophical dualism, then, does not only support sexist dualism. It can contribute to discrimination against homosexuals, that is, it is homophobic.[33]

Both the philosophical and sexist forms of dualism have led to certain general consequences in the shaping of male attitudes to sex and sexuality which even now we are only beginning to understand. I shall sketch some of these consequences very briefly, borrowing some terms from outside theology. It is not of course suggested that *all men* suffer from these consequences. Some may suffer from some of them; others may suffer from none, or from too vigorous a reaction to them. All that can be hoped for is to catch a sense of how deeply ingrained dualistic assumptions have adversely influenced men's attitudes towards women.

1. Androcentrism

The most striking feature of sexist dualism is the androcentrism it encourages. That is why traditional sexual morality is still 'largely founded upon male perceptions and reflecting male interests'.[34] It has been justly claimed that 'who sets the agenda in ethical conversations is the key to their outcome', and 'as women begin to set the agenda, the conversation is shifting away from genital concerns and toward intimacy'.[35] There is a salutary warning here for male writers on sexual ethics. Feminist writers describe how the whole business of thinking and writing about ethics can craftily smuggle in male authorial assumptions which are inimicable to the ethical experience of women. Susan Parsons has shown that the moral tradition deriving from Kant places a high ethical premium on the skill of refined abstract reasoning, well beyond the abilities of most men and women, whether educated or not. 'Understanding God and God's law for human existence is described as a process of increasing detachment from the particularities of the body's concerns, since these will inhibit the appreciation and appropriation of what is universal.'[36]

This criticism is not levelled against rigorous critical thinking but against the belief 'that this capacity for reasoning takes place in a fundamentally unembodied way'.[37] It is in the exercise of mind that people prove themselves as moral beings. From this unembodied approach to the rights and wrongs of ethical conduct, a further nest of unexamined assumptions suggests itself unannounced such that making choices is something done by 'individual isolated beings, locked in with their personal rationality and the privacy of their own will, necessarily related to other individuals, but not intrinsically so'.[38] Choices take place in the private world of thoughts alone. Against this unembodied, male, rational world, radical feminism 'emphasises the truths of the body, first and foremost. We know only in a bodied way.'[39]

2. Repression and rationalization

Once consent has been given to the deep split between soul and body at the centre of one's being, 'I' become separated from my body, and the 'real me' becomes identified with my soul (or mind, will or spirit). I am no longer body, but uncomfortably and uncertainly related to it, as to a thing or perishable object. It is something which 'I' control through prayer or discipline exercised by reason: 'it', being now separate from 'me', resists my control. Body, desire, passion, flesh remain insistent. Ever more strenuous strategies of domination may therefore be called for, in order to bring the flesh into conformity with the spirit, and to repress lingering traces of desire. My body becomes alien to me, an impediment to my relationship with God and constant source of sin.[39] Within single individuals, the relationship between self and body becomes one of domination–subjugation. Reason sees the conquest of desire as something to be pursued by rational means like depriving the body of food, comfort or sleep. The head attempts to rule the heart. The body is first and foremost 'a location for the exercise of will over desire'.[40] If in this relationship, which informs every moment of my waking and sleeping life, I am required to subjugate nature, it will be difficult not to avoid the domination–subjugation pattern of relationship in all other relationships where I am either dominant or dominated. The process of subjecting the body to the control of reason is 'rationalization'.

3. Segmentation

Segmentation occurs when men separate themselves 'from those people and situations that arouse them sexually'.[41] An interesting ancient example is found in the adulterous story of David and Bathsheba. When Bathsheba's husband Uriah is recalled from a holy war, he refuses David's command to visit his wife because sexual pleasures are segmented from military duties. 'How can I go home to eat and drink and to sleep with my wife? By your life, I cannot do this!' (2 Samuel 11.12). Segmentation ends in neurosis, graphically defined by Paul Tillich as 'the way of avoiding non-being by avoiding being'.[42] The neurotic 'surrenders a part of his potentialities in order to save what is left'.[43] Segmentation is the rationale for single-sex communities.

4. Genitalization

Segmentation need not be confined to eliminating contact between the body and the occasions of its arousal. The body itself can be segmented from sexuality, and sexual feeling, instead of being diffused all over the body, becomes instead concentrated in the penis. This is what genitalization means. The male notion that the penis alone is *the* sexual organ is an acquired belief. Under the genitalization of male sexuality, the focus

> is more on sexual acts, acts involving genital expression. In turn, we tend to isolate sex from other areas of life. Sexuality, then, does not mean *in the first instance* loving intimacy, sensuous playfulness, babies, or the *eros* that draws us into communion with all else. It means a happening, a sexual event involving our genitals.[44]

Once sexual feeling is concentrated in the penis, it is easier to make the identification of sexual experience with sexual intercourse. When the intention to have children became the justification for having sex, the genitalization of sex was confirmed.

5. Asceticism

Asceticism is the severe and disciplined avoidance of pleasure, especially sexual pleasure. Ever since the Council of Arles in 309, avoidance of sexual intercourse has been expected of Roman Catholic priests. The main reason for having sex (for most of Christian history) was *reproductive intent*. This gave sexual intercourse a *purpose*. Once it had a purpose, techniques for achieving the purpose could be devised, and all sexual activity which did not fulfil this purpose (e.g. masturbation, same-sex activity, etc.) could be condemned. But the regulatory framework and the purposive attitude to sexuality is at variance with the joy and communion that sexual activity provides. Christian theologians have been generally unable to see sexual activity as playful, yet it is in the experience of sex as *play* that the delight and joy of it become enhanced. Theologians have been accused of a notorious unwillingness to confront their sexuality and to have turned Christian belief into an 'a-sexual experience'.[45] Asceticism, *even in contemporary theological writing*, is evident in the marginalization of sexual experience from mainstream systematic theology.[46]

Play is essential to sex, especially between life-long partners who slide too easily into settled routines. Yet even play has rules, and playfulness in sex does not dispense with rules about who takes part with whom, and what they do. Marital intimacy 'is either playful or it is intolerable'.[47] A 'mature hedonic sensitivity' is rightly said to be 'crucial to Christian identity'.[48] John Macquarrie has observed: 'The Western mind seems to have a tendency towards an almost deadly seriousness. When we do anything, we feel that we have to justify whatever we are doing in terms of some goal at which we are aiming.'[49] Play however is an activity which we do not have to justify, and its lack of having a serious purpose is central to its definition. 'Play has its point in itself, and the player does not need to give a reason for what he is doing. When we begin to look anxiously for a justification for play, then we have forgotten what it means to play.'[50] There is an irony here. Play subverts seriousness, yet here it is, seriously advocated!

Love-making is a spontaneous, playful activity. Seriousness about it can lead to anxiety about performance, with impotence following closely behind. Non-religious ideas of play can also become infected with seriousness. The notion of 'foreplay' as the preparatory sexual activity prior to vaginal penetration already assumes that what comes after the foreplay is the essential thing about the act which the preliminaries make possible. A distinction must be made, however, between play as a quality of a mutual, loving, sexual relationship, and play as a trivializing and demeaning general attitude to women as 'playmates' for male consumers of sex ('playboys'?), reinforced by such expressions as 'scoring', 'playing the field', and 'playing around'. Christian faith offers an alternative vision of sexual relationships, and its foundations are about to be explored. Play must not be seen to cancel the need for chastity within relationships,[51] but neither must the more familiar theme of chastity cancel out the need for play. God is the creator of the body and its enormous potential for pleasure. It is in bodily merrymaking and not in body-denying asceticism that most Christians (but not all) will want to discover the goodness and blessing of God.

The holiness of the body

A contemporary sexual theology which proclaims the liberating reign of God within human relationships cannot avail itself of either anthropological or sexist dualism, and it does not need to. Neither sort is found in the teaching of Jesus. The subordinate status of the body in relation to the soul, and of the female body to the control of men, indicates how far unembodied thinking has strayed from central emphases within Christian faith. These include the created goodness of the material world, the incarnation of God in flesh, the return to life of Christ in the body, the return of Christ to God in the body, and the feeding on Christ's body in the Eucharist until, in his body, he returns. Embodiment must be rescued from dualism so that our bodies can be reclaimed from guilt, embarrassment and religious ambiguity, and reaffirmed as the locus of our being as children of God. In this reclamation of the body from a degrading dualism I make four suggestions.

1. God's continuing incarnation

The incarnation or enfleshment of God in Christ is central to Christian faith. In his 'Hymn to Matter' the great mystical theologian Teilhard de Chardin wrote: 'You who batter us and then dress our wounds, you who resist us and yield to us, you who wreck and build, you who shackle and liberate, the sap of our souls, the hand of God, the flesh of Christ: it is you, matter, that I bless.'[52] It is possible to see God's incarnation as a single, unrepeatable unique event. An alternative way of understanding it is to see it as the chief paradigm or exemplification of what God does, that is, the normal and most usual way of knowing God is in the reality of the body. On this view, the incarnation in Christ remains unique, but becomes inclusive rather than exclusive. In Christ we are given the supreme disclosure of God's grace and power; in our ordinary bodied life, however, we can expect to experience this grace and power for ourselves.

James Nelson has claimed:

> The Heart of the universe continues to be enfleshed. Under the impact of male theology, for centuries we have been led to believe that the divine incarnation really occurred just once, two thousand years ago. We have confined the Christ to that one human figure: Jesus. As I understand him, however, it was not Jesus' purpose to monopolize the Christian experience but, quite the opposite, to release its reality and power in the world - the meeting with God in and through human flesh.[53]

Nelson is right. It is through human flesh that God became supremely known, and through the body that God continues to be known. Part of the patriarchal legacy is the assumption that knowing means knowing abstractly, using concepts to move beyond the individual and the particular to universal ideas and truths. Incarnation subverts this procedure. There is a priceless knowing to be had when flesh meets flesh. It is individual and particular. In its intense joy and mutuality it is also the embodied presence of the divine - an experience of a bodily holiness which contrasts sharply with the bodiless holiness of too much Christian sanctity.

2. The gift of the body – eucharistic presence

Why should Jesus have instituted a memorial of himself which was so physical? The physicality of the Eucharist, in many celebrations of it, seems to be almost deliberately disguised by the substitution of wafery discs that do not remotely look and taste like bread. The substitution in Noncomformist churches of de-alcoholized 'wine' for proper wine, while it reflects the distinguished witness of the temperance movement in earlier times, also signals an alteration of basic symbolism away from the celebration and merriment of the original Passover meal. Does the very consecration of the bread and wine serve to extricate them from the everyday world of eating and drinking and convert them into spiritual food that loses its materiality in order to become holy?

The words 'This is my body' show that brokenness and self-giving are at the heart of the faith. These simple central truths are not abstract truths arrived at by reflecting disembodiedly on the universe, but are affirmed and re-enacted whenever bread is broken and wine poured out by Christians in the name of Christ. Just as incarnation is the paradigm for the presence of God, so eucharist is the paradigm for the experience of God. But the eucharistic meal is 'the gift of a body'.[54] It is surely obvious to anyone who has received the gift of their lover's body in love-making and the gift of Christ's body in the Eucharist that there are many unexplored parallels between these two life-sustaining, life-enhancing, life-creating activities. They engage all our senses, especially the less prominent ones of touch, taste and smell. They are both intensely joyful celebrations, each deeply satisfying. Yet both may also be covenanted pledges of love, richly symbolic, festive and liberating. What is most profoundly spiritual is shown and shared in what is utterly and totally physical. Has the central sacrament of Christian faith been de-materialized, and robbed by a patriarchal priesthood of its erotic, sensual power?

3. The experience of the body – source of spirituality

Patriarchal dualism cuts off the flow of divine grace in and through the body by creating the expectation that divine knowledge is immaterial, abstract and confined to the soul. The rediscovery of the body as a source of spirituality is a liberation for women and men alike. Susan Parsons writes:

> Women understand embodiment not as a danger . . . but rather as opportunity, as possibility, as a continuing source of creativity. Their bodies are experienced as a creative potential of a kind *which can even give birth to God*. Their experience of embodiment is one of togetherness, not detachment, for they know first-hand through their bodies the existence of others, and live in a constant awareness of mutuality and relationship.[55]

There is a danger in picking out reproductive roles in heightening body-awareness, because it can too easily confirm a purely functional account of women as child-rearers. But the opposite danger, of allowing the rhythms and cycles of women's bodies to remain religiously insignificant, is greater and leaves patriarchy unchallenged.

Women, unlike men, are said to 'bear God's image in a dynamic way which is marked by periodicity'.[56] 'Menstruation brings with it the mysterious joy of being able to share in God's work of birthing.'[57] The menopause is a process which is said to bring many spiritual disclosures and is 'a liberation from some of the responsibilities of womanhood in order to find pleasure and fulfilment in others'.[58] There are many women who find no spiritual significance whatever in their periods. Is this because, as one of my friends retorts, they are a 'bloody and painful nuisance'? Or, is it relevant also to suggest that for millenia, patriarchal thought has never allowed women access to reflection on their own bodily experience, and has dismissed menstruation and giving birth as states of ritual uncleanness (Leviticus 15.13–33; 12)?

Several writers claim that, with regard to the enjoyment of sexual experience, 'Women's sexual pleasure . . . derives less from specific sex acts than from a generalized body response to tenderness.'[59] Such generalized tenderness is in sharp contrast with the concentration of sexual feeling in the genitals alone. It is probably a genuine gender difference which has been socially acquired. Men have much to learn from this 'growing understanding of female libido, as diffuse, autonomous, multi-pleasured physicality'. It may help them to forget all they were taught about localized 'erogenous zones' of male and female bodies and realize that there is no turn-on like tenderness.

James Nelson has done more than any other contemporary theologian to revalue the body against dualistic tendencies. He proposes that men generally suffer from an 'erection mentality'.[60] They are too readily obsessed with achievement, performance orientation and anxiety about impotence. They should instead value the penis more when flaccid, and the phallus less. 'Sinking, emptying is a way of spirituality. It means trusting God that we do not need to *do*, that our *being* is enough.'[61] Again there are dangers with this sort of analysis in that it remains genital, but it is part of an important attempt to ground masculine spirituality in a different body awareness, with a particular result that having a penis is just as much about resting and quietude as it is about power and control.

4. Embodied knowing – communion with God

The location of God in flesh, in the giving and receiving of bodies, in the bodily experiences of women and men is no new emphasis in the Christian faith. Recent research on the experience of some late-medieval Christian women indicates the remarkable extent of the physicality of their piety. During the eucharistic raptures of some of them 'the wounds of Christ appeared spontaneously in their hands, feet, sides, and faces'.[62] 'The physical union the women sought and had with Christ was not only that of sharing his agony and passion. They saw often in the host and chalice Christ the baby or Christ the bridegroom and joined him as such.' The physical union experienced by some of these women 'sometimes culminated in what appears to be orgasm'.[63]

These experiences cannot be written off as unbalanced and eccentric, for they provide evidence for an 'embodied knowing' of God which was rooted in the domestic roles and interpersonal situations of the women.

> The experience of women of those times, even more than today, was centered in family life: not just in putting food and drink on the table, but in giving suck and caring for babies, in playing, in hugging, in helping clothe, in sex, in sympathizing with and caring for the hurt or ill or dying, etc.[64]

One of the research questions currently being considered is why medieval theology failed to recognize, assimilate, or reflect upon the intense physical piety of these devout women Christians.

The right answer seems to consist largely of considerations dealt with in this chapter. 'For the theologians, all experience of Christ must be immaterial, noncorporeal.' For them the knowledge of God involves the bodiless intellect and the bodiless will. Touch, or 'tactile knowing'[65] is excluded. 'The pleasures of banquet, sex, and other family life [which] serve the tradition as images of, among other things, richly aware interpersonal union',[66] are not allowed to become a basis for the knowledge of God. The appropriateness of physical desire as a desire also for religious experience is vetoed. Since interpersonal tactile knowledge is knowledge only of particular people, in particular places and so not general or universal, it is knowledge which cannot in principle be knowledge of the divine.

An alternative estimate of the women's experience is that they rediscovered that their bodily needs, their immersion in family life, their giving of themselves in care *was* the source of spiritual life, of encounter with Christ and communion with God. We may not wish their ecstasies, and we must not draw the inference that domesticity is a necessary means towards spiritual fulfilment for women or men. What they show us is the integration of bodily life and feeling in their experience of and response to God. And this must lie at the root of holy, reverent sexual relationships. Knowledge of God must, above all, be 'holistic', involving all levels and dimensions of our being.[67]

Both sorts of dualism considered in this chapter are essential to patriarchy but inessential to living faith in God. The remaking of our perception of embodiment, grounded in incarnation, sacrament, and ordinary bodily and familial life, is simultaneously a rediscovery of our sexual and spiritual life. Its contribution to a renewed understanding of relationships is considered in the next chapter.

Notes

1. T. L. S. Sprigge, *Theories of Existence* (Harmondsworth: Penguin Books, 1984), and Leslie Stevenson, *Seven Theories of Human Nature* (New York and Oxford: Oxford University Press, 1974) indicate the range of views on offer.
2. I have elsewhere argued that the double-aspect theory is more adequate than the other two (and useful for an understanding of traditional Christological claims). See my *Truly a Person, Truly God* (London: SPCK, 1990), especially ch. 2.
3. Carol Christ, 'Reverence for Life' in P. Cooey, S. A. Farmer and M. E. Ross, (eds), *Embodied Love: Sensuality and Relationship as Feminist Values* (New York: Harper & Row, 1987), p. 52.
4. See e.g. Rosemary Radford Ruether, *New Woman, New Earth: Sexist Ideologies and Human Liberation* (New York: Seabury, 1975), p. 46; James Nelson, *Embodiment: An Approach to Sexuality and Christian Theology* (Minneapolis, MN: Augsburg, 1978), p. 46, and *The Intimate Connection: Male Sexuality, Masculine Spirituality* (London: SPCK, 1992), pp. 21–2; Hannah Ward, 'The Lion in the Marble', in Linda Hurcombe (ed.), *Sex and God: Some Varieties of Women's Religious Experience* (New York and London: Routledge & Kegan Paul, 1987), pp. 50–1; etc. The theme is common in feminist analysis.

5. Uta Ranke-Heinemann, *Eunuchs for the Kingdom of Heaven: The Catholic Church and Sexuality*. Translated from the German (Harmondsworth: Penguin Books, 1992), p. 173.
6. Daphne Hampson, *Theology and Feminism* (Oxford: Blackwell, 1990), p. 17.
7. Nelson, *Intimate Connection*, p. 63.
8. ibid.
9. Peter Brown, *The Body and Society: Men, Women and Sexual Renunciation in Early Christianity* (London: Faber & Faber, 1990), p. 10.
10. Thomas Aquinas, *Summa Theologiae* I. 92.1. Quoted from: A Concise Translation edited by Timothy McDermott (London, Eyre & Spottiswoode, 1991), p. 143.
11. Brown, p. 34.
12. Sheila Briggs, 'Sexual Justice and the "Righteousness of God"' in Hurcombe, *op. cit.*, p. 254.
13. John Marshall, 'Sex and Christian Loving' in John Marshall (ed.), *The Future of Christian Marriage* (London: Chapman, 1969), p. 49.
14. See Adrian Thatcher, 'Christian Theism and the Concept of a Person' in Arthur Peacocke and Grant Gillett (eds), *Persons and Personality: A Contemporary Inquiry* (Oxford: Blackwell, 1987).
15. Elaine Storkey, 'Sex and Sexuality in the Church' in Monica Furlong (ed.), *Mirror to the Church: Reflections on Sexism* (London: SPCK, 1988), p. 52.
16. The arguments are well set out by Grace Jantzen, *God's World, God's Body* (London: Darton, Longman & Todd, 1984), ch. 1.
17. A. Kosnik, et al. (eds), *Human Sexuality: New Directions in Catholic Thought* (London: Search Press, 1977), p. 3.
18. Rosemary Radford Ruether, *Women-Church: Theology and Practice of Feminist Liturgical Communities* (San Francisco: Harper & Row, 1985), p. 170.
19. Augustine, *City of God*, (Harmondsworth: Penguin Classics, 1984), Book 14, especially ch. 23, p. 585.
20. Tyndale, *The Obedience of a Christian Man, Works*, (PS), i, p. 171: quoted in D. Sherwin Bailey, *The Man–Woman Relation in Christian Thought* (London: Longman, 1959), p. 200.
21. Bailey, p. 201.
22. Jacques Rossiaud, *Medieval Prostitution* (Oxford: Blackwell, 1988), p. 76.
23. Marina Warner, *Alone of All Her Sex* (London: Weidenfeld & Nicholson, 1976), p. 57.
24. See above, p. 2, and Bryan S. Turner, *The Body and Society* (Oxford: Blackwell, 1984), p. 115.
25. ibid p. 116.
26. Samuel Smiles, 'Over brain-work' in John Murray, *Life and Labour; or Characteristics of Industry, Culture and Genius* (London: 2nd edn 1910), p. 390.
27. ibid.
28. Turner, p. 116.
29. John Ruskin, *Sesame and Lilies* (1865). See J. M. Golby (ed.), *Culture and Society in Britain, 1850–1890* (Oxford: Oxford University Press, 1986), *p. 118*.
30. ibid.

31. ibid. p. 120.
32. See below, ch. 9.
33. See below, especially ch. 9. I am grateful to Elizabeth Stuart for pointing out the connections between dualism and contemporary discussions about orientation.
34. Susan Dowell, *They Two Shall Be One: Monogamy in History and Religion* (London: Collins/Flame, 1990), p. xv.
35. Mary Hunt, 'Friends in Deed', in Hurcombe, p. 51.
36. Susan Parsons, 'Feminist Reflections on Embodiment and Sexuality', *Studies in Christian Ethics*, 4.2 (1991), p. 17. And see Susan Griffin, *Woman and Nature: The Roaring Inside Her* (New York: Harper & Row, 1978), pp. xvi, 188–91; Paula Cooey, in Cooey, et al., pp. 326–7.
37. Parsons, p. 17.
38. ibid. p.19.
39. Nelson, *Embodiment*, ch. 3.
40. Turner, p. 180.
41. Herbert W. Richardson, *Nun, Witch, Playmate: The Americanization of Sex* (New York: Harper & Row, 1974), p. 20. I am indebted to Richardson here for his marshalling together of the terms rationalization, segmentation, genitalization and renunciation in the context of male attitudes to sexuality.
42. Paul Tillich, *The Courage To Be* (London and Glasgow: Collins/Fontana, 1962), p. 71.
43. ibid.
44. 'Homophobia, Heterosexism and Pastoral Practice' in Jeannine Gramick, *Homosexuality in the Priesthood and the Religious Life* (New York: Crossroad, 1989), p. 29; Nelson, *The Intimate Connection*, p. 34.
45. Gareth Jones, 'God's Passionate Embrace: Notes for a Christian Understanding of Sexuality', *Studies in Christian Ethics*, 5, no. 2 (1992), pp. 32–3.
46. ibid. p. 33.
47. Andrew Greeley, *Love as Play* (Chicago: Thomas More Press, 1975), p. 10.
48. Gordon Kendal, 'Christian Spontaneity and the Clarification of Pleasure', *Scottish Journal of Theology*, xxxv, no. 1 (1982), pp. 59–70.
49. John Macquarrie, *In Search of Humanity* (London: SCM Press, 1982), p. 187.
50. ibid. p. 189.
51. See below, ch. 12.
52. Teilhard de Chardin, *Hymn of the Universe* (London: Collins/Fontana, 1970), p. 64.
53. Nelson, *The Intimate Connection*, p. 66.
54. Timothy Radcliffe OP, 'Paul and Sexual Identity: 1 Corinthians 11.2–16' in Janet Martin Soskice (ed.), *After Eve: Women, Theology and the Christian Tradition* (London: Collins/Marshall Pickering, 1990), pp. 62–3.
55. Parsons, p. 26 (my emphasis).
56. Una Kroll, 'A Womb-centred Life' in Hurcombe, p. 94.
57. ibid., p. 98. See also Carol Ochs, *Women and Spirituality* (Totowa, NJ: Rowman & Allanheld, 1983); Margaret Hebblethwaite, *Motherhood and God* (London: Geoffrey Chapman, 1984).

58. Kroll, p. 100.
59. Dowell, p. 185.
60. Nelson, *The Intimate Connection*, p. 37.
61. ibid., p. 96 (author's emphasis).
62. Giles Milhaven, 'A Medieval Lesson on Bodily Knowing: Women's Experience and Men's Thought', *Journal of the American Academy of Religion,* lvii, no. 2 (Summer 1989), p. 346.
63. ibid., p. 347.
64. ibid., pp. 365–6.
65. ibid., p. 360.
66. ibid., p. 363.
67. Thatcher, pp. 137–8.

CHAPTER 4

Sex and Love

In this chapter the question is posed: what is love, and how is it to be approached? Heeding warnings about beginning with abstract concepts and filling them with male experience, I shall answer this question with some historical and psychological observations about courtly and romantic love. These are used to demonstrate a current need for a relational understanding of persons and of love. The heritage of trinitarian faith is then explored. This faith enables us to recover an understanding of the person, of relations between persons, of love, and of God, all of which are post-patriarchal and fully mutual. The divine Persons of God are shown to transcend gender distinctions. The revelation of love which is manifest in the gift and death of Christ and kindled by the Spirit, is the foundation of Christian sexual theology. It addresses, redemptively, worn-out notions of 'person' and 'love'. The Christian doctrine of atonement is taken to be the attempt to show how divine self-giving love or agape has been revealed to us. Yet the practice of unreciprocated self-giving is oppressive. Agape must always be balanced with the other forms of love.

Sexuality

The sexuality of women and men drives them out of themselves to seek relationship with others. Sexuality is 'the way of being in, and relating to, the world as a *male* or *female* person'. It is 'the mode or manner by which humans experience and express the incompleteness of their individualities as well as their relatedness to each other as male and female'.[1] Sexuality is what provides a 'sexual atmosphere'

48

whenever human beings meet.[2] Sexuality, then, overcomes any tendency to remain enclosed, alone, uninvolved or unrelated. It is that dimension of our being which calls people 'to a clearer recognition of their relational nature, of their absolute need to reach out and embrace others to achieve personal fulfilment'.[3]

Our sexuality speaks a powerful message to ourselves as well as to others. It tells us we are incomplete and we are made for relatedness. We are made for communion, not for isolation. Theologically, sexuality is 'God's ingenious way of calling us into communion with others'.[4] Having a sexuality is part of the meaning of being made in the image of God: we are made for relationship and God's nature is Relationship. The fabric of this relationship, between the divine Persons in the Trinity, and potentially between human persons, is love.

Courtly and romantic love

Confident, perhaps, of a self-evident link between sex and love, we may think that this link has always existed. Such an assumption is very misleading. The explicit association of sex with love begins with the ideal of 'courtly love' which developed in Languedoc and spread more widely throughout central Europe in the eleventh and twelfth centuries. Courtly love became 'a dominant model of much medieval literature', summarized recently by B. S. Turner as 'a tradition of sexual passion ... associated with a class of landless, unattached knights for whom the lady of the castle represented an ideal, if distant object of their love'.[5] 'The main themes of courtly love poetry', he continues, were 'humility, courtesy, adultery and the religion of love.'

It is now commonly believed that this strange episode in European history was responsible for a new self-expression which articulated male sexual desire and ennobled it, together with the pain of its unfulfilment. Courtly love was adulterous, at least in intent. It expressed discontent with traditional marriage and sought excitement and danger in challenging fundamental notions of moral, social and ecclesiastical order. It was sexist, and since the women desired were generally unavailable and unobtainable, the desiring males typically wove a web of chivalry, courtesy and general deference in their futile attempts to secure their amorous aims. Yet despite its many imperfections, courtly love became 'purified' and 'Christianized' during the Renaissance period and incorporated as a novel and transforming element into monogamous marriage.[6]

The historical contribution of courtly love to the understanding of relationships in the West can hardly be overestimated, yet little is known or understood about it. Part of *our* problem in understanding courtly love may be our difficulty in appreciating what love was taken to be, prior to early Renaissance times. This problem confronted the great literary scholar C. S. Lewis who observed 'There can be no mistake about the novelty of romantic love, our only difficulty is *to imagine in all its barrenness the mental world that existed before its coming.*. . .'.[7]

We do in fact possess some pointers to some of the likely causes of this barrenness. From the time of Augustine the only justification for having sex was the intention or hope of generating a child.[8] The pleasure and loss of control associated with it was a reminder of the fall of the human race and was to be avoided as far as possible. The biblical celebration of love-making in the Song of Songs had long been buried by layer after layer of spiritual and allegorical interpretation (from which even now it has not fully recovered). The minute questioning of Christians about sexual matters in the confessional was an attempt to enforce ecclesiastical control both of sexual behaviour and the expectations to be derived from it. Clerical celibacy further devalued sexual love. These factors, together with the maintenance of dualistic and misogynistic attitudes described in the previous chapter, make the apparent death of romance and passion easier to understand.

Romantic marriage

Courtly love gives rise to a new sense of individual 'self-consciousness' which articulates feelings of desire and their frustration. By the time of Shakespeare's plays, sex and love, and the difference between them, are explored as comic and tragic themes. In the seventeenth century, Anglicans introduce the 'mutual society' of the partners as one of the purposes of marriage, while Puritans and Quakers become the first Christians to arrive at what came to be called 'romantic marriage'. Romantic marriage was the attempt to combine the excitement and danger of romance with marriage as an institution. Nonconformist Christianity can be credited with challenging and destroying 'the age-old patriarchal subordination of the female to the male' and the unassailable conviction that the purpose of marriage was the avoidance of fornication and the production of children.

> Romantic marriage makes the primary purpose of marriage the love of the husband and the wife for each other, subordinating their intention to have children or to gain economic security to this end. Romantic lovers marry so that they may be, first and

foremost, husband and wife – not so that they may be, first and foremost, father and mother. The primary purpose of their marriage is to facilitate their enjoying an ever-growing intimacy with each other, and this alone is sufficient reason for them to marry.[9]

We have yet to investigate the historical meanings of marriage and the extent to which marriage was observed at all among working-class people. It is important for the present to notice that the association of sex with love, and marriage with romance, was a development. It was a process which historically occurred. Also, the assumption of equality between partners and loving intimacy as itself a justification for marriage were once new and remarkable developments. 'Romanticism' as a period affecting all the arts in the nineteenth century (including theology and philosophy) further strengthened emphases on the expression of feeling (however ambiguous) and on the heroic (and tragic) potential of individuals who, in the search for self-fulfilment would leave no convention undefied.

Two modern myths

The themes of courtly and romantic love demand a separate book. They are included here to suggest that romantic love is associated with radical Christianity and that romantic love has become over-dominant in advanced western societies. The integration of sex and love, a profound achievement, becomes in promiscuity the conscious exclusion of love from sex, with none of the attendant and settled responsibilities which being-in-relation necessarily includes. For some the defiance of sexual convention itself became a convention which, under the weight of its own boredom, sought more extreme pleasure-seeking strategies. Romantic love has been crushed almost to death under the cultural weight that has been placed upon it. A central idea in a recent study on adultery and its causes was 'the Myth of Me', a set of unquestioned cultural assumptions which values individuality, self-actualization, the right to happiness and the satisfaction of sexual need as 'an imperative that had to be pursued'[10] irrespective of the consequences of pursuing these goals on the primary relationship. A pervasive mind-set expects the replacement of obsolescent partners as it does the replacement of obsolescent Cadillacs or microwave ovens.

Recent empirical studies of perceptions of love among American undergraduates led to a useful theory that love for a partner might be composed of three elements.[11] The first is *intimacy*; the second is *passion* ('a state of intense longing for union with another'[12]), and the third is *commitment*, understood both as the decision to love another person, and to maintain that love. 'Romantic love' is a combination of intimacy and passion, but without commitment. 'Companionate love' is 'a blend of the intimacy and decision/commitment components of love' – typically in marriages in which the physical attraction has 'died down': while 'consummate love' is the abiding combination of intimacy, passion and commitment in a long-term relationship. The author concludes: 'A warm, companionable, central relationship is, for most people, a crucial ingredient of a happy and fulfilling life – but love alone will not sustain it.'[13] But it is romantic love, 'the Western myth of romantic love', which does not deliver. It creates false expectations that the initial conditions of a relationship can be sustained; it does not allow for the growth of either party, and it does not prepare for the personal and emotional adjustments which the achievement of 'companionate love' requires.

A good case can be made for saying that western societies need an understanding of love between persons which acknowledges and incorporates romantic love while drawing on theological and spiritual resources which nurture commitment and responsibility. At this point Christian faith speaks incisively. Its trinitarian understanding of God provides a vision of what persons and relations can be when they are united in and by love. The recovery of the doctrine of the Trinity in feminist and systematic theology is the most exciting theological accomplishment of recent years. It has been driven by a socio-cultural need for new symbols of understanding which transcend the individualizing of the human being, the romanticizing of love and the continued dominance of patriarchy in relationships. The time has now come to appropriate the renewed trinitarian vision of God as the basis of a renewed Christian sexual ethic of relations between persons.

Persons – divine and human

There is no space here to describe the development of the doctrine of the Trinity.[14] As the Church sought to hold together belief in one God with belief in the divinity of Father, Son and Spirit, the term 'Person' or *persona* became increasingly central to the task. The gender-specific character of the names of the Persons is discussed presently. This development begins a tradition of thinking which concludes with a variety of modern concepts of the person.[15] Since

God is the creator and we are God's creatures, there is general agreement in the tradition both that the term 'person' has different meanings when used of God and human beings, and that there is sufficient in common between the being of God and human being for the different meanings of 'person' to overlap. This overlapping of meanings is no elaborate word-play, facilitated by the elusiveness of the term. It is based on the overlapping of the being or nature of God with the being or nature of people, created in God's image. There is already a finite reflection of the being of God in human beings and relationships. Human persons in loving relationships finitely reflect, to some degree, those loving relationships of the Persons of the Trinity. But human relationships are precarious. In Christian life the triune God bestows, redeems and sanctifies human personal life, and human life exults in the divine shaping and empowerment which it receives.

The Triune God is 'worshipped and adored as a transcendent Fullness of Personal Being, an ineffable Communion of Persons, in whom the Persons are who they are in their mutual . . . relations with one another in one and the same divine Being'.[16] Part of the problem in grasping the profundity of the trinitarian vision of God is due not to its intrinsic intellectual difficulty, but to the simple neglect it has received in the teaching of the faith, and to the all-pervasive preference in western culture to think of persons as isolated individuals rather than as beings-in-relationship. God's being 'transcends' human being in that God is creator, while we are creatures. All human life is summoned to share in the life of God. The 'Fullness' of God's 'Personal Being' is intended to suggest that God's being cannot adequately be spoken of as something or someone which is purely an individual. For the fullness of God's being to be grasped (insofar as creatures can begin to grasp it), it is necessary to understand that being as *relational*. There are relations in God, as well as relations between God and the world, the Church, etc. These relations are sometimes called 'internal' and 'external' relations. The internal relations in God constitute God's loving nature. They 'overflow' in bringing about other beings who are 'caught up' in this primal source of all life. In particular, loving human relations share in this holy, unfathomable, divine nature.

When the term 'Person' is used of Father, Son and Spirit, it is helpful to keep three essential ideas firmly in view. First, each Person is a distinct divine subject. Second, each Person, although separate from the others, does not break the single divine unity which God is, but contributes to it. And, third, each of the Persons is constituted by its relation to the others. Together they are a 'Communion of Persons'. These features of the 'divine life', albeit from our fumbling human perspective, are features also, at least potentially, of *human* relationships. In loving human relationships each person, while remaining an individual, contributes to the being of the other while the other contributes to him or her in a loving communion of togetherness and separateness.

In summary we may say that three particular characteristics of the trinitarian vision of God which transform sexual theology are *interdependence, interrelation* and *communion*. The Father can only be Father if there is a Son to whom he can be Father. So being a Father is being a Person-in-relation, the Father in relation to the Son. Likewise there can be no Son without the Son being Son of the Father. So being a Son is also being a Person-in-relation, the Son in relation to the Father. Without the Father there would be no Son. Relationality is what makes each Person who they are in communion with the others. Within God, though, the temporal relation implied by the dependence of children on parents in human life is transcended. The Father and the Son are also co-equal and co-eternal; the names 'Father' and 'Son' derive from the most positive experience of parent–children relationships it is possible to imagine, and this experience is a multi-dimensional relationship of love involving giving and receiving, mutuality and reciprocity between the Persons. How is the third Person of the Spirit to be understood within the interrelatedness of the Trinity?

Spirit as shared love

According to one analogy, drawn from human love, the Father may be regarded as Lover, the Son as the Beloved, and the Spirit as the bond of mutual love, the *vinculum amoris* which exists between them. But however convenient this analogy may be in exploring the phenomenology of human love, it has little application in trinitarian thought, because the existence of a bond between two people is quite different from the existence of a third person. Augustine, who plays with the analogy, uses it only incidentally.[17] Fortunately a more adequate analogy, relying still on human love, can be found.

The medieval theologian Richard of St Victor (d. 1173) utilized the insight drawn from human personal relationships that distinguishes between mutuality and sharing. Beyond the mutuality which consists in a committed relationship between two human persons is the desire to share their joint love more widely: 'When I love another person and that love is reciprocated, I also want to share my love with a third person. The joy and the delight which I have in the Beloved has a tendency to overflow, so that I want to share my joy with a third person.'[18] This is a profound insight to which we shall return when developing an incarnate theology of marriage which has as its signature, so to speak, the expression of the partners' love in a wider sharing which may, though it need not, result in the creation of children.

Richard is convinced that love between persons cannot be perfected unless it is shared more widely, and his subtle argument suggests that since God's love is a perfect love, it is a logical requirement that there should be at least three Persons in the Trinity.

> A great accumulation of joy and pleasure builds up for anyone who gives and receives love in fellowship with another. From this, therefore, we clearly gather that the supreme level of that generosity would have no place in Divinity if a third person were lacking in that plurality of persons ... Shared love is properly said to exist when a third person is loved by two persons harmoniously and in community, and the affection of the two persons is fused into one affection by the flame of love for the third.[19]

I do not know whether any sense can be made of the Trinity in an advanced secular society, nor even whether many Christians will find these word-sketches convincing. What is usually called the 'social model' of the Trinity (because it emphazes the plurality of persons) is associated more with Orthodox Christianity than with Roman Catholicism or Protestantism. But the neglect of the Trinity in the West has profoundly impoverished Christian spirituality and led to the loss of the priceless insight that God in Godself is a community of love. God's Being *just is* the relationships of personal mutuality and sharing which together constitute the Divine Life. If nothing else is salvaged from the formulae of trinitarian doctrine, the simple Christian claim that God is a community of persons-in-relation, or just Loving Relationships, can lie at the root of an adequate theology of sex. For it is in the quality of our relationships that we give and receive love, and in our giving and receiving of love that we are drawn into the single Divine Life.

God and her gender

Feminist theologians have been quick to see the 'transforming possibilities' of trinitarian language in overcoming patriarchal concepts of

God, and so of relationship.[20] They have thought that the Trinity, 'as final and perfect sociality, embodies those qualities of mutuality, reciprocity, co-operation, unity, peace in genuine diversity that are feminist ideals and goals derived from the inclusivity of the gospel message'. It 'provides women with an image and concept of God that entails qualities that make God truly worthy of imitation, worthy of the call to radical discipleship . . .'.[21] What, then, is to be made of the difficulty that Father and Son are masculine in gender in the light of the observation that 'the overwhelming weight of the demeaning and destructive historical uses and effects of the father symbol suggest that this primary symbol of God may be irretrievable for many women today'?[22]

The problem here is not that 'Father' and 'Son' are, in earthly life, male, but that in a patriarchal church a male priesthood derives ideological legitimation from a male god. Given the obvious association of Father and Son with the male sex, a case has been made, 'purely by elimination, for referring to the Holy Spirit in feminine terms'.[23] Several assumptions operate here. God is thought to transcend the male/female distinction. Yet clearly 'Father' and 'Son' are masculine terms. It is then thought to follow that, in order to redress the male imbalance, the Spirit must be feminine. The association of the Spirit with creation, conception, nurture, with women and love for children, together with the Old Testament idea of Wisdom who was always personified as a woman,[24] all provide support for this view. However, it is a misleading case to put forward because it concedes the maleness of Father and Son. There is a stronger argument about the gender of the divine Persons yet to be deployed.

A recent study of the Cappadocian Fathers of the fourth century shows that, in their thought, the divine is neither male nor female.[25] Human language about God can do little more than suggest holy hints about the transcendent reality of God, as the Cappadocian Fathers acknowledged. Yet within that limited scope of human thinking about God, Gregory of Nyssa was able to countenance the application of the term 'mother' to the Person of the Father, because, as he says, 'Both terms mean the same, because the divine is neither male nor female.'[26] He argues that gender in God is unthinkable, since in humankind it is a purely temporary feature, belonging to the body but not the soul. 'How could such a thing be contemplated in the divinity', he continues, 'when it does not remain intact permanently for us human beings either?'

We may not want to follow him in his body/soul dualism, but the conviction that gender is a temporary human characteristic led the Cappadocians also to affirm that women and men alike have a common nature and also a common function, namely to lead a Christ-like life. Interestingly, Gregory Nazianzen held that the maleness of the human Jesus was irrelevant to his incarnate state.[27] In assuming a human nature, the Son of God assumed something that is in any case female *and* male. In our terms, we can say that each of the divine Persons, like the human nature which one of them assumes, is *androgynous*, that is, they bring together the 'personality characteristics traditionally or conventionally thought of as masculine with those thought of as feminine so that such characteristics are creatively present in the same individual'.[28] The symbol 'father' can hardly be unaffected by the wild assumptions about how conception happened, (above, pp.31-2) and is reclaimed precisely as its relational character, anchored in human experience between parents and children, is explored and its male signification ignored.

Human persons-in-relation

The renewed understanding of the Trinity in theology has been aided by the parallel recovery of the social character of the person in modern philosophy. This is a movement in philosophy which registers alarm about the modern 'individualization' of the person, and seeks to replace this with a more adequate social or 'communitarian' understanding of the person as a person-in-relation. Once the person is understood as an autonomous, independent, self-assertive human being, the social character of personal being is overlooked and the capacity for loving being-in-relationship is at best problematic. The recovery of the social character of persons emphasizes that persons are inevitably persons-in-relationship. Personal being always consists of two poles, individuality and sociality taken together. But this recovery of the 'social pole' of human personhood *merely confirms* the account of Persons which is central to the Christian doctrine of God. Individuality and sociality are combined within the unity of holy love.

The theme of a person-in-relation, traceable to John Macmurray,[29] is now considerably better known. It conveys the sense that 'I', from my conception onwards, am always in relation-with-others, and it is through the history of my interaction with others that 'I' become whatever I am. I receive my existence from others; I am with others; sometimes I am for others. Alistair McFadyen has provided an excellent Christian theological account of the social character of the person.[30] The structure of personal existence in the image of the triune God, is rightly said to be one where openness and response to others and to God are built in. 'Persons are orientated upon themselves (centred) by moving towards the reality of others ... [They] are what they are for others or, rather, the way in which they are for others.'[31] A relational approach to the human being causes the doctrine of human creation in the image of God to be rewritten.

McFadyen is not the first writer to show that the image of God is a matter of being-in-relation rather than being simply an individual,[32] but his analysis extends further than any other because he has a social concept of a person to start with. 'If, however, the God whom human being images is not a simple, single individual with certain internal attributes, but is more like a community of Persons, then it would seem more adequate to conceive of the image in relational terms.'[33] The themes that 'we live in a relational matrix with one another in the world (regardless of what we may think about it or how we may feel about it)', and that 'we have a common response/ ability to live in mutual relation'[34] command unanimous assent within feminist theology. Carter Heyward helpfully claims that 'To speak of the erotic or of God is to speak of *power in right relation*'[35]. It is in right relation with friends, lovers, husbands and wives, partners and spouses, that love is shared, justice is done and God is acknowledged and adored. Not all right relations, of course, are erotic. Right relations are required throughout the social world.

At-one-ment

Christians claim that 'God is love' (1 John 4.8, 16). God is the answer to the question with which this chapter began. Christian faith can show us what love is and through reflection on the personal triune God, what it is to be made in God's image. This understanding is no cerebral gloss, no second-order reflection on what has a dynamics of its own, no mere intellectual model. We can open ourselves to this love and experience it in our relationships as transforming grace. 'For the redemption of human individuality and sociality what is needed is not a model, but the communication of the energies of true relation and individuation from the Triune being of God.'[36] The central Christian doctrines of incarnation, atonement and trinity tell us what 'God is love' means. The previous chapter emphasized incarnation and the sacrament of communion; the present chapter has emphasized the Trinity because of the contribution to Christian sexual theology that it is able to give and because it is generally less understood than atonement. But there has been little mention of that other exemplification of divine love, the atonement, or process of 'at-one-ment' whereby God and humankind become at one through the life, death and resurrection of Jesus Christ. Something must be said about atonement now if the theological specifications for love-in-relationship are to be completed.

God and humankind have become at one through Christ because, in the life of Jesus, God's nature is embodied and enacted as self-giving, self-sacrificial love. Reflection upon the meaning of the death of Jesus on the cross has led Christians to affirm that 'God is the being who never defends himself. This is the primary quality which distinguishes the divine from the human . . .'. The triune God is symbolically declared by Jesus through his death to be at one with all oppressed, sinful and victimized people. But some interpretations of the doctrine of at-one-ment have been catastrophic for Christian theology. They have depicted it as an internal transaction within God whereby God the Father unjustly punishes God the Son instead of justly punishing the rest of us, thereby freeing us from our sins. Such a doctrine is immoral and grotesque. Some of the personal and psychological consequences of sacrificial theories of atonement, particularly for women, have been bizarre. Women have been encouraged to derive from their devotion to Christ a heightened sense of themselves as martyrs, scapegoats, and victims of violence, [37] confirming their subordinate status and eclipsing any sense of personal self-worth. But at-one-ment need not be viewed like this at all. God's openness and vulnerability in the crucified Christ is the extent of the depth of identity with sinners and victims. This is how at-one-ment happens. This supreme act of self-giving initiates and invites a response, a response of self-surrender in faith. The love which is expressed in the coming of Jesus, in his life, work and teaching, and especially enacted in his death is called *agape*.

The forms of love

A characteristic of divine agape is that it does *not* depend on mutuality or response, but, unlike human love, is maintained irrespective of the preparedness of the beloved to receive it. That is why St Paul stresses that 'Christ died for us while we were yet sinners', and observes, 'and that is God's proof of his love towards us' (Romans 5.8). All Christians agree they are recipients of a divine love which is entirely unmerited. While the term 'agape' is used for divine love, it is broader and can encompass other human forms of love as well.[38] The problem is that the very centrality of agape in the Christian faith has led to an acute imbalance in the understanding of love. Sexual theology must integrate all the forms of love in its account of loving relationships.

Agape, just because it is the centre of Christian faith, is likely to become distorted. It can become a tool of blackmail in the hands of dominant individuals or groups, demanding of the subservient that they sacrifice yet more. It has provided an 'ideological legitimization of powerlessness', and it has elevated the practice of self-sacrifice so that it becomes 'an end in itself, rather than a means to the creation of some other good that might justify it.'[39] *Filial* love, or friendship, just because it may not involve self-sacrifice or even hardship, is scarcely regarded as love at all and is generally emptied of spiritual significance. Within the framework of patriarchal dualism the meaning of *erotic* love is conveniently eclipsed by being unfavourably contrasted with agape which is higher, spiritual and non-sexual. Fortunately a restoration of balance in the Christian theology of love is taking place. Friendship is being restored as a biblical model for both divine and human love with remarkable ethical consequences (which will be explored in chapter 11). 'Friendship with God' is an expression of Christian life in which, as the divine Friend, 'God confirms us, God confronts us, God celebrates us'.[40] The love which is desire or eros and which lies at the root of all human inquiry, art and knowledge, as well as the desire to love and be loved by another human being, is being rightly rehabilitated as a form of human love in the image of the divine. In desiring us and our response, God's love is shown as a blend of agape and eros together.[41]

Enough has been indicated in this chapter, I hope, of the Christian vision of love, of persons, of relationships, and of a God of relationships who becomes incarnate in our relationships with others. But relationships generally are not as they have been described. Too often they are exploitative, oppressive and devalued. And that is because they are distorted by sin. But 'sin', like 'love', is also a distorted term which generates many misconceptions. 'Sex and sin' is the topic of the next chapter.

Notes

1. A. Kosnik, et al. (eds), *Human Sexuality: New Directions in Catholic Thought* (London: Search Press, 1977), p. 82; James B. Nelson, *Embodiment: An Approach to Sexuality and Christian Theology* (Minneapolis, MN: Augsburg, 1978), p. 104.
2. Kosnik, p. 85.
3. ibid.
4. Nelson, *Embodiment*; Kosnik, op.cit.
5. Bryan S. Turner, *The Body and Society* (Oxford: Blackwell, 1984), p. 128. See C. S. Lewis, *The Allegory of Love: A Study in Medieval Tradition* (Oxford: Oxford University Press, 1936), ch. 1; Susan Dowell, *They Two*

Shall Be One: Monogamy in History and Religion (London: Collins/Flame, 1990), ch. 4.

6. Dowell, p. 108.

7. Lewis, p. 4, quoted in Dowell, p. 106. The twelfth century is referred to here. 'Romantic' should not suggest the later 'romantic movement'.

8. See e.g. Gareth Moore, *The Body in Context: Sex and Catholicism* (London: SCM Press, 1992), p. 64.

9. Herbert W. Richardson, *Nun, Witch, Playmate: The Americanization of Sex* (New York: Harper & Row, 1971), p. 68.

10. Annette Lawson, *Adultery: An Analysis of Love and Betrayal* (Oxford: Blackwell, 1989), p. 106; see also pp. 25–6 and ch. 5.

11. R. J. Sternberg, 'Triangulating Love' in R. J. Sternberg and M. L. Barnes (eds), *The Psychology of Love* (New Haven: Yale University Press, 1988) cit. Maryon Tysoe, *Love Isn't Quite Enough: The Psychology of Male-Female Relationships* (London: Harper/Collins Fontana, 1992), pp. 20–5.

12. E. Hatfield, 'Passionate and Companionate Love' in Sternberg and Barnes, op. cit., p. 193.

13. Tysoe, p. 202.

14. See e.g. Leonardo Boff, *Trinity and Society* (Tunbridge Wells: Burns & Oates/Search Press, 1988), chs 1–3; Ninian Smart and Steven Konstantine, *Christian Systematic Theology in a World Context* (London: Marshall Pickering, 1991), pp. 149–62; Edmund Hill, *The Mystery of the Trinity* (London: Geoffrey Chapman, 1985), ch. 2.

15. Adrian Thatcher, *Truly a Person, Truly God* (London: SPCK, 1990), pp. 6–9.

16. Thomas Torrance, 'The Soul and Person in Theological Perspective' in S. Sutherland and T. Roberts (eds), *Religion, Reason and the Self* (Cardiff: University of Wales Press, 1989), p. 115.

17. Leonard Hodgson, *The Doctrine of the Trinity* (Digswell Place: Nisbet, 1964), p. 148.

18. John O'Donnell's summary of Richard's argument in *De Trinitate*, ch. 11. See John O'Donnell, 'The Trinity as Divine Community: A Critical Reflection on Recent Developments', *Gregorianum* 69, no. 1 (1988); see also Smart and Konstantine, *op. cit.*, p. 173.

19. *De Trinitate*, ch. 18, in Grover A. Zinn (tr.), *Classics of Western Spirituality* (London: SPCK, 1979), p. 391.

20. Melanie May, 'Conversations on Language and Imagery of God', *Union Seminary Quarterly Review*, 40.3 (1985), p. 18.

21. Anne Carr, *Transforming Grace: Christian Tradition and Women's Experience* (San Francisco: Harper & Row, 1988), pp. 156–7.

22. ibid., p. 141.

23. Alwyn Marriage, *Life-Giving Spirit: Responding to the Feminine in God* (London: SPCK, 1989), p. 54.

24. ibid., p. 68.

25. Verna E. F. Harrison, 'Male and Female in Cappadocian Theology', *Journal of Theological Studies*, 41.2 (October, 1990), pp. 441–71.

26. *Cant.* 7; ibid., p. 441.

27. Harrison, pp. 458, 465.

28. Nelson, *Embodiment* p. 97.

29. John Macmurray, *Persons in Relation* (London: Faber & Faber, 1961).
30. Alistair I. McFadyen, *The Call to Personhood: A Christian Theory of the Individual in Social Relationships* (Cambridge: Cambridge University Press, 1990).
31. ibid., p. 40.
32. See Emil Brunner, *The Christian Doctrine of Creation and Redemption, Dogmatics*, Vol. 2 (London: Lutterworth Press, 1962), pp. 60–6; and the far-sighted Derrick Sherwin Bailey, *The Man–Woman Relation in Christian Thought* (London: Longman, 1959), p. 271.
33. McFadyen, p. 31.
34. Carter Heyward, *Touching our Strength: The Erotic as Power and the Love of God* (San Francisco: Harper & Row, 1989), p. 16.
35. ibid., p. 3, and see below, ch. 11.
36. Alistair McFadyen, 'The Trinity and Human Individuality: The Conditions for Relevance', *Theology*, xcv, 763 (January/February 1992), p. 13.
37. Mary Grey, *Redeeming the Dream: Feminism, Redemption and Christian Tradition* (London: SPCK, 1989), pp. 118–9, and ch. 7 *passim*.
38. Nelson, *Embodiment* pp. 111–13.
39. Linell Cady, 'A Feminist Christian Vision' in P. Cooey, S. A. Farmer, M. E. Ross (eds), *Embodied Love: Sensuality and Relationship as Feminist Values* (New York: Harper & Row, 1987), p. 140.
40. James Nelson, *The Intimate Connection: Male Sexuality, Masculine Spirituality* (London: SPCK, 1992), p. 65; Sallie McFague, *Metaphorical Theology* (London: SCM Press, 1983), p. 177.
41. Paul Avis, *Eros and the Sacred* (London: SPCK, 1989), ch. 15, 'Eros in God?'.

CHAPTER 5

Sex and Sin

Building on the analyses of love and of relationships in the previous chapter, sin will be identified as the negative, distorting factor which impairs relationships between people and shuts them off from divine grace. First, some justification for continuing to talk of sin *at all*, in the light of general incredulity about such talk outside the church, is offered. Second, sexual sin is defined by five basic concepts: *failure to live in love; selfishness; possessiveness; lust; and dis-esteem.* But the principal justification for retaining talk of sin is that it is a condition which afflicts not simply personal relationships, but the historical, social and cultural contexts within which these relationships are set. This condition is also described.

Sin and judgement

Frequent condemnation of sexual sin has been an essential routine within a patriarchal framework. There are two reasons only why the Church or any Christian should still speak out about sexual sin. First, where there is sin (whether sexual or not), someone is sinned against, and so is a victim. If the Church is faithful to Christ, it will stand with victims, for Christ was himself a victim of human sinfulness. Second, if a person commits sin he demeans himself because his action cannot be a route to wholeness, to human 'flourishing', or to the touch of the divine Spirit. That is why Paul said 'all alike have sinned, and are deprived of the divine glory' (Romans 3.23). Sin inhibits our attaining that full potential God wills for us.

Sexual sins have been grossly overemphasized in the Church, and the impression has been given, not undeservedly, that Christians who decry them lead blameless lives. This is odious hypocrisy, as Jesus pointed out (Matthew 5.20, 28). The Church's emphasis on sexual sin derives from its past power over people's lives. The more people are told that their sexuality, or sexual orientation, or sexual desire, is wrong, and they believe this, the more is control exercised over them, and in areas most intimate, personal and central to their lives.[1] Concentration on sexual sins has also deflected critical attention from other attitudes and practices which biblical Christianity regards as equally sinful, such as 'ruthless greed' (Colossians 3.5), 'fraud, indecency, envy, slander, arrogance and folly' (Mark 7.22). Perhaps the perceived emphasis on personal sins, together with an inadequate theology of sex is the greatest barrier to re-establishing the credibility of the faith among ex-Christian, post-Christian and nominally-Christian people.

Human beings have a propensity to sin, and because they are sexual beings, and because opportunities for sexual arousal and temptation are ubiquitous, there will always be sexual sins. But sin is not just something a person does. Liberation theology has taught us to see that sin is also an historical, social and cultural state in which one cannot fail to participate. Preoccupation with individual sins, 'trespasses' (real or imaginary), has led to the ignoring of sin as an historical reality. Rosemary Ruether has remarked:

> The privatizing and spiritualizing of salvation is the other side of the individualizing of sin. Sin is recognized only in individual acts, not in structural systems. One may be called to examine one's sinfulness in relation to self-abuse or personal unkindness to the neighbor, but not in terms of the vast collective systems of militarism, racism, poverty and sexism.[2]

This view accords well with the description of dualism as the ideology of patriarchy in chapter 3.

Sin has already been provisionally defined as a *failure to live in love*. We have already seen that persons are always persons-in-relation and that personal life is impossible without a network of relationships which constitute it. Only a few of the many relationships we play a part in will be sexual. Loving relationships between persons are marked by mutuality and reciprocity; a closer look at these terms will indicate how readily personal relationships are marked instead by sin. Mutuality is 'an ongoing process of maintaining a rhythm of give-and-take, take-and-give in social and sexual relations. Mutuality is grounded in a shared vulnerability, the capacity both to affect and be affected by one another.'³ It is 'a concept which includes a dynamic flow of passionate energy, capable of being nourished between persons, through sexual relationships or friendships of which sexuality is a dimension . . ., but also in other ways because it is the *fundamental creative and healing energy of existence'*.⁴ Reciprocity is mutual action which in personal relationships is motivated by loving response to the beloved. But relationships are too easily distorted. One partner may do all the giving; the other all the taking. A person may find the other is treating him or her as a convenience, perhaps a means to some selfish end. Shere Hite reports 'Perhaps many women don't really know what it feels like to be loved, since most women (84%) describe the men they live with as loving them in terms of needing them.'⁵ Many women in her research complained that 'men usually do not *love* women so much as *need* them'.⁶

Selfishness and self-love

Second, personal sin may be described as *selfishness*. There is a huge problem here. Some twentieth-century theological accounts of love have so emphasized the self-sacrificial nature of love, exemplified in the willingness of Christ to suffer, that self-sacrifice has become an end in itself, proof of unconditional devotion, irrespective of extreme circumstances where self-sacrifical love may be necessary. An understandable reaction to the overemphasis on selflessness is to emphasize the moral rightness of self-love. 'Self-love is utterly basic to the capacity for friendship. Indeed, self-love and love of the other are of one piece, indivisible.'⁷ For self-denial, now read self-affirmation. And did not Jesus say '"You must love your neighbour as your*self*"' (Mark 12.31)?

The concept of a person developed in chapter 4 enables us to move on from the problem of compatibility between self-love and self-denial because, in God and among ourselves, we exist as selves only as we are constituted and sustained by others. Indeed on the human level we are sometimes de-constituted and exploited by others. The self apart from others is an abstraction from relationships and another example of the cerebral thinking about ethics criticized in chapter 4. Since 'I' cannot extricate my 'self' from my relations with others, talk of self-love risks isolating 'me' from others (which is impossible), or turning my 'self' into an object so that 'I' am simultaneously subject and object of my own thoughts. This too is impossible. The mistake lies in regarding 'self-love' and 'other love' as somehow alternative poles for the 'I', and then making the further assumption that in the interests of balance both must be chosen. The problem for this type of thinking is that 'I' cannot be abstracted either from my thoughts and actions, or from other people as this convenient theory assumes.

Mutuality in relationships requires what has been called 'unselfing', that is, the willingness 'to risk the judgment and disequilibrium that transcending one's horizon entails' so that the beloved can be valued outside 'the distorting prism of one's own needs'.[8] 'Self-love' entails firming up the boundaries, not letting them go. For these reasons I think 'self-love' is in danger of collapsing into selfishness and is unsatisfactory in moral discourse. Writers who use it want to say that 'I' cannot have a mutual relationship with anyone without, say, a sense of confidence in my own worth, an ability to communicate, an acceptance of the person I have so far come to be, etc. This is surely right, and the lack of these qualities is often a key problem for pastoral practice. The experience of God's love has helpfully been described as our appropriation of the proclamation that the self has worth and value whatever the attitude taken to it by others or by itself.[9] This is what talk of self-love in Christian ethics is about, and it is confused because it is God's love for the self, not the self's love for itself, which is the self's empowerment.

This positive 'de-emphasis' on the concept of self is also a clear theme of feminist theology. Many feminist theologians and psychologists 'do not accept the concept of a personal "self" or "identity" apart from the relational matrix in which it is shaped'.[10] The very term 'self' contributes to that understanding of the person as an isolated individual removed from a personal and social context. The term 'identity' has a similar effect. 'I' am not 'identical' with anything, especially some inner essence. Rather when those others with whom I am in relationship are themselves identified, is it possible to identify 'me'.

The relational approach to persons enables us to manage without the category of self-love, and also to affirm without evasion the hard saying of Jesus, '"Anyone who wants to be a follower of mine must renounce self; he must take up his cross and follow me. Whoever wants to save his life will lose it, but whoever loses his life for my sake and for the gospel's will save it"' (Mark 8.34–5). Christ's command is to love God and our neighbour (Mark 12.29–31), and, in the fulfilment of this command, selfhood is acquired. Since love is necessarily expressed in relationships, it 'constitutes a person's identity as a self-transcending participation in the other'.[11] From a relational point of view, self-love must remain the tendency to put one's own interests first, to receive more than to give, to bring about advantage to the disadvantage of the other, and so on. And in this sense, self-love is at the expense of others, and may be regarded as sin. Sexually, self-love may be seen to be the experience of receiving love or of being-in-love for the sake of the experience itself. It is sex without responsibility or regard for the interests of the partner.

Possessiveness and lust

Third, personal sin is *possessiveness*. It brings the all-pervasive sense of private ownership into personal relationships. Because sexual relationships are, above all other relationships, expressed through our bodies, they provide the constant possibility of one or both partners regarding the other as a thing (instead of a person), and reducing him or her to an object. Patriarchal relationships assume the body of a wife is the possession of her husband, and possession is not confined to the legal rights of one partner and, until recently, the lack of these for the other. Possessions are there to be used, but 'to use another person is to violate his personality by making an object of him; and in violating the integrity of another, you violate your own'.[12] A person is treated as an object if her freedom to say 'no' is denied or impaired, or if the pleasure sought in sex is non-mutual. If a person's body alone is desired, apart from the person whose body it is, that person is treated as an object, and the mode of relation to her (or him) is possessiveness. This is likely to happen in the use of pornographic images for sexual gratification, and is the reason why pornography is itself sometimes regarded as a symbol for the oppression of women by patriarchal attitudes.

The contrasts between 'being' and 'having' and 'means' and 'ends' become useful here. 'Having' is the mode of relationship which 'I' exercise towards everything I own. Possessions are 'treasure on earth, where moth and rust destroy, and thieves break in and steal' (Matthew 6.19). Everything I 'have' is expendable and perishable. 'Being' is the mode of relationship between persons where recognition of the other as a person provides the possibility of non-possessive love between them. The German philosopher Immanuel Kant (1724–1804) made the famous distinction between means and ends in the course of stating what he believed about persons.

> . . . their very nature shows them to be ends in themselves, that is, something which cannot be made use of simply as a means . . . Persons are not purely subjective ends, whose existence has a value *for us* as the effect of our actions, but they are objective

ends, or beings whose existence is an end in itself, for which no other end can be substituted.'[13]

Kant put into philosophical form what was in any case the 'Golden Rule' taught by Jesus himself. '"Always treat others as you would like them to treat you: that is the law and the prophets"' (Matthew 7.12). This is a timeless precept, one which applies in ethics generally and sexual ethics particularly. Sinful sex on this view, is any sexual activity which, as it is initiated, one would not also wish reciprocally to receive.

It is appropriate, fourthly, to speak of sin as *lust*. Here again the dominance of agape over other forms of love is a starting point for an analysis of lust. Just as agape led to an emphasis on self-denial which resulted in the over-affirmation of the goodness of self-love, this same dominance of agape has also led to an over-affirmation of the goodness of desire. The argument of the previous chapter followed other writers who have discerned an overlap between erotic experience and the experience of God, and who have found in God both agape and eros. Desire is based on the absence of what is desired, on a lack. This very lack has itself been understood as fundamental to our createdness, for whether we lack sustenance, knowledge, sex or any ultimate necessity for our lives, that lack is what causes us to reach beyond ourselves to seek union with each other, with the world and with God.[14] But there is a danger that emphasis on the goodness of desire may overlook the many distortions to which desire may be prone.[15] It is not that the passion which drives sexual desire is to be excluded from divine goodness, but rather that passion can reach such intensity that its realization becomes an ultimate goal whatever the outcome. 'Lust' may be reserved for such desire.

With lust, eros becomes scheming, overpowering and obsessive. It becomes *epithumia*. Lust is what caused David to rape Bathsheba and, having made her pregnant, to bring about the murder of Uriah, her husband (2 Samuel 11). Lust drove the two judges to attempt the joint rape of Susannah. The narrative describes the destructive power of lust with great accuracy:

> Their minds were perverted; their thoughts went astray and were no longer turned to God, and they did not keep in mind the demands of justice. Both were infatuated with her; but they did not disclose to each other what torments they suffered, because they were ashamed to confess they wanted to seduce her. Day after day they watched eagerly for a sight of her. (Daniel and Susannah, 9–12)

Obsession, furtiveness, secrecy, voyeurism, utter disregard for the victim, blackmail, lies, deception, neglect of faith and community responsibilities all combine in this short apocryphal work to provide a realistic and terrifying picture of male lust. The sickening account of the rape of Tamar by David's son Amnon (2 Samuel 13.1–22) even builds, as we might say, a psychological profile of the rapist and faithfully narrates some of the dreadful consequences for the victim. The rapist is 'tormented' and 'ill with love' (13.2). Yet he finds the victim 'unapproachable'. The seduction is meticulously planned (3–14). Tamar is an innocent and resisting victim (12–14). After the rape the rapist's enormous guilt is conveniently transferred to the victim. 'Then Amnon was filled with intense revulsion; his revulsion for her was stronger than the love he had felt; he said to her, "Get up and go" (15). The distraught woman is told by her brother 'Do not take it to heart' (2)! No action is taken against the rapist when the crime is known (21). There is a sort of moral to the story for Tamar's brother murders the rapist two years later (28–9). What can this incident from holy Scripture tell us, if anything, about ourselves and relationships between the sexes?

One recent writer has movingly compared Tamar's experience with her own experience of sexual abuse when a child. She is able to see the suffering of God in the story, and the ministry of Jesus to her through all those who have helped her through the long trauma that followed.[16] The entire narrative provides an insight into the nature of male lust. It shows that women are not safe from it, especially in houses where they are already known. It shows that peer pressure not to report the rape and inactivity on behalf of the authorities when the crime is known have been going on in patriarchal societies for thousands of years. All these stories say something to men too. They have unpleasant facts to face about their desires and motives which are so unflattering to them they are likely to want to keep them concealed.

Modern liberal thought has made a great mistake in thinking that reason can and does control passion. This is a legacy of Enlightenment thinking which, while admitting the centrality of feelings within human experience, interprets them more as the gentle stirrings of the bourgeois inner sense than a consuming power that will not be denied.[17] The domestication of lust by the complacent assumption that it lies within the control of reason falsifies its character. Paul was acutely aware of the power of sin over resistance to it when he exclaimed 'I do not even acknowledge my own actions as mine, for what I do is not what I want to do, but what I detest' (Romans 7.15). While he did not have sexual sin specifically in mind in this passage,

the identification of lust with 'sin' attempted here, conveys the destructive distortion of passion into naked power.

Dis-esteem

Whenever sexual desire arises in the Bible and tradition alike, it is male
desire that is the problem and women who are the cause, as it was
with Bathsheba, Susannah and Tamar. There is blatant androcentrism
here, in the definition of the problem. That is why it has become
necessary for feminist theologians to show how the general understanding of sin which predominates in Christianity reflects male experience.
'The Christian theology of sin as fundamentally pride, overriding-
self-esteem, or ambition is the result of a totally male-oriented set of
reflections.'[18] A feminist view of personal sin is likely to begin, not
with pride, but with 'dis-esteem'. Christian faith is damnable when
its emphasis on sin robs people of their self-worth. This can happen
to women *and* men, though under patriarchy women continue to feel
crushed by the tradition of male definition that weighs upon them.
More self-denial under these conditions can lead to complete paralysis
of spirit. An incarnational faith should never bring dis-esteem for
anyone because it proclaims the self-giving of God for all women and
men without distinction. 'If there is a God . . . who loves me and to
whom I am lovable, then my first tendency – the tendency to
absolute and unique self-worth – is grounded in fact, and my self-
disesteem is a betrayal of fact, a lie, a sin.'[19] The emphasis on dis-
esteem leads to the construction of sin as an historical condition.

Sin as an historical condition

Floating about in the Gospels is an explosive fragment which eventually found a settled place in John's Gospel, 7.53–8.12. The extraordinary refusal of Jesus in the story to sanction sexual condemnation
of a woman caught in adultery is evidence of its genuineness and
possibly the reason why the earliest manuscripts exclude it. The
woman is brought by her male religious accusers to the temple in
Jerusalem. There is no sign or mention of the male adulterer. The
woman is presumed to be guilty although she almost certainly did
not initiate the adultery. She is of no consequence except that she
provides a few scribes and Pharisees with an opportunity to set Jesus
up as unorthodox for criticizing the Law (John 8.6). How would Jesus
interpret the Mosaic law which said she should be condemned to

death by stoning? Jesus eventually says to her accusers, "'Let which-ever of you is free from sin throw the first stone at her'" (John 8.7). The crowd then slinks off. There is hope in the detail that the eldest left first (John 8.9). Transformation of attitude through grace is sometimes possible despite long experience, not because of it. And Jesus, refusing to condemn the woman, tells her, "'Go; do not sin again'" (John 8.11).

It is a remarkable story. The woman apparently had some measure of responsibility for a sexual sin, which is forgiven. But that is not the issue. In this story Jesus takes issue with gross institutionalized religious prejudice, historically mediated and constituted. The fact that it is Jews who are prejudiced is, mercifully, irrelevant. The point to be made is that damaging prejudices like these are present in the Christian churches today. The ancient text prescribed death for both parties, not simply the woman, and the method of death is not stated (Leviticus 20.10). So the history of the interpretation of the text shows an acceleration of bias against women. Jesus understands this casuistical question among learned religious men as historically grounded prejudice, accumulated over centuries. Perhaps that is why, strangely, he writes on the ground before speaking directly (John 8.6, 8). The woman has to be protected from her male accusers' theology, from a male judiciary which gave her no right even to defend herself, and from a law which, whatever its ancient merits may once have been, was, in the hands of religious literalists, an instrument of terror-ism. In his response to the scribes and Pharisees Jesus shows himself to be the Saviour of religious men afflicted by ingrained traditions of prejudice: in his response to the woman he shows himself to be the Saviour of victims of prejudice, one with them in their defencelessness against the might of historical, social, institutional and religious power.

I have interpreted this story to indicate the historical character of sin, its embeddedness in centuries of prejudice. The men in the story run a patriarchal system. The practice of stoning women for adultery, barbaric even by first-century standards, is evidence for the regulation of women as the sexual property of men, and is, of course, blind to the probable (male) cause of the act. The application of the Law forbidding it provides opportunity for misogyny to operate in the guise of religious righteousness. The structural injustice had become so deeply 'routinized' that it went unquestioned. Jesus however would have none of it. The story shows how prejudice can fester away for centuries as a pious orthodoxy. There is good reason to think that similar prejudice operates in those male attitudes to women which exclude them from ordination, and in the shocking intolerance towards gay men and women which leads at best to their grudging acceptance in the life of the Church.

Homophobia

If this analysis of the historical character of sin should sound smug, it should be acknowledged that rich contemporary Christians like the writer and most of the readers of this book will probably be judged by the next generation to have been equally guilty of historical and structural sin in our neglect of the Third World and of the state of the environment, especially since the information, resources and technology are available to tackle it. The issue here, however, is that *homophobia*, 'the fear that persons may be attracted to persons of the same gender or the fear of being perceived as gay or lesbian',[20] is also a deep-rooted historical sin. Flimsy appeals to proof-texts to justify homophobic attitudes merely mask prejudicial attitudes and transfer the responsibility for entertaining and accepting them to an external, even a divine, authority.

The likely causes of homophobic attitudes among heterosexual people lie in most of us being neither predominantly heterosexual or homosexual in our orientation. We are nonetheless very strongly predisposed towards heterosexual sexual activity since it is proclaimed as normative in most modern societies. Even so, as long ago as 1948, Alfred Kinsey reported that 37 per cent of post-adolescent American males had taken part in homosexual behaviour which included orgasm.[21] Despite the prevalence of heterosexual norms, 'I still get some same-sex feelings. But because of my conditioning, I find them intolerable. So I project my rejection outward onto those visible symbols, gay males, punishing them for what I feel in myself but cannot tolerate.'[22] Other causes include envy of the perceived sexual power of gay men; the threat gay men pose to heterosexual order, the fear heterosexual men have of being found attractive to other men and so 'womanized',[23] and revulsion against the thought of buggery. Since religion provides very powerful legitimization for any attitude at all, by appearing to provide supernatural sanction for it, it is only to be expected that a strong connection will be formed between religion and the self-definition of majorities.

The social construction of sexual dissidence has received much attention recently.[24] In particular it is necessary to explore why it is that

. . . the negation of homosexuality has been in direct proportion to its symbolic centrality; its cultural marginality in direct proportion to its cultural significance; why, also, homosexuality is so strangely integral to the selfsame heterosexual cultures which obsessively denounce it, and why history – history rather than human nature – has produced this paradoxical position.[25]

Answers to these questions are provisional and controversial but, as with other cases of historic prejudice, they have much to do with the over-identity of majorities, using apparent ethnic, racial, doctrinal and gender boundaries to define all that they are not. Having defined the other as other, the majority rationalizes and exercises its power over the other and varying patterns of domination/submission result. Same-sex relationships are discussed in later chapters, where the same criteria for sexual sin will be applied to them as to opposite-sex relationships.

The sin of hiding

Women, whether heterosexual, bisexual or lesbian, have an historic legacy to overcome. The story of the adulterous woman illustrates, before Christian faith even gets started, the claim made recently that 'patriarchal social conditioning has been supported by centuries of theology that have validated male authority and have encouraged men to assert their will over others (chiefly women). At the same time, it has encouraged women to subordinate themselves to the will of others (especially men).'[26] That is why 'dis-esteem' has to be recognized as an historical condition, which, because it mars lives, must be named as sin. This sin has been called 'the sin of hiding'. Speaking of women's experience in patriarchal cultures, Susan Nelson says 'inasmuch as she has poured herself into vicarious living, inasmuch as she has denied her sense of self in total submission to husband/father/boss or in total self-giving to children, job, or family, she has been guilty of the sin of hiding.'[27]

It is appropriate to ask the extent of women's responsibility, and so guilt, for a situation they did not create, but the usefulness of the idea of the 'sin of hiding' lies in the suggestion that to continue to hide within the niches of patriarchal culture *is* a personal, historical and structural sin:

> Women have a legacy of hiding to overcome. Part of this legacy includes hiding from their sexuality, . . . silently assuming disproportionate responsibility for sexual decision-making, for

male sexual pleasure, and for the consequences of sexual behavior. Fearful of speaking their own sexual truth, they fake orgasms, manipulate sexuality with coyness and 'feminine' wiles, and prefer veiled messages to direct communication.[28]

Structural sin

When sin is considered to be a social or structural condition, it is a socio-cultural state in which one cannot fail to participate. Men may find themselves caught up in attitudes which demean women, at work, in the street, at home, in the media and in bed.[29] But men have not been taught to question the injustice of these attitudes (nor how to question them), taking them as 'given' (as well as advantageous). Heterosexuals may be caught up in attitudes which demean homosexuals and encourage caricatures of them. All five areas of personal sin described earlier, lovelessness, selfishness, possessiveness, lust and dis-esteem, are exacerbated by being firmly implanted in the wider social setting.

The failure to live in love is a social condition which tolerates all forms of injustice. Individual young women and men who may wish to exercise sexual restraint through adolescence and perhaps beyond report peer-rejection and ridicule, as worry about 'loss of virginity' (as it was once quaintly put) has been replaced by worry about keeping it. The 'great orgasm hunt'[30] is not conducive to patient sexual growth. Selfishness is institutionalized in 'the culture of narcissism'.[31] Narcissus, of course, was the Greek youth who fell in love with his own reflection in water. Narcissism is another name for 'the Myth of Me'. It is 'the psychoanalytic attitude' which is said 'to foster an amoral or "remissive" culture, in which the need to accept moral responsibility for social conditions is replaced with a therapeutic dissolution of feelings of guilt'.[32] Narcissism is structural selfishness. As long as others contribute to my happiness they are welcome in my home, my company, my bed.

Possessiveness is fuelled by a consumer culture where desire is endlessly stimulated by commodities which make profits and meet alleged needs. Jerome O'Connor thinks the 'commodity form' is a way of life which is in danger of replacing 'the personal form'.[33] Long lists of characteristics of each form are deployed against each other – hedonism with generosity; retention of self with self-donation; body as machine with body as sacral presence, etc. – as the sad but accurate descriptions unfold. The fashion industry is a prime example of 'commodified' structural sin. The construction of women in affluent countries into objects of male desire leads one feminist writer to complain that 'To be a woman is to be constantly addressed, to be constantly scrutinized – in the kitchen, on the streets, in the world of fashion, in films and fiction.'[34]

The desire to be pleasing to men is inflated by the promise of achieving ideals, all of which can be purchased – 'ideal legs, ideal hair, ideal homes, ideal sponge cakes, ideal relationships'. The fashion industry, she continues, is nothing but 'the narcissistic construction of women as objects for "the look"', and doubtless the connivance of women in presenting themselves in accordance with pre-defined images of allurement and perfection is further evidence of an all-pervasive ideology which carries on patriarchal domination by other means.[35] Here is a paradox. When speaking of structural sexual sin it became necessary to speak of the sin of hiding, whereas the message of the fashion industry is the opposite – 'if you've got it, flaunt it'. Yet this dualism of privacy and publicness is also patriarchal dualism carried on in other ways. The increased purchasing power of women in capitalistic societies, evidence of emergence from 'hiding', is met by endless commodities for reducing women back into objects for the look. This is a terrible trap for women and men alike.

All three types of sin inhibit human flourishing and undermine that essential relatedness of people in and for each other. Christ overcame human sin by his relation to God, by the absence of those personal sins just described in his historical life, and by his challenging of the historical and social status quo by redeeming love. The benefits of his victorious life are made available to us through the Spirit. Since the Church is no more than a community of sinners proclaiming the news of divine forgiveness, its common life should be the place where sinners are welcome and at home. Awareness of the historic dimension of sin should make Christians critical of their own past traditions instead of being critical of the pasts of sinful individuals. Awareness of the social dimension of sin should make us all more understanding, more forgiving of people whose lives go wrong. Since sexual desire is God-given, those who are in a hurry for sexual experience and eager for sexual experiment do not place themselves outside the community of faith. Their sexual activity already provides them with precious experience within which the Christian vision for sex within love can take root.

Notes

1. I am grateful to Elizabeth Stuart for reinforcing this point.
2. Rosemary Radford Ruether, 'Spirit and Matter, Public and Private: The Challenge of Feminism to Traditional Dualisms', chapter 4 of P. Cooey, S. A. Farmer, M. E. Ross (eds), *Embodied Love: Sensuality and Relationship as Feminist Values* (San Francisco: Harper & Row, 1987), p. 66.
3. General Assembly Special Committee on Human Sexuality, *Keeping Body and Soul Together: Sexuality, Spirituality, and Social Justice* (Presbyterian Church, USA, 1991), p. 176; and see John Lansley, 'Reciprocity', *Modern Churchman*, 33.3 (1990), p. 41.
4. Mary Grey, *Redeeming the Dream: Feminism, Redemption and Christian Tradition* (London: SPCK, 1989), p. 87.
5. Shere Hite, *The Hite Report: Women and Love* (London: Penguin Viking, 1988), p. 83.
6. ibid, p. 84 (author's emphasis).
7. James Nelson, *The Intimate Connection: Male Sexuality, Masculine Spirituality* (London: SPCK, 1992), p. 53; and see David K. Clark, 'Philosophical Reflections on Self-Worth and Self-Love', *Journal of Psychology and Theology*, 13 (Spring 1985), pp. 3–11.
8. Linell E. Cady, 'A Feminist Christian Vision' in Cooey, et al., *op. cit.*, p. 142.
9. Donald F. Driesbach, 'On the Love of God', *Anglican Theological Review*, 59 (January 1977), pp. 32–43.
10. Carter Heyward, *Touching our Strength: The Erotic as Power and the Love of God* (San Francisco: Harper & Row, 1989), p. 47.
11. Edward C. Vacek, 'Scheler's Phenomenology of Love', *Journal of Religion*, 62, (April 1982), pp. 156–77. From the abstract.
12. John Macmurray, *Reason and Emotion* (1936), cit., H. W. Montefiore, in D. M. MacKinnon, et al., *God, Sex and War* (London and Glasgow: Collins/Fontana, 1963), p. 76.
13. I. Kant, *The Metaphysic of Morality* (1785), iv, 276; see S. Korner, *Kant* (Harmondsworth: Penguin Books, 1970), pp. 146–7.
14. See e.g. Thomas Acklin, 'The Resonance in Religious Language of the Word Summoning Human Desire to Symbolic Transformation', *Bijdragen: Tijdschrift voor Philosophie en Theologie*, 45 (1984), pp. 183–205.
15. See J. Chryssavgis, 'Love and Sexuality: An Eastern Orthodox Perspective', *Scottish Journal of Theology*, 40.3 (1987), pp. 322, 325, for confirmation of the view in that tradition of the goodness of erotic love reduced by 'contemporary individualism' to 'purely physical activity'.
16. Tracy Hansen, 'My Name is Tamar', *Theology* (95), 767, September/October 1992, p. 376; originally in *Priests and People* (September 1990). I think Hansen's appropriation of the story is a profound example of the method of biblical interpretation proposed in ch. 2.
17. Ernest Gellner, *The Psychoanalytic Movement, or The Coming of Unreason* (London: Paladin Books, 1985), ch. 1.
18. Anne Carr, *Transforming Grace: Christian Tradition and Women's Experience* (New York: Harper & Row, 1988), p. 58.
19. Lyndon Reynolds, *The Downside Review*, (106), 364 (1988), p. 219.

20. *Keeping Body and Soul Together*, p. 176.
21. Alfred Kinsey, et al., *Sexual Behavior in the Human Male* (Philadelphia: W. B. Saunders Co., 1948), cit., Nelson, *Intimate Connection*, p. 61. And see below, ch. 9.
22. Nelson, *op. cit.*
23. ibid.
24. See Jonathan Dollimore, *Sexual Dissidence: Augustine to Wilde, Freud to Foucault* (Oxford: Clarendon Press, 1991), and the many works cited therein.
25. ibid, p. 28.
26. *Keeping Body and Soul Together*, p. 68.
27. Susan Dunfee Nelson, 'The Sin of Hiding: A Feminist Critique of Reinhold Niebuhr's Account of the Sin of Pride', *Soundings*, 65.3 (February 1982), 321–2: cit. *Keeping Body and Soul Together*, p. 68.
28. *Keeping Body and Soul Together*, p. 69.
29. Anne Borrowdale, *Distorted Images: Christian Attitudes to Women, Men and Sex* (London: SPCK, 1991).
30. See Eugene Kennedy, *The New Sexuality: Myths, Fables and Hang-Ups* (Garden City: Doubleday, 1972), ch. 4.
31. Christopher Lasch, *The Culture of Narcissism: American Life in an Age of Diminishing Expectations* (New York: W. W. Norton, 1978; see also Robert N. Bellah, et. al., *Habits of the Heart* (New York: Harper & Row, 1985).
32. David H. Fisher in Edith Wyschogrod, et al., *Lacan and Theological Discourse*, (1989), p. 3.
33. Jerome Murphy O'Connor, in Mary Anne Huddleston (ed.), *Celibate Loving: Encounter in Three Dimensions* (New York, Ramsey: Paulist Press, 1984), pp. 196–7.
34. Rosalind Coward, *Female Desire: Women's Sexuality Today* (London: Paladin, 1984), p. 13.
35. For criticisms of this view see Elizabeth Wilson and Juliet Ash (eds), *Chic Thrills: A Fashion Reader* (London: Pandora, 1992).

CHAPTER 6

A Christian Vision for Marriage

The Christian faith has an unparalleled vision of marriage. At the same time attitudes and expectations towards marriage are rapidly changing, inside and outside the Church. This chapter describes some of these changing social attitudes and their connection with the declining influence of patriarchy. It makes a firm theological distinction between a marriage as a permanent relationship into which two people grow, and a wedding as a temporal point in a couple's history involving a ceremony. The standard identification of one with the other is criticized, but the theological and moral implications of this criticism are deferred to chapter 7. The teaching of Jesus about marriage is described and defended. The medieval view of marriage as a sacrament is upheld, but for very different reasons. The giving and receiving of Christ's body in incarnation and eucharist is compared with the giving and receiving of lovers' bodies in love-making, and sacramentality claimed for each. It is also suggested that marriage provides experience of God's faithfulness, creativity and worship.

Marriage and patriarchy

The popularity of marriage as a social institution is declining sharply. The marriage rate in England and Wales has fallen by more than half since 1971. In the twelve months to September 1990, the rate of people marrying for the first time fell to 39.6 per thousand single people aged over 16. This compares with a rate of 82.3 in 1971 and 51.7 in 1981. In the same period 28.7 per cent of all births were outside of marriage, and 153,000 marriages were dissolved.[1] One very general reason for this decline may lie in a greater awareness of feminist criticisms of marriage as a patriarchal, oppressive institution, with a deeply ambiguous history. But marriage was oppressive even in the time of Jesus (see below) and his teaching offers a vision of what it might become. Because marriage is also a civil institution covered by the laws of nation states, theological thinking about marriage has also been dominated by a legal framework, and this has too often undermined the understanding of marriage as a moral and personal relationship. Engels rightly traced the inseparable relationship between the institution of marriage and the adoption of the principle of private property.[2]

Marriage has until recently ensured the economic dependence of women on men. Women, from earliest times, have had no legal entitlement to property of their own once they married men. They were themselves the property of their husbands (as adultery laws indicate). The valuation of women's virginity has had more to do with the goods of property than the goods of religion. Jesus' teaching about the one-flesh union of the couple served very different ends: 'In England until the present century, the doctrine of unity prevailed: that at marriage man and wife became one, and he was it.'[3]

Marriage has been used since Roman times to perpetuate social class. Unofficially marriage has not always been required to provide a justifying religious framework for legitimate sexual relationships. 'Prostitutes, servants, lower-class women, and women of oppressed racial minorities' have been regarded traditionally as fair game for socially powerful males.[4] Working-class and peasant people, with no property to dispense have had no great need for marriage. In seventeenth-century England the great majority of couples who brought their children to be baptized were recorded in English church registers as having common-law marriages. 'Without benefit of clergy, lower-class men and women simply began living together. The church, at least in England, participated in these patterns for centuries. In the past, the world was not as concerned about sexual morality as many of today's moralizers imagine.'[5] Only in this century have marriages not been arranged by parents.[6]

Theological thinking about marriage until the Reformation was dominated by a double need – procreation and the avoidance of fornication. It is to the great credit of the Anglican divines of the seventeenth century that the 'mutual society' of the partners became 'one of the principal aims of matrimony'.[7] The advent of courtly and, later, romantic love, have enriched marriage. The expectation that the couple should already be 'in love' prior to marriage belongs to the modern period (and as we have seen in chapter 4 leads to unrealistic expectations). At the present time a deepening sense of equality between men and women is leading to the new and exciting possibility of partners regarding themselves as equals and becoming life-long friends, no longer held in relationships of domination and submission, or bound by conventions of male superiority.

Changing attitudes to marriage

Attitudes towards marriage as an institution have also changed. It is probably true that from the early eighteenth century citizens have felt increasingly free to criticize all institutions which they think serve them badly (for example, the monarchy, the Church, Sunday trading, unjust taxes, wages and laws, etc.). In short, an earlier view was that institutions were there to be served, and the emerging view was that institutions were there to serve. Those who marry no longer need to marry in church, or of course to read into marriage any Christian meanings or convictions. The liberalization of divorce laws in Protestant countries could not have happened without the immense social pressure for change, further evidence that institutions eventually mould themselves to the public will. Indeed one of the greatest social changes of all, implanted unannounced in the consciousness of most young individuals in western societies, is the sheer secularization of society, the decline of influence of religious institutions and the loss of the meaning-giving function of traditional religious belief.

Attitudes towards marriage may also have been influenced by a more modest assessment of the institution of the family that supports it. Freud and his followers have drawn attention to the tension and neuroses that accompany 'family life'. It is beginning to come clear that sexual abuse and violence are deeply entrenched in families. The ease with which divorce can be obtained undoubtedly effects a further change in attitude to marriage. Partners entering a marriage are now fully, if tacitly, aware that if 'things don't work out', extrication is always available, and when things begin not to work out, extrication can be an easier option than perseverance. The availability of effective contraception in the present century and the virtually unanimous support among the public for its use (including most of the laity within Roman Catholicism) has finally separated the procreative and the recreative elements of sexual intercourse. People who marry for the first time generally marry later than was customary in earlier generations. Most western countries and North American states have lowered their ages of majority in recent years. Sexual decisions are left to individuals. It is more or less inevitable in these circumstances that partners will engage in sexual activity before marriage, and if they do, then logically, they cannot simultaneously be looking forward to marriage as the approved state which makes full sexual relations licit.

The well-known Roman Catholic writer on marriage, Jack Dominian, thinks that 'perhaps the greatest achievement of recent times is the move by western society to celebrate sexuality', and 'the second major event in this recent history is that ... society has moved significantly from seeing the basis of sexuality as biological to being personal.'[8] These are great gains, and gains they remain even when balanced against much promiscuity, abortion and some breakdown of family life. It is suggested that it is the demise of marriage as a patriarchal institution which, by bringing about greater emancipation for women, has led inevitably to an increase in divorce, just as women's control of their own reproductive capacities has led to greater promiscuity. These gains now need to be consolidated in post-patriarchal ways of relating between women and men, both before and during marriage.[9]

Marriages and weddings

Readers of the Bible and the Christian theological tradition will know that, officially, marriage is the only context within which sexual intercourse can take place. Marriage therefore assumes a 'hegemony'[10] over all other sexual relationships, with the consequence that any sex outside the matrimonial state is forbidden, and single people, post-married people, together with gay and lesbian people whose covenanted unions the churches will not officially recognize, are profoundly alienated. As more liberal attitudes developed towards sex before marriage throughout this century, but particularly in the 1960s, an issue for a generation of engaged Christian couples was whether the traditional teaching could be modified to legitimize sexual intercourse prior to the wedding. This dilemma explicitly assumed a temporal framework of 'before' and 'after', with the marriage ceremony providing the dividing line, the legitimizing episode within the sexual history of a couple. But the theology of marriage which regards a wedding service as a licence for love-making is deficient. 'Sex before marriage' or 'pre-marital sex' is an issue only for theologies of marriage which identify marriages with weddings. This point must be strongly emphasized because it will influence the treatment, in chapter 7, of sex which is technically and temporally 'pre-marital'.[11]

When does a marriage take place? At least three answers to this question could be given: consent, ceremony, consummation in coitus, or a combination of some or all of these. The issue was intensely disputed in the eleventh to fourteenth centuries. Under ancient Roman law 'consent alone sufficed to create the union'.[12] This still remains the official but little-recognized teaching of the Roman Catholic Church. That is why a person seeking the annulment of a Roman Catholic marriage even today is likely to argue that the initial consent was defective, and so the resulting ceremony invalid.[13] 'Marriage is based on the will of two people and . . . all external forms are historically conditioned and of secondary importance.'[14]

It was not until the Council of Trent in 1563 that the Roman Catholic church insisted that marriages should be performed within the context of a Christian ceremony.[15] One reason for this development was the need to confirm that consent had actually taken place, by ensuring that witnesses were present. Up to that time, no witnesses were required. Consent could be obtained by proxy and there was no minimum age below which consent could not be given.[16] Another less obvious reason for the Christian ceremony was that the Church was able to control marriage. It made it impossible for men who had been secretly married to continue to become priests.[17] Even with these new restrictions, no one suggested that the sacramental grace of marriage was conferred by the priest or the Church. The sacrament of marriage still did not require the administration of a priest. It was administered by the couple to each other, provided there were no legal reasons against it.[18]

Among northern European people marriage seems to have been publicly recognized by 'the transmission of *mundium* or authoritative guardianship of the bride from her father to her husband',[19] with the payment of any dowry. These two elements, consent and transfer, survive through the Reformation to Christian liturgies of the present day. The making of consensual vows before witnesses who must sign a marriage register is necessary in civil and ecclesiastical ceremonies. Transfer was accomplished (in the Book of Common Prayer) by the demeaning and derogatory question, 'Who giveth this Woman to be married to this Man?' The question is a reminder of an ancient custom which has everything to do with property and little to do with faith. But the 'Giving Away' has still not disappeared. It remains an optional part of the 1980 Alternative Service Book rite.

The question as to when a woman and man become wife and husband can therefore be answered: when they exchange public consent within the context of a (religious) ceremony. This answer gets further support from the recognition, in the twelfth century, of marriage as a sacrament. Once marriage came to be regarded as a sacrament the further question arose, 'By what agency and at what moment is the supernatural gift bestowed?' The answer to that question, confirmed by Aquinas, was that 'the ministers of the sacrament of marriage are the bride and bridegroom themselves, and the form of the sacrament is their reciprocal consent'. The 'sacramental moment' then, given that one had to be identified, is the exchange of consent. The priest does not marry the couple. He rather pronounces, after the consent, that they are married. 'The fact that the "sacramental moment" in the nuptial rite was thus identified with the mutual exchange of *consensus per verba de praesenti* ['consent by the spoken word in the present tense'] undoubtedly facilitated recognition of the latter as the moment at which the marriage was believed to come into existence.'[20]

Pre-ceremonial marriages

I think this view that a couple are married, both in the eyes of the Church and of the state, when they exchange vows in public, remains a standard view. It is reinforced by the power of a public event, at which the families and friends of the marrying couple are usually present, to determine a sense of 'pre-history' and 'post-history'. Nation states require reliable documentation on the marital status of their subjects, and in many countries churches continue to act as agents of the state in recording information. For legal and financial reasons, a temporal point at which a couple become husband and wife, is required. This temporal point also provides an extremely simple and convenient function in appearing to signal exactly when sexual intercourse is right and when it is wrong.

Unfortunately there are overwhelming reasons why 'the cere-monial theory' of the origin of marriage won't do. In the first place, it ignores the teaching of Jesus about the couple becoming one flesh. If the essence of marriage is public consent, sexual consummation of it is unnecessary, as Hugh of St Victor and others believed.[21] Yet the Church has consistently taught that sexual consummation is necessary to a marriage. Lack of it is often a reason for the Vatican to grant an annulment, right up to the present day.

Second, public consent is only possible on the basis of the pre-history of the marrying couple. The consent represents a stage in the development of a relationship, and prior consent is needed by both parties to proceed to the public stage. Since the parties are themselves the ministers of the sacrament of marriage, and the role of the

Church is to recognize, solemnize, pronounce and bless, the parties may regard themselves as married prior to any wedding that subsequently takes place. Any sex they have will be pre-ceremonial but not pre-marital.[22] The ceremony is the means of public recognition of a marriage relationship that already exists '. . . a *wedding* does not in itself necessarily create a *marriage*, but is rather the legitimation by and before society of a marriage.'[23] The church service 'solemnizes' what already exists.

This conclusion, correct though it is, is likely to shock many Christians. Those anxious to defend marriage as a hallowed state within which alone sexual intercourse can happen will not take kindly to the view that marriages do not have tidy beginnings, and that the marriage ceremony is an event within the history of a couple growing in a mutual relationship which is in the process of becoming a marriage, not the event which makes them married. That there is a huge difference between pre-ceremonial and pre-marital sex is likely to prove at least a disconcerting thought.

Third, following from the view that marriage is a growing relationship of two people toward each other, Christians will want to distinguish the profound personal meanings of marriage from the legal, financial and administrative details which accompany the married state. Relationships are, for the people living in and through them, living, growing, changing interpersonal processes. Only for lawyers, bankers, Inland Revenue officials and bureaucrats is it necessary to regard the marriage as a contract with dates and times. Ethics is always more complex than law.

> Ethics often takes its metaphors from the juridical order out of a hunger for simplicity . . . Either you are married or you are not. There can be no discussion before the law of how married you are, or how deeply you are into the marital process. Law is too blunt an instrument to enter into these nuanced responsibilities of interpersonal life . . . Happily, however, legality is not exhaustive of reality.[24]

'Sexual property'?

A recent and influential writer has argued that marriage should not be solemnized until some years after its inception. William Countryman observes that in the patriarchal order women are sexual property, goods purchased by a man from another man. In these circumstances 'the first act of sexual intercourse, with its accompanying proof of the bride's virginity, was sufficient'.[25] The hymen, on this view, was a sort of kitemark of virginal quality assurance. The sexual property which modern individuals seek, however, is different. It 'lies in the interior goods'[26] which include intimacy, companionship, love, and so on. Technical virginity is no longer an issue; indeed prior sexual experience may be an advantage: 'It is very difficult to specify the date, even in the most successful of marriages, when it became clear that the property transactions involved were indeed in good order.'[27] It follows, thinks Countryman, that the Church 'would perhaps be better advised not to solemnize marriages at the inception of the relationship itself, but to wait a period of some years before adding its blessing'.[28] I don't think the notion of sexual property is sustainable: even 'goods' is compromised by an economical and transactional view of relationships. But the analysis recovers by a different route, the insight that a couple grow into a marriage, without any decisive before and after on a temporal scale. The suggestion to be considered in the next chapter is that sexual intercourse can become the temporal point at which marriage becomes a firm intention.

The teaching of Jesus about marriage

The view that marriage is a state conferred on consenting parties by their public vows supplanted the earlier view that marriage is a one-flesh union of a man and a woman. Within this union a primary symbolic meaning of 'one flesh' is the act by which physical union is obtained. This is of course the teaching of Jesus. This teaching is inseparable from his teaching about divorce, but that must be postponed until chapter 8. Here the hermeneutic framework described in chapter 2 is doubly useful, for the text we shall be looking at (Mark 10.1–12) itself contains three references to what we now call the Old Testament. Jesus is himself reader and interpreter of these texts, and he interprets them in a particular social situation and in the light of his inauguration of the kingdom or reign of God. All this must be unravelled before we take as our text his interpretation of still earlier texts and try to interpret them for ourselves. Despite this complexity success is still possible.

Husbands, in the Jewish and Gentile worlds, were able to divorce their wives with great ease in the time of Jesus. According to Deuteronomy 24.1 a man could write a certificate of divorce if the woman he had 'taken' in marriage 'does not win his favour because he finds something offensive in her'. Rabbi Hillel argued that 'something offensive' could be as trivial as 'spoiling a dish'.[29] When Jesus was asked about the practice of divorce, he explains the Deuteronomy passage and goes on to give reasons for its inadequacy.

> 'It was because of your stubbornness that he [Moses] made this rule for you. But in the beginning, at the creation, "God made them male and female." "That is why a man leaves his father and mother, and is united to his wife, and the two become one flesh." It follows that they are no longer two individuals: they are one flesh. Therefore what God has joined together, man must not separate.'
>
> When they were indoors again, the disciples questioned him about this. He said to them, 'Whoever divorces his wife and remarries commits adultery against her; so too, if she divorces her husband and remarries, she commits adultery.' (Mark 10.5–12)

This teaching, within the context of easy divorce of women is little short of amazing. The law allowing divorce is not revised or tightened; it is abolished. In the reign of God men are forbidden to divorce women at all. Their property rights over their wives are suspended because wives are no longer the property of their husbands but full and equal partners in the marriage. This is one of several passages where the attitude of Jesus to women is extraordinary and anticipates modern concerns for equality and sexual justice. The position of the wife becomes changed from one of unilateral submission to her husband to that of partner in a marital union where mutual submission of each partner to the other is the norm.[30] Next we might note the reasons Jesus gave for setting aside the divorce law in Deuteronomy; he appeals to the creation accounts in Genesis believing these to override the temporary concession in the Mosaic Law. There is some primordial fact about the constitution of human beings 'at the creation' on which the new teaching of Jesus is based. It is an appeal to some element of basic 'given-ness' about the way, in God's mercy, each of us is. Recollection of the discussion of human persons-in-relation in chapter 4 will help us to reclaim it.

Jesus quoted two passages which appear in our Bibles as Genesis 1.27 and 2.24. The second of these is, 'That is why a man leaves his father and mother, and is united to his wife, and the two become one flesh.' Jesus interprets the passage by drawing out a particular meaning of 'one flesh'. This term is a metaphor which has its home in the Hebrews' unabashed acceptance of the body and bodily union, yet because it is a metaphor, open to subtle application and development, it has been taken as little more than a tasteful euphemism for sexual intercourse within marriage (and, as we have seen, it eventually became omitted from some accounts of marriage altogether). Yet to become 'one flesh' with the marriage partner is to become one in being with him or her and so to undergo a transformation of one's own being as an individual person. But Jesus' comment on the passage is: 'It follows that they are no longer *two individuals* [my emphasis]: they are one flesh.' The insertion of 'individuals' in the New English and Revised English Bibles draws out a missing emphasis in earlier versions. Jesus' vision for women and men in marriage is a full sharing of each life with and for the other such that the individual identities are transcended in the single shared life in which each is fully 'from' and 'for' the other and is fulfilled 'in' and 'through' the other.

The 'one flesh' teaching of Jesus is based on his understanding of how God made men and women for each other, and of the fruitful possibilities that lie in the growth of individuals toward each other in their common life. It is a positive teaching *about* marriage, not a prescription *for* marriage. This is why the churches regard marriage as an institution ordained by God and why the Alternative Service Book calls marriage 'a gift of God in creation'.[31] There is a potentiality in the life of a couple in which their physical union is a symbol of their personal life union in commitment and mutuality. This growth into union is, for Jesus, something intended by God, and is why their 'joining together' is attributed to the work of God. 'Therefore what God has joined together, man must not separate.' The entire passage is about the transcending of a narrow self-interested legalism by a broader vision of the married state based on the created and creative possibilities of human relationships with which the will of God is identified. Sadly, the biblical text which proclaims the removal of legalism, has become instead another absolute law, one with dominical authority, forbidding divorce altogether without reference to the life circumstances and situation of the couple. We return to this perplexing question in chapter 8.

The sacrament of marriage

Marriage has been regarded as a sacrament in the Roman Catholic Church since the second Council of Lyons in 1274, but was never so regarded in Protestantism. This is not surprising. Marriage was the latest and the least of the seven sacraments and the grace it was thought to bestow was largely conceived in negative terms, that is, it prevented fornication, and maintained the church by producing children. Since celibacy was regarded as better than marriage, a further ambiguity arose. If celibacy was superior, why was marriage sacramental at all, since celibacy wasn't? Despite these ambiguities the teaching that marriage is a sacrament is fruitful and a fresh beginning must be made in the reconstruction and commendation of it.

According to the Book of Common Prayer, a sacrament is 'an outward and visible sign of an inward and spiritual grace given unto us, ordained by Christ himself, as a means whereby we receive the same, and a pledge to assure us thereof'. Through the word and sacraments, 'The divine presence is focused so as to communicate itself to us with a directness and intensity like that of the incarnation itself.'[32] The foundations for asserting that marriage is just such a case of holy communication have already been laid in earlier chapters. Human beings are 'persons-in-relation', and in marriage persons are so closely related that they 'are no longer two individuals: they are one flesh'. The intimate union of husband and wife led the writer of Ephesians to observe: 'Men ought to love their wives, as they love their own bodies. In loving his wife a man loves himself' (Ephesians 5.29). Marriage, then, is a state within which each peron finds fulfilment as he or she contributes to the fulfilment of the partner. To live within the marriage relationship is, potentially, to receive back one's personal identity enriched from having shared it with one's beloved.

The incarnation of God in Christ enables Christians to expect that they will experience the holy in and through the flesh. When lovers are committed to each other and are able to make love without fear of exploitation, anxiety about being vulnerable, guilt about bodily pleasure or shame about abandonment to passion, the meaning of their sexual encounter in all its depth, intensity and significance requires the language of the holy if it is ever to be articulated satisfactorily in words. But to speak of sex as holy is not merely to borrow religious words in order to sacralize pleasant experiences. There is no more obvious and immediate way whereby God mediates divine grace through the medium of the material, created order, in this case the giving and receiving of the bodies of lovers covenanted to each other in marriage. Pope John Paul II comes close to saying this. He observes: 'The first and immediate effect of marriage is . . . the Christian conjugal bond, a typically Christian communion of two persons because it represents the mystery of Christ's incarnation and the mystery of his covenant.'[33]

A common criticism of monogamous marriage is that it can degenerate into a cosy 'coupleism'[34] or 'coupledom' whereby the two partners become an enclosed, self-sufficient unit confining their interests to the private spheres of home, children and leisure. The understanding of God we are given through incarnation and trinity expose coupleism as a travesty. The incarnation and self-giving of God in Christ is God's way of revealing the divine love for the whole world. Incarnate love is made 'particular' in the person of Christ, but the particularity of it is the means of its universality. The love of God is certainly focused and concentrated upon the Son, but the Son is not merely the recipient of the Father's love: he is the means whereby that divine love is made available to all humanity. If the love which is embodied in flesh is divine, it drives beyond itself to be ever more widely shared. It is in the nature of divine love to spread itself ever more broadly.

The expansive nature of holy love is the reason why reference was made in chapter 4 to the doctrine of the Trinity in the thought of Richard of St Victor. Unless the love of two persons results in being shared more widely, he held, selfishness cannot yet have been overcome. The love which is the uniting bond of the couple, which so to speak has the spiritual, emotional and physical resources of each partner behind it, contains a dynamic which reaches beyond the couple in its drive to share itself more widely. When directed outwards, their love can become a creative, healing power throughout the couple's social and personal world. A marriage which is brought to the incarnate triune God for consecration will be one where divine love, incarnated in the particular couple, becomes a source of enrichment in the lives and loves of others. Agape cannot be contained by any institution, whether a marriage, a church, or a religious orthodoxy.

Eating flesh

Love-making in the context of the bond of marriage resembles the Eucharist of Christian worship since in the Eucharist the body of Christ is given and received and in love-making the body of one's beloved is given and received. The giving of one's body to one's partner can be a profound act of trust which makes the receiving of it a sacred joy. The receiving of the beloved's body in one's arms, mouth or vagina is literally a receiving. Indeed many of the intimacies of love-making are fairly literally an eating of the body of the person one loves. Kissing, especially deep kissing; the use of the tongue in caressing and stimulating; biting, sucking and nibbling; these are all patently ways in which we eat the bodies of our lovers, receiving them, affirming them, receiving pleasure in them and in giving them back. We rejoice in the taste and smell of consecrated bread and wine at the Eucharist and in the taste and smell of the body of our partner which she or he has consecrated to us. Is it enough merely to say that love-making 'resembles' the Eucharist? No. The God incarnate in the Christ who gives his body in a supreme act of self-giving love for the world is the same God who is incarnate in the love which married partners share and in the physical way that love is expressed. That is a further reason why the sacramentality of marriage must be upheld in the Christian theology of marriage.

Christ's passion is his *suffering*, not the strong emotional *love* which is the more common meaning of that term today. Yet there is a clear convergence between those two meanings in his death. Talk of human passion expresses the strong, emotional, insistent, physical side of love which is expressive, wholly self-involving, yet distinguishable from what has earlier been described as lust. All these elements are present in the life of God as it has been expressed in God's Son, culminating in his death, and are 're-presented' in the Eucharist. The cross is the symbol of God's passionate love.

The experience of 'embodied knowing' described in chapter 4 gives added weight to the sacramental interpretation of love-making within marriage. The bodily knowing of those medieval women was contrasted with the cerebral knowing of the male theologians. One way of knowing God was through the intense involvement in the physical detail of daily family routine which, when combined with the physical detail of the Eucharist produced an ecstasy, a summation of their devotion to Christ and to their families and Christ's devotion to them. The other way of knowing God was through abstraction from all particulars to the bodiless knowing where minds encounter timeless truths. One is immediate; the other is inferential. These ways of knowing confront us in both types of love-making, the Eucharist and marital intimacy. As the worshipper prepares to receive the body of Christ, she or he may well wish to use the different items of the liturgical activity to make inferences from what is going on to something else which is spiritual and tantalizingly elsewhere, like the mystical body of Christ or spiritual food for the soul of which the bread and wine is but a sign. The alternative view is that Christ can be trusted to reveal himself in the particulars of the Eucharist so that there is no need to infer anything. The meanings are already there, in the celebration. And so it is with the making of love. Inferences from love-making to a divine source of love are not only unnecessary; they are pointless. The presence of God is there already.

Faithfulness, children and worship

The faithfulness of each spouse to the other is a life-long commitment to their joint flourishing. It seems, for whatever reason, that most married partners are at least tempted at some time during their marriages by the possibility of an adulterous liaison. Appeals to the seventh commandment, 'Do not commit adultery' (Exodus 20.14), or to the ethics of promise-keeping in these circumstances, are less likely to be efficacious than a drawing upon the spiritual resources which faith makes available in situations where infidelity beckons. What exactly might these resources be? Each partner is God's own means of cherishing the other. Betrayal of the partner can be a double breach of trust, confirmed perhaps in the overwhelming sense of nullity that betrayal brings. Faithfulness is not merely a desirable human quality. It is a quality of God's relationship with the world, the Church and all humanity. 'The human symbol of God's faithfulness to us is our faithfulness to other people.'[31] There is more than a vague parallel to be discerned between frail human faithfulness and assured divine faithfulness. In exercising human faithfulness a partner expresses the faithful love that God is. The issues of fidelity and 'open marriages' are discussed in chapter 8.

Marriages may produce children. For most of Christian history this has been the primary justification for having sex at all. The Second Vatican Council is insistent: 'Marriage and married love are by nature ordered to the procreation and education of children.'[36] Children may be the beneficiaries of the fruitful agape which is their parents' union, and parents who lovingly choose to bring children into the world are likely to experience for themselves the love and creative power which is God's own activity in creating and sustaining the world. Children, according to Augustine, were one of the goods of marriage,[37] and most married couples who are able to have children would agree with him. The patriarchal family has placed a disproportionate responsibility for children on mothers, but this is a stubborn characteristic of patriarchy, not necessarily a characteristic of marriage. Once it has been agreed that there are many thriving well-balanced children of single parents and many unthriving unbalanced children of married parents, it is still true that marriage remains the context where children are more likely to receive the care and nurture they need to become confident and affirming.

Marriage is the only context where it is possible to offer worship to someone or something other than God.[38] The Book of Common Prayer acknowledged this in the words (but said only by the bridegroom during the giving of the ring), 'With this Ring I thee wed, with my body I thee worship, and with all my worldly goods I thee endow . . .'. In the 1980 Alternative Service Book, 'with my body I thee worship' becomes 'With my body I honour you, all that I am I give to you . . .', and can be said by bride and bridegroom.

'Worship' derives from the Anglo-Saxon *weorthscipe*, 'honour'. The honorary title 'the Worshipful the Mayor' in British civic life confirms that worship may be offered to distinguished people. Jews and Christians, however, are clear that, in a theological sense, God and God alone is the sole and appropriate object of worship, and must not be confused with any creature. That is the teaching of the first three of the ten commandments (Exodus 20.3–6). How, then, without idolatry, could anyone conceivably offer worship to his or her spouse?

German Martinez has recently sketched a detailed analogy between marriage and worship. Marriage is described as 'the total validation of the other in the devotion and service, celebration and mystery of a relationship'.[39] Worship is also this, for in worship Christians believe themselves confirmed or validated in their relationship with God, and God also becomes confirmed and affirmed in the devotion, service and celebration offered. Marriage and worship both require 'symbolic action, depth of meaning, and self-transcendency'. The symbolic action involved in sexual relations must be postponed to the next chapter. For the present, while agreeing with the parallels to be found between marriage and worship, the emphasis in this book has been on human participation in divine love, not in exploring analogies between divine and human love. In serving each other and renewing the unconditional commitment which each has for the other in marriage, the expression of devotion and dedication is not simply analogous to an act of worship: it is an act of worship. When a partner in marriage is affirmed and honoured by his partner, that partner is God for him, and affirms and honours him as God does.

Strong theological reasons can therefore be given for continuing to insist that within marriage 'the divine presence is focused so as to communicate itself to us with a directness and intensity like that of the incarnation itself'. In this sense marriage is a sacrament. It is a vision of what God may have for us. Keeping in view the danger that a strong emphasis on marriage can eclipse all other possible sexual relations, what remains is to examine whether marriage is the only way in which the sacramental grace of God can enter into the sexual experience of women and men. That is what the rest of the book is about.

Notes

1. *Population Trends 66* (HMSO, 1992).
2. Friedrich Engels, *The Origin and History of the Family, Private Property and the State*, quoted in Susan Dowell, *They Two Shall Be One: Monogamy in History and Religion* (London: Collins/Flame, 1990), p. 1.

3. Annette Lawson, *Adultery: An Analysis of Love and Betrayal* (Oxford: Blackwell, 1989).

4. John Shelby Spong, *Living in Sin? A Bishop Rethinks Human Sexuality* (San Francisco: Harper & Row, 1988), p. 48.

5. ibid., pp. 48–9.

6. Lawrence Stone, *The Family, Sex and Marriage in England 1500–1800* (London: Weidenfeld & Nicolson, 1977), pp. 270–1.

7. D. Sherwin Bailey, *The Man–Woman Relation in Christian Thought* (London: Longman, 1959), p. 199.

8. Jack Dominian, *Sexual Integrity: The Answer to AIDS* (London: Darton, Longman & Todd, 1987), pp. 43–5.

9. See Spong, p. 53.

10. Mary Hunt, *Fierce Tenderness: A Feminist Theology of Friendship* (New York: Crossroad, 1991), p. 118: and see Susan Dowell, 'A Jealous God? Towards a Feminist Model of Monogamy' in Linda Hurcombe (ed.), *Sex and God: Some Varieties of Women's Religious Experience* (New York and London: Routledge & Kegan Paul, 1987), p. 217.

11. Greg Forster makes the suggestion, but only very tentatively, that cohabiting couples should be regarded morally and socially as married, in *Marriage before Marriage?* Grove Ethical Studies no. 69 (Bramcote: Grove Books, 1988).

12. Bailey, p. 117.

13. Uta Ranke-Heinemann, *Eunuchs for the Kingdom of Heaven: The Catholic Church and Sexuality* (London: Deutsch, 1990), pp. 339–40.

14. ibid., p. 338.

15. Dowell, p. 106.

16. Bailey, p. 131.

17. Ranke-Heinemann, p. 100.

18. I am grateful to Frank Gillies for pointing this out.

19. Bailey, p. 117.

20. ibid, p. 141.

21. ibid., p. 127.

22. The distinction is found in e.g. A. Kosnik et al. (eds), *Human Sexuality: New Directions in Catholic Thought* (London: Search Press, 1977), pp. 160–1, and discussed further in ch. 7 below.

23. Peter Forster, 'Weddings Don't Always Make Marriages', *Church Times*, 13 March, 1992 (author's emphases).

24. Daniel Maguire, *The Moral Revolution: A Christian Humanist Vision* (San Francisco: Harper & Row, 1986), p. 78.

25. L. William Countryman, *Dirt, Greed and Sex: Sexual Ethics in the New Testament and their Implications for Today* (London: SCM Press, 1989), p. 261.

26. ibid., p. 253.

27. ibid., p. 261.

28. ibid., p. 263.

29. Don T. Smith, 'The Matthean Exception Clauses in the Light of Matthew's Theology and Community', *Studia Biblica et Theologica*, 17, no. 1 (1989), p. 59. The Mishnah, *Gittin*, 9:10 is cited.

30. See Kenneth J. Thomas, 'Husband–Wife Relations: A Hermeneutical Case Study', *Theological Review*, 3, no. 2 (1980), pp. 20–30.

31. *The Alternative Service Book 1980* (London: Clowes, et al., 1980), p. 288.
32. John Macquarrie, *Principles of Christian Theology* (London: SCM Press, 1966), p. 398.
33. Pope John Paul II, *Familiaris Consortio* (1981); text in Austin Flannery OP (ed.), *Vatican Council II: More Post Conciliar Documents* (Leominster, Hereford: Fowler Wright, 1982), p. 825.
34. Dowell, in Hurcombe, p. 217.
35. James B. Nelson, *Embodiment: An Approach to Sexuality and Christian Theology* (Minneapolis, MN: Augsburg, 1978), p. 149.
36. *Gaudium et Spes*, §50. See Austin Flannery OP (ed.), *Vatican Council II: The Conciliar and Post Conciliar Documents*(Leominster, Hereford: Fowler Wright, rev. edn 1988), p. 953.
37. *De genesi ad litteram* 9.7, quoted in Ranke-Heinemann, pp. 94–5.
38. I use 'marriage' here in an extended sense yet to become apparent (in chs 9–11).
39. German Martinez, 'Marriage as Worship: A Theological Analogy', *Worship*, 62 (July 1988), p. 332.

CHAPTER 7

Beginning with Sex, or Sex before Marriage

In this chapter five views about sex before marriage are outlined and assessed. A previous conclusion, that marriage has no fixed temporal beginning, is introduced into the discussion about beginning with sex and allowed to destigmatize so-called 'pre-marital' sex. Sexual experience is distinguished from sexual intercourse, and the urgent universal need for 'safe sex' is allowed to reinforce the independent conclusion that sexual routines which end up with ejaculation inside a vagina are the product of social history and culture. They can and should be changed, especially for those beginning with sex, and education in safe sex points the way. Alternatives to sexual intercourse, past and present, are commended, and 'a theology of waiting' is suggested, but not prescribed, for couples intending marriage. The theology of marriage outlined in the previous chapter is shown to support the introduction of betrothal as a liturgical rite, and enables some types of cohabitation to be positively viewed.

Sex and symbols

The human species is sometimes called *homo symbolicus*, a term which conveys the insight that people are symbol-makers and symbol-users, able to express themselves through symbolic meanings.[1] The term 'body-language' expresses how meanings may be conveyed through bodily movements and gestures. 'Love-making' suggests that voluntary sexual acts may also convey the feelings which partners have for each other. This is where difficulties arise. An act of sexual intercourse can be an exploitative, dehumanizing, violent act expressing misogyny and contempt; it can be an overwhelming, pleasurable expression of deep, committed, married love; and it can be an expression of a whole range of meanings in between.

'Sexual intercourse' is a wholly inadequate term to describe committed symbolic sexual relations. Together with a host of other ugly polysyllabic euphemisms (like 'masturbation', 'homosexuality', 'fellatio', etc.), 'sexual intercourse' belongs to the nineteenth-century process which Michel Foucault has called 'the medicalization of sex'.[2] Whatever merit this vocabulary may have in a medical context, it is inadequate and misleading in an ethical one. The location of love-making within a permanent covenant relationship optimizes the symbolic meaning which love-making can convey. The tricky question, prompting many others, is whether such a relationship is the only context where sexual intercourse should take place.

Five views of sex before marriage

There is a useful spectrum of five views about the moral legitimacy of sex 'before' marriage which will aid our discussion of beginning with sex.[3] According to the traditional view, all sexual pleasure, if it occurs outside marriage, is sinful. Intercourse belongs within marriage where its purpose is procreative. A Roman Catholic manual of 1936 forbids any 'sexual excitement' even to engaged couples: ' . . . it is certainly not allowed to these persons to intend or consent to even the smallest degree of venereal pleasure.' Even, 'Mixed hiking parties of young people, Catholics and non-Catholics are fraught with danger of sin.'[4] Since all sexual activity is licit only when it aims at a procreative end, and sexual pleasure is regarded with, at best, suspicion, I shall call this the *biological* view.

Second, and only slightly more permissive, is the Vatican's 1975 'Declaration on Certain Problems of Sexual Ethics' which insists that 'sexual intercourse may take place only within marriage', and that 'Sexual intercourse is not lawful . . . save between a man and a woman who have embarked upon a permanent, life-long partnership.'[5] This view confirms the teaching of the Council that 'the acts proper to marriage' are 'noble and honorable; the truly human performance of these acts fosters the self-giving they signify and enriches the spouses in joy and gratitude.'[6] This position is a great step forward in the admission of the goodness of sexual pleasure and its contribution to the quality of the marriage, while excluding completely sexual intercourse for those 'who have a firm intention of marrying and whose love for one another, already conjugal as it were, is deemed to demand this as its natural outcome'.[7] I call this the *exclusive* view. While marriage now affords mutual enjoyment of each in the other, irrespective of propagation, sex outside of marriage is excluded.

Third, there is the view that pre-marital sex is wrong, but 'pre-ceremonial' sex might not be. The argument of the previous chapter has already warned against regarding weddings as legitimizing episodes in relation to a couple's sexual expression. This view reaffirms the exclusive view that sexual intercourse belongs within marriage but extends it either by making an exception in certain cases, for example, betrothed or engaged couples, or by regarding the marital state as a personal union of the couple prior to the ceremony which solemnizes it. This view might well be called the *intentional* view, since what legitimizes sex is the intention to solemnize, at some future time, the married state which may have started or be about to start.

Fourth, sex may be licit if it is 'an appropriate expression of the quality and depth of a relationship, whether marriage is intended or not'.[8] A more recent example of this position is that taken by the Presbyterian Church (USA) Report (1991) which advocates a 'Christian ethic of common decency'.[9] This ethic 'honors but does not restrict sexual activity to marriage alone',[10] and has 'justice-love or right-relatedness' as 'the appropriate norm for sexuality'.[11] This might be called the *appropriateness* view, since, in accordance with certain criteria, couples decide for themselves when it is responsibly appropriate to have sex.

Fifth, sex is 'a natural human function which serves functions other than procreation or expression of intimacy'.[12] A context of commitment is not required and no symbolic meanings need be ascribed. Sexual experience is the pleasant fulfilment of a human need. This view might be called the *indulgent* view.

The biological and indulgent views while at opposite ends of the spectrum have at least one common feature. They are both open to the charge of 'reductionism', that is, of reducing sexual experience to a particular function, in the one case the begetting of children; in the other the fulfilment of needs. What of the other views? The Vatican Declaration adduces several arguments for excluding pre-marital sex among couples who intend to marry, from which four are relevant here. First, 'Such liaisons can scarcely ensure mutual sincerity and fidelity . . . nor, especially, can they protect it from inconstancy of desires or whim.'[13] Second, 'Love must be protected by the stability of marriage if sexual intercourse is really to meet the demands of its own finality and of human dignity.' Third, stable marriage is inaugurated by a 'marriage contract'; and, fourth 'Pre-marital liaisons often exclude the expectation of a family.'[14]

But this defence of the exclusive view makes no concessions to young people beginning sexual experience in novel circumstances such as earlier puberty, later marriage, greater mobility and affluence, unchaperoned dating, extended education, greater sexual knowledge, and, most significantly, the availability of a range of contraceptive practices still officially forbidden to Roman Catholics. The arguments don't add up. To suggest that committed couples in the pre-ceremonial stage are incapable of fidelity undermines and insults them. The protection which marriage is thought to afford to couples seems apparently unable to stop too much adultery. The claims that marriage is a contract and that the contract inaugurates the marriage seem to be at variance with earlier Catholic teaching. And the desire of couples to postpone having children whether in early marriage or before marriage, is usually a sensible and honourable one. For non-Catholics and a majority of Catholics, contraceptives are one of the gifts which God has provided through technology, and which make responsible family planning possible. The further argument that 'if children are born to partners in such a union it will be to their detriment', draws on the likelihood that children born in secure homes where both parents live are more likely to thrive. But this is by no means universally true and the confident, almost complacent assumption that children are automatically disadvantaged if their parents have not been through a ceremony is easily falsified by common-law marriages which work and Christian marriages which do not.

New beginnings and safe sex

These reasons lead me to think that the 'exclusive' view cannot be the last word. But perhaps the strongest argument against it is provided by the finding of the last chapter that the beginning of marriage is a process of growth, not a ceremonial event conferring entitlements. That being so, the route from initial limited commitment of one partner to another, to life-long union with him or her, should be compared with the route 'by which a monk or nun arrives at the point of taking life vows. In no religious community can one avoid the path of being an aspirant, postulant and novice. Even at one's profession, the vows taken are usually simple, life vows coming some years later.'[15] The comparison invites the suggestion that early in a relationship the possibility of an eventual life commitment is present, but there are stages to go through before that commitment becomes irrevocable. These stages provide opportunities for withdrawal.

I return to this comparison in connection with the practice of cohabitation later in the chapter. A theological analysis of marriage has reduced the importance of a wedding ceremony as a temporal point before which couples can have sex. I think this is an important development in thinking about so-called 'pre-marital sex' in a more positive way. A second development, equally necessary, is the removal of the assumption that having sex and having sexual intercourse are the same thing. A basic rethink must be done about the whole way in which sexual intercourse is posed as a problem in both Christian and secular thought. That might help us overcome the influence of genitalization and procreation in both theory and practice. It could also contribute originally to theological thinking about beginning sexual experience.

Since the arrival of HIV and AIDS, attempts have been made to provide education in 'safe sex'. A consideration of safe sex will provide the opportunity to formulate a different view of what sexual relations are about. The HIV virus can be transmitted by an infected person to another through body fluids, in particular semen and blood. Vaginal or anal penetrative sex without using a condom correctly, especially with someone whose sexual history is unknown, is very risky. The condom, however, provides substantial protection for both parties. A leaflet distributed to all women students in the college where I work advises them never to have penetrative sex with a man without ensuring that he wears a condom, and then goes on to suggest that sex can be enjoyable without penetrative sex at all:

> There are many ways to enjoy sex without penetration. Try penis to body contact, but not between your buttocks or your thighs. Penis to breast contact is safe and fun. Talking dirty, exploring fantasies, mutual masturbation, massage and showering together are other alternatives to penetrative sex. In fact, all sexual activities that do not involve the exchange of body fluids, so use your imagination – many men are worried about AIDS too, so make safer sex fun for them.[16]

Some Christians have criticized safe sex and AIDS-awareness campaigns. One criticism is that continence not condoms is the answer. That Christians should criticize others for trying to prevent suffering and save lives is too damagingly ironic to dwell on. Nonetheless this leaflet assumes its readers will have penetrative sex either casually or very early in a relationship. There are moral reasons why people should not have casual sex and a Christian vision of sex as an expression of love can be offered as a genuine alternative. Education in safe sex raises a very deep question. Penetrative, unprotected sex outside the context of prolonged intimacy and mutual trust is dangerous and anxiety-generating. So why have it anyway? Why not do something else, especially if it is more fun and helps to recover a sense of play?

A different sexual repertoire

One reason why having sex and having sexual intercourse have come to mean the same thing may be that in the West we have been taught for most of Christendom that the goal of sex was procreation and the pleasure associated with it was a sin. This led to the genitalization of sex, the relegation of intimacies and expressions of tenderness as secondary to the main business of discharging semen into the vagina as quickly, sinlessly and productively as possible. Men were taught that for this to be physically possible, a woman needed to be aroused (though not too much). It was a predictable repertoire in three short acts – foreplay, penetration and orgasm (his). Michel Foucault and others have shown that sexual repertoires as well as sexuality itself is historically and socially constructed,[17] and the repertoire just described is a prime example.

I take 'repertoire' here to mean the range of sexual activities between partners which may, but need not, include penetration of a vagina by a penis. (While a repertoire has to be *performed*, as in an orchestra's repertoire, I emphatically do not wish to suggest the idea of a lover as a self-conscious performer.) Penetrative sex between fertile people, with a condom and outside a committed relationship is a sexual repertoire open to the charge of absurdity. It is the climax (!) of a set of activities which aims at procreation yet with the additional aim of frustrating it! Why not change the repertoire? A change of sexual repertoire is already an urgent necessity in sexually permissive societies where AIDS is a threat, and entrenched models of patriarchal sexual behaviour, with their emphases on domination, conquest, activity, performance and so on, are obstacles in the way. But fear of AIDS and unwanted pregnancy is neither the only nor the chief reason for a change of practice. A host of writers has shown that these sexual practices, which pass themselves off as entirely natural, have been constructed by men to maximize male pleasure while women bear the risks.

Shere Hite reported in 1976 that '70% of women do not have orgasms from intercourse, but *do* have them from more direct clitoral stimulation.'[18] Vaginal orgasm was shown to be a 'myth'. That women readily have clitoral orgasms but do not readily have vaginal orgasms is central to the argument of this chapter for at least four reasons. First, it is an example of open and candid sexual knowledge which was not generally available to earlier generations, and is a valuable source for a credible sexual theology. Second, the assumption that women generally find sexual intercourse pleasurable is patriarchal. Patriarchal definitions of women's sexuality could not separate reproduction from pleasure. Third, women's bodies are made by God in such a way that the capacities for orgasm and reproduction are different, and the organs needed for each are separate. The envelopment of a penis is essential for reproduction (artificial insemination excepted) but inessential for pleasure – inessential to her orgasm and also to his.

Fourth, the discovery that patriarchal definition of women's sexuality and pleasure has imposed itself on women further reinforces the contention that sexual repertoires are social constructions. This has enormous implications for sexual theology. Hite showed that 'within the dominant pattern of heterosexual interaction male pleasure is primary'. She views 'sexual patterns as social constructions' and raises the possibility of 'noninstitutionalized sexuality'.[19] The 'sexual pattern' of foreplay, penetration and male orgasm is a cultural phenomenon, not a biological one, combining the age-old procreative intention with the exercise of 'conjugal rites'. The pattern remains, even though its historical 'site', patriarchal marriage, is increasingly no longer normative for sexually active people. Women who do not enjoy these arrangements do not need recourse to psychological theories about their inadequacies, their natures or unhappy childhoods to explain their frustrations. These feelings are, rather, 'a logical reaction to the fact that many men are treating women as if they indeed do *not* love them, no matter what they say'.[20]

The leaflet referred to earlier suggested an alternative sexual repertoire for couples which left the vagina out of bounds for the penis. The reason for this advice is the avoidance of AIDS. But there is a healthy congruence here between safe sex practices and the meanings Christians give to sex, in particular that sexual intercourse is experienced most profoundly when it is an expression of love between married partners. Sexual procreation belongs to marriage, but sexual recreation can take place outside marriage provided procreative activities do not form part of it. There are complementary theological and socio-cultural reasons for this conclusion. A new sexual repertoire is an urgent social requirement, and out of this social need, a Christian vision of sex and sexuality acquires an unexpected relevance.

Alternatives to sexual intercourse

One predictable response to the suggestion of an alternative sexual repertoire is that procreative sex (with or without contraceptive barriers) is too firmly and universally entrenched as a social habit, and that the advocacy of sex without penile envelopment is Utopian. (The term 'penetration' is rightly criticized as sexist. So also is 'envelopment', so I use both.) In reply, mention might be made of alternatives already introduced and practised in different parts of the Church. Three will be briefly considered. The American groups of Shakers were Protestants who shared their possessions, believed in complete equality between the sexes and renounced sexual intercourse. Nonetheless the dance from which their name is derived was 'a heterosexual "shaking dance" that provided regular "orgasmic" release'.[21] One of their immense achievements was that 'They enjoyed and appreciated the natural world and the human body, yet they did not do so by glorifying genital sex and idolatrizing the biological family.' Their communal dance has even been called 'total intercourse, rather than merely genital intercourse',[22] because in rejecting genitality it is said they were able to 'resexualize' the whole body and share a sexual activity together with all the members of the community.

The Oneida Community, founded in the nineteenth-century by the Congregationalist minister and revivalist John Humphrey Noyes, practised 'complex marriage'. Complex marriage allowed sexual intercourse between members of the community provided men did not ejaculate. Noyes called this 'Male Continence', a practice which shifts the purpose of intercourse:

> from excitation and tension release – a purely private pleasure – to the continued communion, heightened mutual awareness, and shared enjoyment of the partners . . . The goal of the sexual union is not orgasm, tension release, something *else*. The goal of sexual union is that very union, communion, and mutual contemplation . . . [achieved by] . . . the heightened control over the instinctual sexual processes by the human intelligence and will.[23]

Complex marriage is more readily recognizable in Catholic thought as *coitus reservatus*. Male ejaculation is withheld or 'reserved' whereas in *coitus interruptus*, the penis is withdrawn from the vagina prior to ejaculation. The practice has been zealously discussed in Catholic moral theology from the thirteenth to the twentieth centuries, and a whole chapter of Uta Ranke-Heinemann's classic study *Eunuchs for the Kingdom of Heaven* is devoted to it. The parameters of that discussion are unedifying – Was it 'unnatural'? Did men find it pleasurable? Was it a subtle form of contraception? Was it not really *coitus interruptus* after all, tactfully omitting the sticky end? Ranke-Heinemann thinks 'the entire debate illustrates the disaster of Catholic sexual morality', but in exposing 'such absurdities'[24] she may have overlooked the creative (but not procreative) possibilities in this practice which was 'frequent' at the end of the twelfth century.

Today *coitus reservatus* or 'complex marriage' would be regarded as a high-risk activity. It is envelopmental sex, and since there may be seepage of semen prior to or without ejaculation, it is an unsatisfactory defence against conception or infection. But that is to lose the point. The intensity and intimacy of the experience are likely to have been found highly pleasurable and may well have contributed to that great cultural achievement of the thirteenth century whereby sex and love began to be permanently linked. The practice belonged to the repertoire of the courtly lovers.[25] It also attempted to separate making love from making babies. By contrast with the modern standard sexual repertoire of arousal-penetration-male orgasm, it represents both a heightening of pleasure and of control.

'Petting'?

Can an alternative sexual agenda be suggested from these fragments and rediscoveries which, when combined with our theological analyses in chapters 3 to 5, and the vision for marriage in chapter 6, 'connect' with young people beginning with sex? What would its ingredients be? Given the presence of what was called 'structural sin' there will be countless influences, peer expectations and practical opportunities to acquire sexual experience in ways which are dishonourable, distressing and dangerous. It is difficult to remain a virgin at a time when 'losing one's virginity' is generally regarded as a gain.

I take it for granted that during their early teens (if not before) most teenagers will have become involved in that dubiously named practice, 'petting' (derived apparently from sixteenth-century Scottish and northern English dialect where it meant 'to fondle, especially erotically'). The mutual kissing, fondling and gradual tactile exploration of the body of the partner with whom one is declared to be 'going out' provides essential sexual experience in the process of sexual awakening and curiosity to sexual maturity. Anxious interventions to prevent this from happening will almost certainly be counter-productive. Petting is an invaluable feature of adolescence.

Teenagers learn the deep pleasures of sexual contact and at the same time how to exercise control over physiological instincts in the name of intimacy and eventually love. They also learn how to interact with each other as persons. Much sexual experience falling short of intercourse can be gained in this way.[26]

Petting deserves to rank as a fourth example of non-procreative sex. But 'going out with' can become 'going steady with', and 'going steady with' can become a longstanding, intimate and developing friendship with marriage and even the thought of marriage years away. Petting by this time (and probably long before) will have resulted in orgasm (especially his, since the penis is more exposed than the clitoris). The relationship may be fraught with difficulties, since one partner may be more committed than the other or regard the relationship in a more exclusive way. Higher education and/or scarce employment opportunity may put physical distance between the partners (and create opportunities for developing new, and potentially sexual) friendships. The more established a relationship becomes the greater the desire (and the pressure) to 'go further'. At this point, the practices called 'safe sex' can be encouraged. Since old fears about wasting seed (or running out of it) or contravening natural law by depositing it anywhere else than in the vagina have been finally overcome, and since female orgasm through the stimulation of the clitoris can be physiologically, conceptually and pragmatically separated from penis-envelopment, the repertoire can develop to a genital stage with each responsible for and sharing the orgasm of the other.

Waiting

It is likely, nonetheless, that the closer a couple grows towards each other, the more they will want to become 'one flesh' in a total physical way. Given the God-given goodness of sexuality this is unsurprising. There is still value in restraint. If a couple regard their sexual contacts as symbolic of their whole relationship, they may still feel that uninhibited sexual intercourse might be reserved to symbolize a state of permanence, mutual self-giving and commitment that the relationship as a whole has yet to achieve. A 'theology of waiting' is available to them in this situation. St Paul regarded the presence of the Spirit as a foretaste of a more complete future state (Romans 8.14–30) and so taught that the entire Christian life may be viewed as a state of anticipation. It is open to a Christian couple to regard their committed but technically unconsummated relationship in a similar way. 'It is God also who has set his seal upon us and, as a pledge of what is to come, has given the Spirit to dwell in our hearts' (2 Corinthians 1.22). Interestingly the Greek for 'pledge' (*arrabon*) in modern colloquial Greek means 'engagement ring'. This thought may sustain the couple further in their waiting. If they refrain from what they both badly want, this refraining itself becomes a symbol of the waiting.

It is to be hoped that in this lengthy process each partner will clarify for themselves whether they wish to commit themselves for life to the other. It is important that the Christian community *discourages* marriage unless the partners have given it long and critical consideration, precisely because of its total irrevocable nature. The Church of England Alternative Service Book expressly does this in warning that 'it must not be undertaken carelessly, lightly, or selfishly, but reverently, responsibly, and after serious thought'.[27] During this process the couple may in any case make love whatever their thoughts, doubts or intentions are. It is important for them also to anticipate the possibility of this happening by having available a reliable contraceptive method even if its possession hastens its use. Technically they are likely to have had 'pre-ceremonial' sex. I doubt whether, under such circumstances it is 'pre-marital' at all. It may be true that many couples will anticipate marriage by having sex and, having had sex, reconsider the intention to marry. They may also come to regret some of their sexual experiences. But sex is surely an area where almost everyone makes mistakes, and since sexual mistakes are the most obvious mistakes people are likely to make and the Christian community is itself one of forgiven sinners, pre-ceremonial sex should be greeted with understanding and prayerful gratitude for the joy each has already found in the other.

Betrothal

The analysis of beginning with sex sketched here may throw some light on contemporary arguments among Christians over betrothal and cohabitation. John Spong has proposed 'betrothal' as 'a relationship that is faithful, committed, and public but not legal or necessarily for a lifetime'.[28] It could be 'preliminary to marriage' or 'a relationship complete in and of itself and that has meaning for both partners in a particular context in which a lifetime vow is neither expected nor required.'[29] There would be a betrothal liturgy and within a betrothal 'the conception and birth of children would not be appropriate'.

A basic distinction would need to be made between a relationship which intends or is open to become a marriage and one in which the partners declare themselves to be one flesh physically while apparently foreclosing a marital possibility. The first of these is covered by the 'pre-ceremonial view', the second by the 'appropriateness' view. Any liturgical proposals would do well to avoid strengthening bourgeois courtship procedures, in particular 'engagement', for engagement cannot hide the function of a 'no trespassing' sign affixed to the bridegroom's prospective property (on her finger, where it creates the duty of admiration by all her friends).

A better argument for betrothal can be made from our earlier analysis of the beginnings of marriage as a process. When this process is compared with the analogous process of becoming a monk or nun, the temporal events of exclusivity, betrothal and marriage in a couple's relationship, might have their parallels in the stages of aspirant, postulant and novice. Exclusivity might indicate an early stage in the couple's relationship when they agree to be sexually active with each other and no one else. The period between exclusivity and betrothal is the stage when sexual intimacy is developed but sexual intercourse is not practised. Betrothal is the point marking the decision to express a commitment to each other, of which sexual intercourse is the symbol and the seal. That commitment is open to becoming a commitment for life. If so, it will be confirmed in a future marriage ceremony. If not, it will be allowed to come to an end. Right up to the point of the ceremony, opportunities for withdrawal are available.

There are difficulties with betrothal. Perhaps the most obvious one is that a betrothal would be a temporal point in a couple's history, like a wedding, but earlier (and provisional). If betrothal became the legitimating point after which intercourse was acceptable, would not the question of 'pre-betrothal' sex arise, much as weddings have given rise to the question of 'pre-ceremonial' sex? How serious would couples about to become betrothed have to be? Is it realistic to expect any major Christian church to authorise such a ceremony?

Despite these difficulties (which opponents can be expected to press), betrothal also has clear advantages. It retains marriage as the context for having children. Betrothal gives theological recognition to the availability and use of contraceptives. It honours the responsibility of millions of couples who are sexually active, non-promiscuous, and in no hurry to marry. It would help to deter couples from marrying too hastily or unsuitably. It acknowledges the far-reaching social changes and trends which stand between the experience of marriage in the present day, and marriage in the time of Jesus. It would not matter too much if the liturgical content of a betrothal were left informal. Betrothal would not be a substitute for marriage and should not look like one. It should be regarded as a resource for Christian couples, as they seek to thank and honour God for the gift of each other. For these reasons Christian communities everywhere should give betrothal serious thought.

'Trial marriages' and cohabitation

Would betrothal be equivalent to 'trial marriage'? No. The term 'trial marriage' belongs too obviously to a consumer-culture where goods can be sampled and returned prior to purchase. A trial presupposes doubt, whereas a marriage demands total commitment.[30] This term was probably designed by opponents of cohabitation to misrepresent the intentions of the majority of people who come to practise it. Cohabitation is a majority practice in Britain among prospective married couples, and a recent study predicts that four out of five couples in Europe are likely to live together before marriage by the year 2000.[31]

Researchers have placed people who cohabit in three broad types: those who live together as a casual arrangement; those who are preparing for a future marriage or living together as an alternative to marriage now; and those who choose cohabitation as a conscious substitute for marriage, with no intention of becoming married in the future.[32] The third type is likely to contain people who think the patriarchal character of traditional marriage is unreformable or who, having experienced the loveless marriages of their parents, earnestly hope to achieve something better. Some people in the second category will be awaiting or contemplating marriage just because they are determined not to enter into it 'carelessly, lightly, or selfishly'. At least some in the first category will not bring to their relationship, at least initially, any of the meanings associated with abiding commitment. There is therefore a very wide spectrum of intention to be found in cohabitation. It is a disgraceful slur on cohabitees to regard cohabitation as a single state or type of relationship, pejoratively and dismissively labelled 'living in sin'. This is quite as bad as labelling all pre-ceremonial sex 'fornication'.

Couples who married for the first time in the early 1980s and who cohabited before marriage were 50 per cent more likely to have split up within five years than those who did not.[33] These are sad figures and they are seized on by supporters of the traditional view as evidence of the consequences of the rejection of traditional Christian teaching. Perhaps cohabitation still attracted less conventional people at the time of the cohabitation studied in the survey, and the choice of a register office wedding which many opted for was indicative of a less total commitment to the marriage.[34] Perhaps some cohabitees who do not intend future marriage succumb to pressure from society, family and friends, marry 'under duress', and regret it later. The issue remains to be settled whether Christians who are beginning with sex may in good conscience do so without the intention to marry. In other words, is the 'appropriateness view' an acceptable one?

Sex without marriage

The liberal defence of sex as soon as people are ready for it is superficial. It ignores the realities of structural sin, and assumes both that sexual 'decisions' can be made in a cultural and moral vacuum, and that reason can control passion. It operates out of a covert philosophical dualism. The Presbyterian Church Report which advocates 'justice-love' and 'right-relatedness' (among other criteria) as principles for sexual conduct has been roundly criticized as abandoning, not simply developing, Christian traditions and creating confusion.[35] The appropriateness view is open to most of the difficulties facing 'situation ethics' which flourished in the 1960s. Most particularly, young people are very vulnerable during adolescence and simply may be unwise to become involved in deep emotional attachments in this period of their lives.

Young people beginning sexual activity are best served by Christian families and groups who offer an alternative and partly countervailing vision of sex and sexuality in which sex is celebrated as a gift of God, brought into a context of mutual love, and openly and frankly discussed. What was called an alternative sexual repertoire could be placed high on the agenda in this situation. That long stage from puberty to life-long commitment to another person (if that ever happens) can then be shared with mature Christian friends who are there to be alongside, listening, understanding, remembering and affirming. Tragically, such support is hardly ever available. Increasingly it may be expected that young people will opt for sexual intercourse without prospective life-long union as a justifying framework.

It must be frankly said that this is a practice which necessarily falls short of the Christian vision for sex and marriage outlined in chapter 6. It means that the symbolic meaning of love-making does not reach the heights of total commitment. The sexual centre of the relationship lacks even the intention of eventual life-long union. But Christians fall short continually in their vision of everything else, like the unity of the Church or the realization of God's kingdom. Signals of disapproval at this stage will be received as the experience of rejection. Many couples who take full responsibility for their sexual decisions, including contraception, testify in the quality and depth of their relationships that the Spirit of God is not the sole property of Christians or the guardian of fixed distinctions. Such couples are more likely to constitute a problem for a judgemental Church than for themselves. The challenge for the Church in such cases is that of showing how the Spirit of God is already in the couple's lives and how that relationship can more fully share in that divine love which shows itself in the sacrament of marriage. So while I cannot fully endorse the 'appropriateness' view I think it is a grave pastoral mistake to use the Christian vision for marriage as a means of alienating couples from the life of the Church, whose sin, if it is a sin at all, is one of impatience. However, experience of the love of God is not confined to the sacrament of marriage. Life-long same-sex unions and sexual friendships have yet to be explored in subsequent chapters.

Notes

1. The social theory which emphasizes *homo symbolicus* is 'symbolic interactionism'. See e.g. Herbert Blumer, *Symbolic Interactionism: Perspective and Method* (Englewood Cliffs, NJ: Prentice-Hall, 1969), p. 2.
2. Michel Foucault, *The History of Sexuality: Volume 1, An Introduction* (Harmondsworth: Penguin Books, 1981).
3. Borrowed loosely from A. Kosnik, et al., *Human Sexuality: New Directions in Catholic Thought* (London: Search Press, 1977), pp. 158–63.
4. H. Davis SJ, *Moral and Pastoral Theology: A Summary* (London and New York: Sheed & Ward, 1936), p. 76.
5. Austin Flannery OP, *Vatican Council II: More Post Conciliar Documents* (Leominster, Hereford: Fowler Wright, 1982), pp. 489–90.
6. *Gaudium et Spes*, §49. See Austin Flannery OP, *Vatican Council II: The Conciliar and Post Conciliar Documents* (Leominster, Hereford: Fowler Wright, rev. edn 1988), p. 952.
7. Flannery, *More Post Conciliar Documents*, p. 489.
8. Kosnik, pp. 161–2.
9. General Assembly Special Commitee on Human Sexuality, *Keeping Body and Soul Together: Sexuality, Spirituality and Social Justice* (Presbyterian Church, USA, 1991), p. 39.
10. ibid., p. 38.
11. ibid., p. 39.
12. Kosnik, *op. cit.*, p. 163.
13. ibid., p. 489.
14. ibid., p. 490.

15. From a letter by the Rev. E. J. Penny to the *Church Times*, 19 June, 1992.
16. '*1. Prevention*', from a series of leaflets about HIV and AIDS and how they affect women, published by Positively Women.
17. Foucault, *op. cit.*, part 2, 'The Repressive Hypothesis', and the discussion of Foucault in e.g. B. S. Turner, *The Body and Society* (Oxford: Blackwell, 1984), *passim*.
18. Naomi Weisstein, speaking of the first Hite Report (1976), in the preface to the third Hite Report, *Women and Love* (London: Penguin/Viking, 1988), p. xxxiv (author's emphasis).
19. Rhonda Lottlieb, 'The Political Economy of Sexuality', *Review of Radical Political Economics* 16, 1, pp. 143–65: cit. Weisstein, in Hite, *op. cit.*, p. xxxiv.
20. Hite, p. 119.
21. Herbert Richardson, *Nun, Witch, Playmate: The Americanization of Sex* (New York: Harper & Row, 1971), p. 129. I am particularly indebted to Richardson's insights here, even though his more general theory about the evolution of sexuality may, after twenty years of hindsight, be questionable.
22. ibid., p. 130.
23. ibid., p. 132-3.
24. Uta Ranke-Heinemann, *Eunuchs for the Kingdom of Heaven: The Catholic Church and Sexuality* (London, Deutsch, 1990), pp. 176–7.
25. Richardson, p. 132.
26. A recurring theme in Richardson, especially pp. 24, 41, 98.
27. *The Alternative Service Book 1980* (London: Clowes, et al., 1980), p. 288.
28. John Shelby Spong, *Living in Sin? A Bishop Rethinks Human Sexuality* (San Francisco: Harper & Row, 1988), p. 177.
29. ibid., p. 178.
30. On whether cohabitation can 'teach skills for a later marriage', see David A. Scott, 'Living Together: Education for Marriage?', *Journal of Pastoral Counseling*, xviii (Spring/Summer 1983), pp. 47–55.
31. Duncan J. Dormor, *The Relationship Revolution* (One Plus One: Marriage and Partnership Research, Central Middlesex Hospital, 1992).
32. Gary Jenkins, *Cohabitation: A Biblical Perspective*, Grove Ethical Studies No. 84 (Bramcote: Grove Books, 1992), pp. 4–5. He draws on the earlier work of M. D. Newcomb, 'Heterosexual Cohabitation Relationships' in S. Duck & R. Gilmour (eds), *Personal Relationships 1: Studying Personal Relationships* (Academic Press, 1981), p. 132.
33. John Haskey, *Population Trends* (London: Office of Population Censuses and Surveys, HMSO, June 1992).
34. John Haskey, quoted in the *Evening Standard*, June 18, 1992.
35. See e. g. Gary L. Watts, 'An Empty Sexual Ethic', *The Christian Century*, 108 (May 8, 1991), pp. 520–1.

CHAPTER 8

Sex and Marriage – Inside, Outside and After

The present chapter celebrates uninhibited love-making within marriage, noting, that in having children, love-making becomes a surging intimation of the creative presence of God. The widespread practice of adultery is analysed from the point of view of the corrupting effect of 'bourgeois values' which simultaneously regularize marriage while undermining it. The 'non-possessive devotion' which is the marriage relationship is understood as a sharing in God's covenanted faithfulness towards humanity. Marriage expects sexual exclusivity. In the second half of the chapter, a detailed look at the teaching of Jesus on divorce is undertaken. The surprising conclusion is reached that the New Testament permits exceptions to the rule that marriage is life-long and indissoluble. These exceptions generate others which must be recognized by today's churches. The position that only separation and not divorce is permitted by the teaching of Jesus is set out and shown to be untenable. The conclusion is then reached that remarriage can be an option for divorced people to take.

Sex in marriage

Throughout the history of Christendom there have been restrictions imposed on when, where and how sexual intercourse between married couples could take place. The counsel of the Desert Fathers to married people was to avoid intercourse on Saturdays, Sundays, Wednesdays and Fridays, throughout the forty days of Lent and before all feasts at which they might take the Eucharist.[1] Bailey, speaking of a later period in European Christianity, mentions abstinence 'on Thursday in memory of Christ's arrest, on Friday in memory of his death, on Saturday in honour of the virgin Mary, on Sunday in honour of the Resurrection, and on Monday in commemoration of the departed'.[2] Even two days a week were too many: 'The married must abstain for 40 days before Easter, Pentecost, and Christmas; each Sunday night, and on Wednesdays and Fridays; and from the manifestation of conception until after the child's birth.'[3] Intercourse during the wife's period, and for seven days after it was forbidden.

Ambrose held that married intercourse 'through love of sensuous delight'[4] was equivalent to adultery. Adultery *within* marriage became a constant fear thereafter. Notoriously, Augustine taught that assent to any pleasure in the sex act was confirmation of the original sin that had brought doom on humanity, and was proof of the fatal inability of the will to control the body.[5] The sole legitimizing purpose of sex was procreation, a purpose which lapsed as soon as the desired number of children had been reached or the ability to conceive disappeared. 'Emergency sex' was tolerated, that is, if either partner was judged about to fall into fornication, then it was the duty of the other to provide sexual relief.[6] Only the missionary position for sex was allowed (because it was thought to maximize the chance of conception); any deviation from the missionary position was ranked as an 'unnatural vice'.[7] Couples could expect to be questioned minutely about these matters in the confessional.[8] Any 'disordered act', that is, one executed with too much ardour or in an 'unnatural' position, or too soon after an earlier one, was thought to lead to the conception of malformed children or girls.

Lovers today, whether believers or not, should rejoice that sex is no longer subject to patriarchal control, biological misinformation and religious repression. Jack Dominian has written of marriage as 'the context of a continuing, reliable and predictable relationship',[9] within which alone the full potential of sexual intercourse can be realized. Among the meanings that couples will discover within this secure and permanent context are that sex is 'a body language of love' through which each affirms the other. It 'can act as a reconciliatory, healing language', sometimes after days or weeks of pain, and be a joint celebration of life.[10] This is a valuable way of describing some of the meanings of sexual experience. Nonetheless there is a bolder, more theological approach to the meanings of sexual love which does not necessarily replace this body-language description but instead names the ultimate founts of meaning which make sexual love communicative at all. These have already become apparent in some of the analyses undertaken in this book. We might now recall some of these.

First, belief in an incarnate God expects to discover the presence and power of the holy in flesh. Second, the sacramentality of marriage was located in the gifting of each partner's body to the other, as Christians are accustomed to receiving the gift of the body of Christ in the Eucharist. Third, the recovery of 'embodied knowing' helped us to discern and know the holy in the immediacies of ordinary bodied life. Fourth, the Spirit may be discerned in the mutual self-giving of each partner in deepening love which, as it deepens, also becomes more widely available to become a source of joy and healing to others. And fifth, commitment to one's married partner is a form of worship: 'When a partner in marriage is affirmed and honoured by his partner, that partner is God for him, and affirms and honours him as God does.' Two further elements of this theological approach to the meanings of love will be considered shortly: the spirituality of birth and the experience of faithfulness.

Having children

Procreation remains one of the meanings of married love. While it has been important to emphasize that married love need not be procreative in a physical sense, it is very probable that at some stage of a couple's life they will want to have children. When there is a conscious decision to try to have a child, love-making is likely to be particularly intense, frequent and uninhibited. Profound religious meanings suggest themselves out of the process of conceiving children. When children come into the home their parents' relationship to each other changes. Each will require the agape-commitment of the other as new demands for attention create new priorities and frustrations.

The work of God in all theistic traditions is to create, and in conceiving a child, a couple may well experience their life-producing, life-bearing and life-nurturing creative powers as a surging intimation of the creative presence of God. The distinction again needs to be made between a cerebral and a full-bodied apprehension of these deep truths. Theoretical knowledge can provide important conceptual connections between divine and human creativity. But embodied knowledge offers a more direct and immediate participation in God through the experience of the mingling of the life-providing physical powers of the lovers' bodies. As already suggested, women may experience their bodies 'as a creative potential of a kind which can even give birth to God'.

A child is the fulfilment of the couple's love. A child is not necessary for the fulfilment of love, but if one comes, she may be the direct product of the love of her parents. In desiring a child, the prospective parents must desire each other, and this desire is a sign of that eros-love which has been described as 'a form of human love in the image of the divine'. The growing of the child in the womb and the stirrings there, the preparation of the home to receive him, the arrival of gifts, the knitting of baby clothes, and so on, all generate a 'theology of waiting' which, as we have already seen, is that open, receptive, expectant state of mind which is a gift of the divine Spirit and an intimation of her creative work throughout creation. The arrival of a child, herself a creation of the love which kindles a sacramental marriage, is a peak experience of life.

Sex outside marriage

Seventy per cent of women recently surveyed by Shere Hite who were married more than five years were having or had had sex outside marriage, although almost all also believed in monogamy.[11] A recent analysis of adultery in Britain shows that nearly as many married women as men have extra-marital affairs, and describe them similarly as 'one-night stands'.[12] The greater economic independence of wives from husbands is held to be a major cause. Depressingly, it seems that equality in marriage extends to equality in adultery, and the ugly phrase 'masculinization of sex'[13] has been coined precisely to indicate the ugly trend not towards the infusion of feminist values into marriage, but the appropriation by married women of those double standards which previous generations of women rightly condemned in men.

One in three marriages contracted in Britain will on present trends end in divorce. In the US the figure is one in two. Marriage as a relationship may, ideally, be permanent, but marriage as an institution certainly is not. Generally, until almost the present century, marriages were arranged and did not touch large sections of populations at all. One of the changes now occurring is the 'de-patriarchalization' of marriage. The prospect is attractive, consistent with, and an outworking of Christian values. Equality within marriage introduces the possibility of the partners becoming life-long *friends*, with domestic and child-care arrangements being matters for genuine negotiation. But another obvious change happening to marriage is that it is no longer so obviously a life-long commitment. The easy availability of divorce inevitably introduces an option unavailable to earlier generations. In fact there are advocates of two kinds of 'open marriage'. In one the marriage is open to the possibility of being permanent, depending on how things go; in the other the marriage is open for each partner to pursue 'secondary relationships' which may or may not be intimate. These are revisionary proposals of a very different character.

Bourgeois values

Adultery and the premature ending of marriages require analysis which takes seriously the social conditions giving rise to each. The Frankfurt School of sociologists, or 'critical theorists', has generally been neglected by British and American theologians but their analysis of modern marriage is a great help in the development of a sexual theology.[14] Social attitudes to marriage are themselves the products of history. The Frankfurt School discerns three particular currents of thought: those of natural law, perpetuated by Roman Catholicism down to the present day; the eighteenth-century 'bourgeois enlightenment'; and the romanticism already discussed in chapter 6. By 'bourgeois' I mean the capitalist class and their interests, and by 'enlightenment' I mean eighteenth-century European philosophy which emphasizes reason and individualism above tradition. According to Rudolf Siebert, in replacing natural law the 'bourgeois enlighteners' regarded marriage as a contract. '[They] degraded marriage into the form of a mutual contractual use of the partner's sexual organs, a kind of exchange process dominated by the equivalence principle.'[15] Romantic marriage quickly followed which 'posited marriage merely into love'. But love, unless it is more than just an intense feeling, and manifests itself instead in unconditional obligations, soon collapses. As a continuation and correction of this unfortunate history of marriage, the Frankfurt School proposed marriage as 'socio-ethical love'. This form of love was the means by which 'transitoriness, moodiness and merely subjective arbitrariness is to be superceded and unconditional mutual recognition is made possible'.[16]

These three currents of thought have powerfully regulated and predisposed the thinking of millions of people past and present in the industrial and post-industrial West. The values shaped by material conditions attached to labour, production, consumerism and commodification are, among others, precisely these values. We have already met that sense of hurt surprise when the thrill of romantic love exhausts itself and there appears to be nothing left but the pursuit of pleasure and 'the Myth of Me'. But new experiences beckon, new partners become available, new commodities fill the consciousness as well as the home. 'That most divorced people remarry again one or two years after their divorce, shows . . . how shallow their marital relationship and individualities were in the first place.'[17]

This apparently perfunctory criticism of early remarriage after divorce should be seen as a criticism, not of those who undertake it, but of societies where individuality has become excessive and relationality has become partially eclipsed. What is lost, these writers say, is the strict monogamous relationship in which 'The life of the one marital partner is held together by his or her reflection in the other partner with whom he or she lives and grows older.' This is as good a description of the 'one flesh' teaching of Jesus as can be found anywhere. They call it *mimesis*.[18] Individualism has by now become so overemphasized that it is often difficult to convey what a marriage undefined by implicit contract theory, shallow romanticism and possessive individualism looks like. Adorno called the married relationship 'non-possessive devotion'.

What has been called socio-ethical love is intended to confront shallow bourgeois values with deep and lasting personal commitment. The critical theorists regarded 'socio-ethical love' as:

> The beginning of a new, post-bourgeois form of concrete, living universality, in which the lovers are not only emancipated, but also fulfilled. Ultimately there is no unconditional, mutual recognition, mimesis, reconciliation, victimless inter-subjectivity and non-possessive devotion without resurrection and the Reality who guarantees it.[19]

Support can be found in critical theory for absolute truth, objective morality, and even, in some of their writings, a transcendent God who guarantees it. While they were mainly Jewish, their support for marriage was remarkably congruent with the best that Christian ethics could provide. They help to confirm two imperatives for Christian faith and practice.

First, they help to preserve and to cherish the Christian vision for marriage along the lines suggested in chapter 6. Second, they help to develop an informed and compassionate understanding of individuals who marry in a culture where support for marriage as a life-long union has been substantially withdrawn. The institution of marriage, our thoughts about it and our expectations of it, have already largely been shaped for us in a way which is quite difficult to retrieve, and among the invisible influences upon us there are corrosive and destructive assumptions which already undermine the institution they define. This is a remarkable example of what was earlier called structural sin. Under the conditions of structural sin, which hide themselves even while influencing our conscious choices, it becomes inevitable that many marriages will not work. The reasons for the casualties will be social and not merely individual ones. In this climate deep, Christian, non-judgemental understanding is necessary.

Open marriages or exclusive faithfulness?

In the light of this kind of analysis, calls for open marriage in either of the senses suggested earlier should be resisted. A genuine openness within marriage occurs when the bond of love between the spouses is turned outwards towards, and shared with, friends, neighbours and community. Not all changes to marriage are to be encouraged. The stronger the marriage, the greater is the likelihood of each partner developing friendships outside the marriage which are deep but non-threatening. Susan Dowell convincingly argues that a 'sexually open marriage' would 'militate against any real openness we try to seek with others in our life together . . . I would hate to be for ever taking jealousy readings, tenderly checking on the feelings of insecurity and exclusion of the one in the outside corner of the triangle, which is what seems to happen to people who try to be "civilized and caring" in their practice of non-monogamy.'[20]

We are now in a position to take further the theology of faithfulness discussed in chapter 6 and to provide reasons for the view that the faithfulness of partners to each other should be sexually exclusive. Faithfulness to one's partner was understood as a sharing in God's covenanted faithfulness towards all humanity. What, then, is to be made of the suggestion that if marital permanence is to be secured, sexual exclusivity should be relaxed? For example, if a partner has sexual needs that the other partner in the marriage does not meet, the needy partner cannot flourish if his or her needs remain unmet. Exclusivity on this view actually prevents the co-flourishing to which each of the partners is committed.

Extra-marital sexual relationships, if unknown to the spouse, are a betrayal of trust. If known they are likely to subject the marriage to considerable strain. Even if consent is given by a spouse to the other to pursue a sexual relationship, the consent may be given unwillingly. Since sexual feelings are very powerful and cannot be controlled, outcomes cannot be controlled either, and this uncomfortable fact is almost certain to ensure that anxiety will be introduced into the relationship. But the most powerful criticisms of 'love-triangles' are provided by the social criticisms just discussed. The illusion that sexual feelings can be managed and controlled without hurtful or unintended outcomes, and indeed, to the mutual flourishing of every-one involved, belongs to the inflated power of reason. The freedom to pursue extra-marital interests looks too much like the freedom to pursue economic interests in the market place, and the transfer of sexual attention to someone else looks too much like the freedom to consume new economic goods or acquire new sexual property. Sexual responses outside marriage to people one finds sexually attrac-tive exploit the romanticism that popular culture thrusts upon us. In effect they extend the marriage contract by adding a further name to the list of persons to whom one's sexual organs may be legally joined.

'Adultery' and 'faithfulness' are words that imply norms of sexual exclusivity within marriage, and that is a reason for continuing to use them. But they should be used to support faithfulness within marriage, never to condemn partners when things go wrong. It is sometimes pointed out that monogamy in the sexual sense is an 'unnatural' state to which most people in most periods of history, especially men, are undisposed to practise. On this view, monogamy conveys a set of unrealistic expectations. Accordingly, an honest and responsible sexual morality would prepare husbands and wives to anticipate and live with each other's inevitable, extra-marital, sexual interests.

The view taken here is that many people *do* have a predisposition against monogamy. Jesus himself may have recognized this. That is why his teaching on easy divorce was uncompromising and was resisted by his disciples. It is right to recognize this and to prepare to live with it. But it is also right to resist it. The demand of sexual fidelity to a single partner throughout life may be a striking example of conflict between gospel and social values.

After marriage – the teaching of Jesus on separation and divorce

Christians have a vision of marriage as a life-long sacramental union which should be commended, defended and lived. On the other hand, some marriages must end and will already have ended before the necessary papers get signed. In some cases divorce is simply demanded by the ghastly circumstances which prompt it. In many other cases divorce will occur simply because it is there, and the opportunities available for repentance, forgiveness and reconciliation will not have been tried. In order to be clear about the very possibility of divorce for Christians, and so to avoid guilt and even loss of faith at having contravened the alleged teachings of Jesus about ending marriage, it is now necessary to look in some detail at his actual words. Heeding once more the warnings in chapter 2 about the difficulties involved in reading the text of the Bible, we quickly discover that whatever our expectation, there is no unambiguous teaching about divorce in the New Testament.

There are five short passages to consult, four of them from the Gospels. These are arranged in parallel columns above so that they may better be contrasted with each other. Our purpose will be to uncover differences, not to impose on the passages a unity which is not there.

Mark 10.11–12 (1)	Luke 16.18 (2)	Matthew 5.31–2 (3)	Matthew 19.9 (4)
Whoever divorces his wife and remarries commits adultery against her; so too, if she divorces her husband and remarries, she commits adultery.	A man who divorces his wife and marries another commits adultery; and anyone who marries a woman divorced from her husband commits adultery.	If a man divorces his wife for any cause other than unchastity he involves her in adultery; and whoever marries her commits adultery.	If a man divorces his wife for any cause other than unchastity, and marries another, he commits adultery.

Mark 10.5–12

This passage has already been discussed in connection with Jesus' teaching about marriage.[21] We may recall that Jesus overruled contemporary divorce practice. There is to be no divorce at all. The remarriage of the husband is primarily an offence against the ex-wife ('adultery against her'). Only in Mark is this reason for the wrongness of remarriage given. At the time adultery could only be committed by a wife against her husband, or by a man against the husband of the wife he has seduced. It could not be committed by a husband against his wife. Jesus insists that divorce harms women and for that reason should not happen. Only Mark has Jesus raise the possibility of women divorcing men ('if she divorces her husband'). This saying causes further difficulty since wives were not then permitted to divorce their husbands. Does Jesus look forward to a time when equality of access to divorce was to become possible?

Luke 16.18

This verse may be from a collection of sayings which the final authors of Matthew and Luke had available to them (which modern scholars call Q), and which was unknown to Mark. (I assume with the great majority of scholars that Mark was written first.) Unlike the saying in Mark it has no context. It is not about divorce but about divorce and remarriage which, taken together, are wrong. Separation is not wrong.[22] The saying in Luke adopts a male perspective only. Remarriage entails adultery, and so would appear to be excluded by the seventh commandment (Exodus 20.14). Mark's 'against her', making it an offence against the divorced person, disappears.

Matthew 5.31–2

This saying is found in the Sermon on the Mount in the context of six examples (the 'Six Antitheses') which illustrate how the teaching of Jesus takes further the obligations of the Old Testament Law. Commentators generally believe it too derives from Q and that Matthew has altered it. There are important changes. Divorce by itself, not divorce and remarriage, is the issue. More important, there is now an exception to the 'no divorce' teaching. A wife's unchastity is a clear exception to the apparently exceptionless rule. We shall return to the whole question of exceptions in a moment.

Matthew 19.9

This saying belongs to Matthew's re-working of the story he found in Mark 10.1–12. There are several changes to that earlier version.[23] The one that concerns us at present is the addition of another exception clause like that already inserted in 5.32, but not found in Mark 10.11. The unchastity of a first wife exempts a husband from the charge of adultery if he subsequently remarries.

There is one more passage to be fitted into this complicated jigsaw. When Paul discusses marriage and divorce in 1 Corinthians 7 he shows a direct knowledge of Jesus' teaching about the permanence of marriage. (The background to Paul's sexual teaching has already been mentioned in chapter 2.) Some married Christians there wanted to renounce marriage altogether in their fervour to prepare for Christ's return. Paul makes a 'ruling' which, he says, 'is not mine but the Lord's': they must stay married (1 Corinthians 7.10–11). But another exception to the 'no divorce' principle quickly emerges, for Paul next makes a further ruling about cases where believing spouses are married to unbelieving partners and the unbelievers want a divorce. In such cases Paul rules the marriage is void: 'If however the unbelieving partner wishes for a separation, it should be granted; in such cases the Christian husband or wife is not bound by the marriage. God's call is a call to live in peace' (1 Corinthians 7.15).

So far we have arrived at three different positions about divorce: divorce is always wrong; divorce is not wrong but remarriage is; divorce is generally wrong but exceptions are permitted to it. The argument will be taken forward by concentrating next on the exceptions. This will initially be difficult because in the case of unchastity there is surprising lack of agreement about what the term means.

Exceptions to the rule

The Greek word for 'unchastity' is *porneia* which earlier versions of the Bible translate 'fornication'. According to one view, 'unchastity' refers to incestuous marriages[24] which, while prohibited in Judaism, were more common in the Gentile world of expanding Christianity. On conversion to Christianity separation from a spouse to whom one was closely related would be permitted, while remarriage would not. According to another view, unchastity could be no more than the discovery upon marriage that the bride might have already had sexual intercourse. A third view is that the term might refer to a wife's sexual misdemeanour. None of these candidates for the meaning of *porneia* advances modern discussion about whether or when a marriage might end. In the first case incestuous marriages are illegal in most countries. The second view confirms the right of a husband to return his sexual goods to their former owner if they are damaged before use. And the third rests on a double standard. A man can divorce his wife for adultery, but she can't divorce him. The point to take forward from this rather sterile discussion of unchastity is that an exception is made *at all*. The teaching of Jesus is already being modified in Matthew's community as the church grows and expands.

One imaginative writer has recently proposed that the exception of fornication be extended to cover other equally destructive elements within a marriage such as violence. The infidelity of a wife, according to Matthew's exception clause, is a sufficient reason for divorce. But why is infidelity wrong? One partly empirical way of showing it to be wrong, which carries credibility today, is to examine all the 'interpersonal elements necessary for full marital intimacy' and to show how adultery violates them. But if adultery violates these elements, so also does marital violence, with the result: 'If battering can be found to violate the marital relationship to the same, or greater degree that adultery does, then wife battering deserves recognition as an acceptable reason for divorce.'[25] The argument is sound. But that is not the point. The fornication exception generates other exceptions. It is inevitable and right that it should.

Paul is very clear what he is doing in allowing Christians married to unbelievers to divorce if the unbelieving partners want it. He shows he knows that, according to the teaching of Jesus, divorce cannot happen. He then addresses a particular and difficult case that has been drawn to his attention. Paul is obliged to engage in a process of interpretation of Christ's teaching like the process of interpretation of Scripture described in chapter 2 of this book. He distinguishes his own view from that of Jesus (1 Corinthians 7.12). Presumably he knows he could be wrong. The Jesuit writer Stanley A. Marrow observes that if Paul 'took the bold step of going contrary to what was clearly an absolute command of the Lord, and did it in full awareness of what the Lord himself had taught, then he did so for a profoundly theological and deeply Christian reason.'[26] That reason is the freedom from law which Jesus secured for us (Galatians 5.1; 1 Corinthians 15.54–6). A further reason is the more immediate, peaceable one – 'God's call is a call to live in peace.' (v.15) Constant conflict between partners is too much to bear. But if these are genuine reasons for divorce at all, then they are genuine reasons for divorce in other cases than this one.

Separation, but not divorce?

So the New Testament already includes two exceptions to the rule forbidding divorce. The churches were required to interpret the teaching of Jesus in the light of prevailing difficulties, just as they are today. If the reasons justifying the exceptions are valid, they are valid for other exceptions too. One can readily think of more grave exceptions – the one permitted at Corinth is trivial compared with some of the grounds for divorce which are heard today, especially those to do with violence and abuse. The conclusion that Christians are free to remarry after divorce is gaining ground, and some may find it disturbing. It is easier to assimilate the wider social practice of divorce than to find genuine theological reasons for it. Some will want further reassurance that divorce and remarriage, not merely separation, is a genuine option.

We will let Jerome Murphy-O'Connor speak for the standard 'no divorce' position. He thinks the texts we have already considered in this chapter from Matthew and Mark clinch his case. He writes:

> The text concerns the fidelity that is demanded of the abandoned partner in a marriage that has broken up ... The radicalism of Christian love means that if one partner defaults the other is not freed ... Christian love ... does not accept the faithlessness of one as sufficient justification for the other to break the original commitment.[27]

This stern conclusion is said to derive further support from the private conversation between Jesus and the disciples. Jesus, we recall, had ruled out divorce and remarriage for any other reason than the wife's 'unchastity'. The incredulity of the disciples at his teaching leads them to remark: 'If that is how things stand for a man with a wife, it is better not to marry' (Matthew 19.10). Jesus replies:

> 'That is a course not everyone can accept, but only those for whom God has appointed it. For while some are incapable of marriage because they were born so, or were made so by men, there are others who have renounced marriage for the sake of the kingdom of Heaven. Let those accept who can.' (Matthew 19.11–12)

The enforced celibacy which this passage is thought to demand of divorcees is deemed to be the required Christian witness to 'the permanent possibility of return and forgiveness for the sinner'.

This text has a long and strange history of interpretation because of the support it allegedly provides for celibacy. Those issues must not detain us now. Using again our general rules for interpreting biblical texts, I offer four reasons why the 'no divorce' interpretation of this passage is wrong. If these reasons are valid the important conclusion follows that the text *places no requirement on partners in wrecked marriages today to testify to the wreckage by refraining from further life-long commitments.*

First, the 'course' which 'not everyone can accept' is not celibacy at all, but life-long and faithful monogamy. There is a remarkable realism here with which modern readers can identify all too well. Life-long and faithful monogamy is an extremely difficult course to take, so difficult in fact that 'only those for whom God has appointed it' should sign up at all. Far from marriage being the biblical norm in the New Testament, Jesus taught that it should not be embarked on at all unless the intending partners have a divinely-given and life-long propensity to faithfulness. It is better not to marry than to decide at some future time during the marriage that the whole thing was a mistake. The ultimate cause of all divorce is marriage! Some cohabitees may be understood to be exercising responsibility in *avoiding* marriage, resisting the once common social expectation that life-long monogamy was their only decent option. I do not think that Jesus, or the New Testament, teaches that those 'who have renounced marriage' must refrain from all sexual activity, but the arguments for this, another unsettling conclusion, must await chapter 11.

Second, Jesus taught a radical shift away from the contemporary practice of divorce on demand, with men the divorcers and women the divorcees. The teaching is aimed at patriarchal men. That is why the disciples tackle Jesus about it afterwards. Women are simply not disposable in the manner they and their contemporaries had come to think. It is the behaviour of men accustomed to divorce their wives for any cause they please that is reprimanded here (Matthew 19.3).

Third, in Matthew's account Jesus says, 'If a man divorces his wife for any cause other than unchastity, and marries another, he commits adultery' (19.9). But the earlier version of this saying in Mark (10.11), which Matthew alters, is 'Whoever divorces his wife and remarries commits adultery *against her* . . .'.[28] Now there is considerable difference between committing adultery *against one's former partner*, and committing adultery against God. Again it is the patriarchal order which is being destroyed, not the life prospects of women divorcees. A man who puts his wife away and marries someone else is sinning against *her*; that is where the wrongness of his action lies. The full authority of the divine commandment is directed against him.

Fourth, the situation addressed by Jesus did not require that the wife be consulted, still less that she give her consent. The possibilities that both partners might want divorce, or that the woman might want divorce, or that a marriage might simply be unrevivable, are not addressed by this text, and the text should not be misused by being applied to them. Matthew's handling of Mark's narrative is awkward. He still assumes that divorce is a male prerogative, and (if 'unchastity' means adultery) his insertion of exception clauses overlooks completely the contributory behaviour of the husband which may have led a wronged spouse to seek solace elsewhere.

Re-marriage?

It is time to draw conclusions. From the second half of this chapter, the conclusion follows that there are exceptions to the rule that a wife and husband must remain married whatever their circumstances. From the first half of the chapter, the conclusion follows that Christian marriage is a life-long, exclusive, sacramental union which is undermined, among other reasons, by the declining sociocultural estimation of it, and, as the present Pope has said, 'To bear witness to the inestimable value of the indissolubility of marriage is one of the most precious and most urgent tasks of Christian couples in our time.'[29] How is it possible to reconcile these conclusions?

These two conclusions represent the genuine polarity which must exist when the Christian vision for marriage is brought to any social context where 'all alike have sinned' (Romans 3.23). That vision for marriage is lived out under the potentially destructive effects of personal, historical, social and cultural sin described in chapter 5, and in part of this present chapter. Within this general milieu, the pressure on marriage is immense. The teaching of Jesus about marriage and its experienced sacramentality will confirm and strengthen the resolve of many partners to remain together: others for whatever reason will drift apart. There is an urgent Christian ministry to the pre-married, the married and the pre-divorced where the indissolubility of marriage will be emphasized. Even then some partners will opt to end their relationship.[30] For those who do, new beginnings are open to them.

No assumption should be made that if a marriage fails, another should be attempted. One possible conclusion to be drawn from a failed marriage could conceivably be that God has not 'appointed' marriage for that person. A divorcee might decide to devote his or her life exclusively to Christian discipleship (Luke 14.26). Alternatively the post-married may explore relationships from another perspective, that of friendship, where commitment is less intense but sexual expression still possible. (We shall discuss this further in chapter 11.) But a further option is remarriage. In cases where one has been wronged, the option of remarriage is a legitimate one. Not all the churches have arrived at this conclusion, but it is nonetheless consistent with Christian teaching.

Notes

1. Peter Brown, *The Body and Society: Men, Women and Sexual Renunciation in Early Christianity* (London: Faber & Faber, 1989), p. 256.
2. D. Sherwin Bailey, *The Man–Woman Relation in Christian Thought* (London: Longman, 1959), p. 133, n. 2.
3. Sources in Bailey.
4. Brown, p. 362.
5. Uta Ranke-Heinemann, *Eunuchs for the Kingdom of Heaven: The Catholic Church and Sexuality* (London: Deutsch, 1990), ch. 6.
6. ibid., p. 195.
7. ibid.
8. For the impact of this on the modern period, see Michel Foucault, *The History of Sexuality Volume 1: An Introduction* (Harmondsworth: Penguin Books, 1981), part 3.
9. Jack Dominian, *Passionate and Compassionate Love: A Vision of Christian Marriage* (London: Darton, Longman & Todd, 1991), pp. 31–2.
10. ibid. pp. 94–5.
11. Shere Hite, *The Hite Report: Women and Love* (London: Penguin/Viking, 1988), p. 395.
12. Annette Lawson, *Adultery: An Analysis of Love and Betrayal* (Oxford: Blackwell, 1989), pp. 28–9 and ch. 7.

13. ibid.
14. The literature is extensive. Alas, my source here is confined to Rudolf Siebert, 'The Frankfurt School: Enlightenment and Sexuality', in G. Baum and J. Coleman (eds), *The Sexual Revolution,Concilium* 173.
15. ibid., p. 30.
16. ibid.
17. Habermas, in Siebert.
18. *Mimesis* 'signifies a relationship between persons, in which the one leans upon the shoulder of the other or nestles to him or to her'. It 'indicates gestures of mutual, unconditional recognition, generosity, tenderness, exuberance, creative love and freedom without revenge' (*op.cit.*, p. 35.)
19. ibid.
20. Susan Dowell, *They Two Shall Be One: Monogamy in History and Religion* (London: Collins/Flame, 1990), p. 64.
21. See above, pp. 86-7
22. If Mark 10.11–12 is taken as a separate saying not belonging originally to the incident to which it became attached, then it is both divorce and re-marriage taken together which is wrong there as well.
23. The position is further complicated by the fact that the verb for divorce in Matthew 19 is used both for 'simple separation' and 'complete divorce with the right to remarry'. See William Heth, 'The Healing of Divorce in Matthew 19.3–9', *Churchman: Journal of Anglican Theology*, 98, no. 2 (1984), p. 140. I have allowed for this ambiguity in developing a different conclusion to Heth's.
24. Strongly supported by Don T. Smith, 'The Matthean Exception Clauses in the Light of Matthew's Theology and Community', *Studia Biblica et Theologica*, 17, no. 1 (1989), pp. 66–78.
25. From the abstract of Gary P. Liaboe, 'The Place of Wife Battering in Considering Divorce', *Journal of Psychology and Theology*, 13 (Summer 1985), pp. 129–38.
26. Stanley A. Marrow, 'Marriage and Divorce in the New Testament', *Anglican Theological Review*, 70 (January 1988), p. 13.
27. Jerome Murphy-O'Connor, in Mary Anne Huddleston (ed.), *Celibate Loving: Encounter in Three Dimensions* (New York: Paulist Press, 1984), p. 200.
28. Emphasis added.
29. John Paul II, *Familiaris Consortio*. See Austin Flannery, OP, *Vatican Council II: More Post Conciliar Documents* (Leominster, Hereford: Fowler Wright, 1982), p. 830.
30. For an agenda of questions to ask in this position, see Edward Collins Vacek, SJ, 'Divorce: Making a Moral Decision', *Anglican Theological Review*,70 (1988), pp. 310–22.

CHAPTER 9

From Homophobia to Neighbourly Love

In chapters 9 and 10 an attempt will be made to apply the sexual theology of earlier chapters to the experience of lesbian and gay people. Unfortunately some of the attitudes of heterosexual Christians still make this difficult, so the present chapter tackles these directly. Homosexual orientation and the current state of causal knowledge about it are discussed with a view to stating Christian principles for thinking about them. These include neighbour-love, the 'golden rule' and the refusal to give false evidence. Some of the causes of homophobia are suggested, and some myths surrounding homosexuals exploded. The gospel is interpreted as liberation for gay Christians. The gifts they bring to the wider Christian community are acknowledged, and continued discrimination towards them is noted as a matter of much sadness. Then in chapter 10, with the ground prepared, work begins on appropriating the sexual theology for lesbian, gay and bisexual people.

Homosexual orientation

The term 'homosexual' first appeared in English in 1891.[1] 'Gay' derives from the thirteenth century Provençal word *gai* where it referred to courtly love, and later, same-sex attraction.[2] A 'homosexual' person is one who is erotically attracted to people of the same (Greek *homos*) sex. The term 'heterosexual' (one who is erotically attracted to people of the 'other' (Greek *heteros*) sex) is later still. The Greek prefixes are misleading, for the ancient world made no attempt to distinguish between people on the grounds of their sexual preferences.

This pair of terms has allowed contemporaries to think that people can be safely allocated to one or other of these self-announcing, clear-cut, categories of person. This is just not true. Alfred Kinsey found that '37 per cent of the male population after adolescence had had some homosexual contact, that 13 per cent had been more homosexual than heterosexual for at least three years between adolescence and 55, and 4 per cent were exclusively homosexual after adolescence.' 'Contact' meant activity leading to orgasm. If orgasm was excluded, 50 per cent had had some 'homosexual dealings'.[3] There has been recent criticism of the composition of the sample used by Kinsey.[4] The critics have themselves been criticized for allowing their dislike of liberal sexual attitudes to interfere with their analyses.[5] Kinsey's conclusions have also been confirmed by others.[6]

In these circumstances it is wise to take Kinsey's conclusions cautiously. He and his researchers produced what is now regarded as a 'classic' 7-point continuum which moves from an exclusive heterosexual orientation (point 0) to an exclusive homosexual orientation (point 6). It is repeated here. There is no need to revise the scale in the light of the recent criticisms, although the exact numbers of persons occupying each point can be expected to receive further scrutiny.

0 fully heterosexual, with no homosexual experience.
1 predominantly heterosexual, with incidental homosexual experience.
2 basically heterosexual, with significant homosexual experience.
3 bisexual, with significant heterosexual and homosexual experience.
4 basically homosexual, with significant heterosexual experience.
5 predominantly homosexual, with incidental heterosexual experience.
6 fully homosexual, with no heterosexual experience.[7]

At least 50 per cent of adult males find themselves at point 1 or above on the scale, and 37 per cent are at point 2 or above. Thus a working assumption is established: substantial numbers of males are neither fully heterosexual nor fully homosexual. Some are bisexual. Since the homo/hetero divide is not yet a century old, and same-sex attraction has been known in every generation, this assumption should entail no surprise. A homosexual male on this view is someone who finds his place somewhere on the continuum between 4 and 6. Same-sex attraction, to some degree, is diffused throughout half of whole populations.

Causes of homosexual orientation

It can be stated with confidence that the ancient world simply assumed that some men would love other men.[8] 'Since very few people in the ancient world considered homosexual behavior odd or abnormal, comments about its etiology were quite rare.'[9] In the modern world the literature on the causes of homosexuality is daunting, weighty enough for any gay or lesbian person to feel stigmatized by it. The search for causes can be an expression of homophobic anxiety. It can intensify the impression, unknown to the ancient world, that homosexuals suffer from a pathological condition.[10] Nonetheless, despite the paucity of any settled conclusions so far, some reference to it now will help both the fight against homophobia and the informing of appropriate Christian attitudes towards homosexual people.

There appear to be three main types of explanation – psychoanalytic, biological and social. Each type has several variations. Freud held that (male) homosexuality occurred when a boy failed to 'transfer his heterosexual libidic attraction from his mother onto other mature females',[11] perhaps because of the strength of the attraction, or some misdirection of it which may be environmentally caused. The theory therefore assumes retarded, arrested or impaired development.[12] According to the 'adaptational' or 'phobic' theory, the child acquires incapacitating fears of the opposite sex, due to unresolved tensions with either parent, or for some other reason.[13] Alternatively the fear may be acquired by the mother and passed on. In 'foetal-distress syndrome'[14] a mother's fear of abandonment by her husband during their pregnancy, or his traumatic failure to support her, leads to her transferring the trauma to the child.

Biological explanations abound. On one account male homosexuals have an excess of the female hormone oestrogen; lesbian women an excess of the male hormone androgen.[15] On another, 'The relative quantity of testosterone available during critical periods of fetal brain development stamps the yet to be born infant with a masculine or feminine orientation, usually but not always in accordance with the genetic sex of the fetus.'[16] Homosexual men are said to have a larger nerve cluster connecting the left and right sides of the brain, called the 'anterior commissure' than their heterosexual counterparts. Alternatively they have a smaller 'interstitial nucleus', another nerve bundle, in the hypothalamus, than heterosexuals.[17] Other studies suggest strong genetic influence. One, based on gay men who are also twins, shows that 52 per cent of identical twin brothers had brothers who were also gay, compared to 22 per cent of fraternal twins and only 11 per cent of adoptive brothers.[18]

Other explanations attempt to understand homosexuality as 'a function of adaptation brought about by natural selection',[19] while yet another kind of explanation denies there is any phenomenon to explain. The 'social constructionists' hold: 'The homosexual is rather an artefact, a "social construction". It was an idea invented in the late eighteenth and nineteenth centuries, primarily by the medical community, so that physicians and associate workers could assume control over a particular segment of society, previously controlled by the Church and the courts.'[20] There were homosexual acts before the nineteenth century, but only in this century is there a distinct personality type with his or her unique 'case history', problematic childhood, etc.

Risky applications

There are incautious theological attempts to proceed as if one or other of these theories were true. Elizabeth Moberley is convinced that lesbian women and gay men have been 'unable to meet the normal developmental need for attachment to the parent of the same sex . . . If the attachment-need later emerges from repression, it seeks fulfilment in a renewed same-sex relationship.'[21] Her approach differs from standard Christian counselling tactics which advocate celibacy or heterosexual marriage, since 'Same-sex love is the *solution* to unmet developmental needs. It is not the problem.'[22] But this well-intentioned position is still not radical enough. It assumes that to be gay is to be in deficit. No sexual expression of homosexual love is allowed. The goal of the counsellor is that ultimately the counsellee is to become heterosexual.

Another notable analysis assumes, with Freud, that all women and men are fundamentally bisexual. Rosemary Ruether writes:

> We are not born heterosexual. We are taught to become heterosexual, through the immense pressures of patriarchal and heterosexual socialization. For some people this heterosexual conditioning fails to 'take'. They grow up feeling themselves attracted primarily to the same sex, although at the same time sinful and perverse because of these feelings.[23]

Why some people resist social conditioning while others do not is not known. If this theory were true, it would render any deficit theories

about gays superfluous, and confirm the spectrum of sexual orientation like that just cited, except for the crucial difference that bisexuality is the norm, and homosexuality and heterosexuality represent
tendencies towards either end of the scale. The theory would completely undermine traditional assumptions about the normativity of
heterosexuality. It would show that heterosexuality was socially
constructed and therefore that it lacked any theological or biological
foundation. However, if the theory is to be understood as expressing
certain basic facts about human sexuality, evidence alone will establish
it, and it cannot so far be said to have been established. If instead it is
floated as a possibility, and one which would lead us simultaneously
to accept more readily all expressions of sexual orientation on Kinsey's
scale 0 to 6, then it may be welcomed. But that position is a moral,
not a scientific one, and reasons supporting it must be stated.

Neighbour-love

What is to be made of this theorizing? Where do we start? Heterosexual readers might want to stand in the shoes of homosexuals and
ask: 'What does it feel like to be told one has suffered an impaired or
defective development as a child? or is in the grip of fear? or is
traumatised? or apparently has bigger or smaller nerve bumps than
heterosexuals?' What if some of the theories are as implausible as they
look? None of them is yet strong enough to be conclusive; some look
to be at best unlikely; some are clearly incompatible with others;
combinations and variations provide almost limitless scope for speculation. And laced with them all is the danger that the very treatment of
lesbian and gay people as pathologically odd maintains the differences
on which homophobia thrives. The saying of Jesus about the speck of
sawdust and the plank applies to the treatment of minorities of any
sort, and so is especially relevant here:

> 'Why do you look at the speck of sawdust in your brother's
> eye, with never a thought for the plank in your own? How can
> you say to your brother, "Let me take the speck out of your
> eye," when all the time there is a plank in your own? You
> hypocrite!' (Matthew 7.3–5)

Christians need a framework for thinking about lesbian and gay
sexuality which is true to the gospel of Christ. The conclusion to be
worked towards is that while homosexual acts, like heterosexual acts,
are sometimes wrong, homophobia is always wrong; homophobia, not
homosexuality, is the plank that needs removal. But that is to anticipate.

The diversity of theory should warn us that while we have much observation, investigation, interpretation and speculation about lesbians and gays, we lack knowledge. This lack of knowledge prompts several further observations. First, ignorance is usually a rampant source of prejudice, so no assumptions about homosexuals being sick, defective or disordered in advance of evidence should be allowed to find shelter in apparently dispassionate aetiological discussion. The principle which suggests itself here is the ninth of the ten commandments: 'Do not give false evidence against your neighbour' (Exodus 20.16). Many assumptions are made about homosexuals which are false and which, under the rubric of this commandment, Christians are simply forbidden to make.

Second, since the causal knowledge sought is genuinely scientific, it will inevitably be of homosexual people considered as objects, whose presence in a predominantly heterosexual world has caused them to be regarded with pathological and behavioural curiosity. The followers of Jesus, while welcoming the dispassionate approach of science will always want to treat people as subjects, ever mindful of the dangers of misrepresentation and victimization which helped to crucify their Lord. The principle which suggests itself here is the second commandment of Jesus: 'You must love your neighbour as yourself.' (Mark 12.31). Homosexual, bisexual and heterosexual people are all our neighbours, and homophobic attitudes towards our neighbours are simply incompatible with the love which Christians will want to extend instead. Loving our neighbours means putting ourselves in their place. It includes being grateful to God for their sheer diversity, whether of race, colour, interests, ages, customs, religious faiths and, of course, sexual orientation. It includes the prayer that with the plank removed from our own eye we may be enriched, not threatened, by diversity and undeterred by specks of difference.

In biblical perspective, 'The faithfulness of the community is best tested by how well the least powerful members of the community are faring.'[24] There can be no serious love without the pursuit of justice. Merely listening to the homosexual neighbour is likely to lead to the simple conclusion that his or her attraction towards people of the same gender does not feel unnatural, dishonourable, phobic, retarded, or sinful, at all, but is just different from how others feel. It is like being left-handed in a right-handed culture. *Sinister* means, of course, 'the left hand', long before it came to mean 'suggestive of evil'. It is hard for minorities *not* to arouse suspicion. There is nothing sinister about being left-handed! And there is nothing sinister about being lesbian or gay. The Golden Rule of Jesus, 'Always treat others as you would like them to treat you: that is the law and the prophets'(Matthew 7.12.), is as applicable here as it is anywhere. But many people, perhaps a majority, *do* think that homosexuals are sinister. This too needs aetiological investigation. We need to know the causes of homophobia, just as much as we need to know the causes of homosexuality.

Causes of homophobia

James Nelson cites several reasons why homophobia is very wide-spread among heterosexual men.[25] First, erotic feelings towards men, which our culture teaches us to disown, get projected onto overtly gay men and disowned there. Second, since gay men are culturally identified as being sexually and successfully active, their apparent sexual prowess becomes envied. Third, gay men who behave as if they were women undermine the patriarchal order. Fourth, since gay men fancy other men, the heterosexual male is afraid of being regarded as an object of sexual attraction. He is accustomed only to meting out this treatment to heterosexual women. And, fifth, 'To seek validation, love, and affection from other men, however, is a fearful thing, for we have been taught to relate to other men on a different basis – competition.'[26]

There is, I think, much psychological realism in these suggestions, which needs to be supplemented by the assessment of the influence of certain biblical passages upon the homophobic mind. Some of these passages were discussed in chapter 2. Inasmuch as they exclude the practices of pederasty, prostitution, promiscuity or homosexual rape, they are vigorously affirmed by gay Christians themselves. These passages have been extensively, not to say exhaustively discussed.[27] Clearly Coleman is right to conclude:

> In estimating the importance of St Paul's teaching for today, the churches face the awkward fact . . . that there is a considerable difference between the ancient institution of pederasty and the freedom gay men and women now seek to commit themselves, within the Christian family, to the only kind of permanent loving relationship, and a physical expression of that relationship, open to them.[28]

> The Bible never speaks of homosexual love nor of homosexual orientation. That a minority of persons are created homosexual and may find spiritually fulfilling love relationships with the same gender was unknown to the biblical writers.[29]

Is there not some more explicit exclusion of homosexuality in the Genesis statement that 'God created human beings in his own image; in the image of God he created them; male and female he created them' (Genesis 1.27)? This verse was used, as we have seen, by Jesus himself, in his teaching on the permanence of marriage. In our time it has been used to point out both the equality of men and women as bearers of God's image, and the dynamic interrelation of the sexes as a reflection of the divine life. But we are occupied here with a narrower, more specific problem, whether the image of God is exclusive to heterosexual relationships, and the answer is plainly not. The context is a creation narrative. The writer is accounting for the origins of things, including people.

> In order to account for the origins of the human race the writer
> . . . would inevitably describe the creation of the separate sexes
> which produce offspring and would comment on the nature of
> the union which brings about procreation. One would no more
> expect an account of gay love than of friendship in Genesis:
> neither could produce offspring.[30]

Even if there is in the text a heterosexual norm, that norm should not be understood to cover the sexual orientation of every single individual.

Obstacles to sexual justice

The dominant heterosexual culture has found it convenient to assume several falsehoods about homosexuals. Now that homosexuals are no longer criminalized, fragmented and silenced, they have been able to organize themselves and challenge the myths. In particular the Lesbian and Gay Christian Movement in Britain, and kindred movements in other countries, testify to a vibrant faith in Christ coupled with a godly intolerance of institutionalized homophobia from their 'straight' heterosexual brothers and sisters in Christ in the mainstream churches. Encounter between Christians of different sexual orientation can be very like that other encounter between Christians and people of other faiths. Meeting them usually makes one aware of their depth of faith, insight and spirituality, and this in turn makes prior judgements about their godlessness and estrangement from God ignorant and unchristian. Since Christians are bound to reject any false evidence against their neighbours, it is important to remove the filter of falsehood through which homosexuals are likely to be viewed. Here are some of the best known myths.

Unnatural?

Plato argued that homosexual acts were unnatural because animals do not perform them. If 'unnatural' means 'contrary to the behaviour of other species within nature', he was wrong. 'We know that in species after species, right through the animal kingdom, students of animal behaviour report unambiguous evidence of homosexual attachments and behaviour – in insects, fish, birds, and lower and higher mammals.'[31]

Sick?

Michael Ruse discusses the issue exhaustively.[32] There is plenty of unhappiness around among homosexuals (loneliness, depression, despair, etc.) but nothing to suggest that unhappiness is caused intrinsically by being gay, as opposed to being gay in a suspicious, intolerant, heterosexual society. A widely recognized study has shown there is no greater incidence of mental illness[33] among homosexuals than among heterosexuals.[34] The study was one of the factors leading both the American Psychiatric Association and the American Psychological Association to remove homosexuality from their official lists of mental disorders. What is left is the filter of heterosexual disapproval. The accusation that someone is sick is no more than a powerful expression of disgust.

Perverse?

A perversion 'involves going against one of culture's values or ends or things considered desirable, and other members of society cannot understand why one would want to go against the value'.[35] I do not know what to say about this. Sodomy is apparently a minority interest among gay men, and the need to wear a condom when engaging in it is by now well understood. It should certainly not be assumed that heterosexual couples do not practise anal intercourse and that when they do, they do anything wrong. Its association with humiliation and violence may account for some of the horror with which many have come to regard it. It could never be right if those were the accompanying intentions, yet for some it is capable of becoming part of a private repertoire of giving and receiving love. Dislike of anal sex, like dislike of oral sex, is more an aesthetic preference than an obvious moral wrong, and, says Ruse wisely, 'one ought to persuade people not to confuse their disgust at a perversion with moral indignation'.[36] Another manifestation of perversity, it is said, is that gay men seek sex in toilets and go 'cottaging'. Well, this illegal and anti-social activity is not confined to homosexual men. All men who do this need help, for they are probably seeking out a place 'where their sexual activity gives rise to intense guilt and shame and where there is always the possibility of their being mugged or arrested – in other words, a real possibility of being punished'.[37] But the assumption that all gay men are, even potentially, 'cottagers', is just the sort of 'false evidence' the ninth commandment forbids.

There is also a fear that some homosexual people have confirmed or even established their orientation by perversely choosing homosexual behaviour, and so perversely forsaking their original heterosexual identity. Some think that Paul had this in mind in Romans 1.27. The suggestion amounts to yet another causal theory – homosexuals are heterosexuals who make perverse choices. To a heterosexual such conduct would plainly be perverse (in accordance with the above definition), and that is a reason for thinking the suggestion groundless. No heterosexual, at least from those on point 0 of the Kinsey scale, would think of having sex with another man.

Promiscuous?

Are gay men and lesbian women more promiscuous than heterosexuals? Some surveys suggest so.[38] Normal rules and constraints may fail to apply in a sub-culture, and that is what some gay bars and clubs have become. Also, permanent relationships are by their nature public, and these are still difficult (if not impossible) to form in some societies where a consequence of being discovered to be gay may be dismissal from employment or physical harm. Promiscuity is an evil whether among gays or straights. Many gay people, perhaps especially Christians, do not condone it.

A threat to the family, to society, etc.?

Lesbian women and gay men often become a reason for division within their families, but do not otherwise threaten them. As more gay people 'come out' and so become more visible, the more likely will heterosexual couples come to see that the nuclear family is not the only way of living together. If this is in turn perceived as a threat, it is so only in the weak sense of some people feeling disconcerted by other people who are different from them.

Child-abusers?

This is surely the most wicked of all the allegations made about gay people. We can in fact be sure that child abuse occurs disproportionately among heterosexuals.

Obsessed with sex?

Perhaps, but no more than heterosexuals. Since gay men and lesbian women are defined by their sexual interests, everything else about them comes second.

Sinful?

A whole catalogue of sexual sins such as those discussed in chapter 5 is open to gays, as it is to straights. There is no good theological reason why, given the groundwork of earlier chapters, same-sex expressions of love should be in themselves sinful at all.[39] It is of course well known that according to Jewish law, 'If a man has intercourse with a man as with a woman, both commit an abomination. They must be put to death; their blood be on their own heads!' (Leviticus 20.13). But Christians know perfectly well that, if they are faithful to the teachings of the New Testament, they are entitled to set aside the legal prescriptions of the Old, as of course they generally do. There is no outrage in the Old Testament against the relationship between David and Jonathan. 'Your love for me was wonderful,' grieved David on hearing of Jonathan's death, 'surpassing the love of women' (2 Samuel 1.26). Since none of the biblical references to homosexuality also refer to homosexual love (except perhaps this one) there are no biblical grounds for concluding homosexual love is sinful.

Christian liberation for lesbian women and gay men

Lesbian and gay Christians have come to see themselves in the light of the gospel and outside the homophobic attitudes by which the gospel message is stifled. From this liberation perspective, a particular emphasis may be placed on God as the creator of all things: 'Without him no created thing came into being' (John 1.3). From a Christian liberation perspective, a person's sexuality and so sexual orientation is a divine gift. It does not need to be renounced, concealed, pronounced sick, or regarded as deficient. Indeed, to do this is to disown what God has given.

Second, the gospel is the good news that God accepts us as we are. This was the fundamental issue of sixteenth-century controversies over what was then called 'justification'. The sinner is made right with God neither by believing right doctrines nor by performing good works but simply on the basis of that gracious love which was revealed in Jesus Christ. The human response is to accept that we are accepted. Paul Tillich, the great Protestant theologian, often used to speak of the experience of the gospel as a voice saying to us, 'Do not seek for anything; do not perform anything; do not intend anything. *Simply accept the fact that you are accepted!*' 'If that happens to us', he went on, 'we experience grace.'[40] Our need of divine grace is a human need, and God meets it unconditionally in Christ.

Third, just because the acceptance of the sinner is without condition and without qualification, the trustees of the gospel message are in constant danger of reducing it to something more manageable, restricted and human. Conditionalizing strategies like, 'God loves the homosexual but hates his sin', 'God accepts the person but not the orientation', or 'Gays are accepted as long as they pretend to be straight', or 'Homosexual orientation is not sinful but homosexual acts are', etc. are all variations on a reductive theme, reducing the gospel to a merely human message and reducing homosexual people to how heterosexual people would prefer them to be. These strategies are sinful attempts to let some people off loving other people they have chosen not to like.

Fourth, a consequence of receiving the good news of God's empowering love is that one has already chosen life, 'life in all its fullness' (John 10.10). Sexuality is too much a part of a person's totality for it to be separated out from the rest of him or her, and repressed. It is hard to see how sexual repression and salvation are compatible:

> For many people, in an effort to repress their sexual feelings, crush out all feeling whatsoever and live lives devoid of warmth and intimacy . . . The unloving suppression of the self's erotic needs frequently leads to the destructive acting out of those needs. What we reject in ourselves, we tend to project outward: sexism, heterosexism, homophobia, hatred of women or hatred of men, racism.[41]

God has made us to become lovers, and sin is primarily a failure to live in love. Some homosexual people, like some heterosexual people, may well have the gift of celibacy, but the majority will have a God-given desire for same-sex love, and only through the realization and expression of this love will fulfilment arrive. In all this, lesbian women and gay men are subject to the same standards of self-discipline and personal holiness as everyone else, no greater, no less.

The gifts of lesbian and gay Christians

John McNeil holds that there is a 'special providence' in the emergence of visible gay and lesbian communities within the Church at present.[42]

He is right. Those Christians who have accepted their same-sex orientation as part of their created goodness and who have risen above the inhibiting and stultifying propaganda of heterosexism are living witnesses to that incarnated spirituality of the body which challenges the inherited body-spirit dualism and causes it to retreat, defeated. The confident sense of embodiment which lesbian and gay Christians resonate in their lives mark them out as 'a resurrection people'.[43]

We have often had cause to mention the need to overcome the excessive emphasis on individuals in western culture, leading to 'the Myth of me' and 'the culture of narcissism'. Lesbian and gay Christians have had to struggle against the procreative ethic of the past and to forge instead 'a new understanding of sexual relations based on an interpersonal ethics of love' and on 'the equality of the partners. Since gay couples have been obliged to form such an ethic, there is a providential aspect to the emergence of a christian gay community at this point in history.'[44] With patriarchal marriage in deep trouble, the conventionally married and those contemplating marriage now have alternative unions to learn about and learn from. The loneliness and alienation which gay and lesbian people have had traditionally to endure is at last being overcome within communities where hurt and anger can be expressed, where people are accepted despite their intense self-rejection and where the grace of God is sacramentally available. The sense of community which the spiritual needs of lesbian and gay people have created is often deeper than the sense of community in mainstream congregations. The experience of rejection and the care of people dying of AIDS has led to the claim that hospitality and compassion are particularly to be found in the gay community.

There must be no suggestion that the emerging lesbian and gay spirituality is valuable only for what straight Christians can learn from it; rather, it is full of riches beyond the imaginations of those who are homophobic, and it is a living reminder that like other evils which have divided the body of Christ, bigotry, sexism, racism, and the like, homophobia has no permanent reality. At the same time it is important not to idealize the achievement of lesbian women and gay men, both inside and outside Christian communities. The broader gay community has a great need for the restorative grace of God which lesbian and gay Christians can mediate to them. There is deep unhappiness among some homosexuals, with self-hate and self-mockery, problems with alcohol and drugs, demeaning attitudes to the opposite sex and a destructive self-preoccupation.[45] The gospel of Christ addresses this, not in judgement and rejection, but in divine acceptance and love.

Limitations on gay rights

God has made us all to be lovers (whether or not our love is sexually expressed), and some of us will fulfil our created natures in same-sex unions. The form of these, and the pastoral problems surrounding them are considered in the next chapter. However the Roman Catholic Church has a different view. The Vatican continues to uphold the natural law tradition, to proclaim that every sexual act must be open to procreative intention, and to regard itself as above all criticism in such matters. The Vatican Declaration on Sexual Ethics spells out that 'homosexual acts are intrinsically disordered'.[46] The Pastoral Letter of 1986 extended the accusation of disorder more or less to the heart of the homosexual person: 'Although the particular inclination of the homosexual person is not a sin, it is a more or less strong tendency towards an intrinsic moral evil; and thus the inclination itself must be seen as an objective disorder.'[47]

The psychological impact of the Vatican teaching on most Catholic Christians who take it seriously is, of course, disastrous. If one conforms to the church's teaching, even one's inclinations are an objective disorder.

> One must then repress all sexual feelings (and with them, all other feelings). Any person who does this necessarily hates an essential part of him- or herself, and this self-hatred frequently spills over in a paranoid hatred of all homosexuals. It is these self-hating gays within the church's power structure who frequently become our worst persecutors.[48]

In June 1992, a further letter from the Congregation for the Doctrine of the Faith to the US bishops warned against forthcoming legislation which would extend legal rights to gays: 'There are areas in which it is not unjust discrimination to take sexual orientation into account, for example, in the consignment of children to adoption or foster care, in employment of teachers or coaches, and in military recruitment' (para. 11). Many of the pernicious myths already dismissed in this chapter are now assumed as sacred truths. Gays undermine 'the family and society' (Foreword, and para. 9). Children, physical education students and soldiers, are clearly not safe where there are gays about. The rights of homosexual persons 'can be legitimately limited for objectively disordered external conduct', as 'in the case of contagious or mentally ill persons, in order to protect the common good' (para. 12).

This gross offence continues throughout the letter. Closeted gays, that is 'the majority of homosexually oriented persons who seek to lead chaste lives', represent no threat to the church because their sexual orientation is concealed. But the church must be wary of liberated gays, because 'from this quarter' will come 'those who judge homosexual behaviour or lifestyle' to be, in the words of the 1986 letter, 'either completely harmless, if not an entirely good thing'. It is remarkable that such attitudes should persist in the church. Fortunately there are other Christian voices to listen to, and some of these are more faithful to the gospel of liberation and love.

Notes

1. John Boswell, *Christianity, Social Tolerance, and Homosexuality: Gay People in Western Europe from the Beginning of the Christian Era to the Fourteenth Century* (Chicago and London: University of Chicago Press, 1980), p. 42.
2. ibid., p. 43, n. 6.
3. Michael Ruse, *Homosexuality: A Philosophical Inquiry* (Oxford: Blackwell, 1988), pp. 4–6.
4. Judith Reisman and Edward W. Eichel, *Kinsey, Sex and Fraud: The Indoctrination of a People* (Lafayette, Louisiana: Huntingdon House, 1990).
5. See e.g. the review in *The Lancet* 337 (2 March 1991), p. 547.
6. References in Ruse.
7. ibid., pp. 5–6.
8. Peter Brown, *The Body and Society: Men, Women and Sexual Renunciation in Early Christianity* (London: Faber & Faber, 1990), p. 30; Robin Lane Fox, *Pagans and Christians* (Harmondsworth: Penguin Books, 1986), p. 346; Boswell, p. 59.
9. Boswell, p. 49.
10. But see Ruse, pp. 19–20 for proper, and moral, reasons why scientific study of homosexuality should continue.
11. See Ruse, p. 23.
12. The clinical details and post-Freudian developments of the theory must be consulted elsewhere, e.g. Ruse, chs 2–4.
13. Sources in Ruse, ch. 3.
14. Frank Lake, *Tight Corners in Pastoral Counselling* (London: Darton, Longman & Todd, 1981), pp. 150–2.
15. Described, though not endorsed, by Ruse, p. 97.
16. John Shelby Spong, commenting on the work of Gunter Dorner, in *Living in Sin? A Bishop Rethinks Human Sexuality* (San Francisco: Harper & Row, 1988), pp. 73–4.
17. Both reported in *The Guardian*, 3 August 1992.
18. Reported in *The Guardian*, 18 December 1991. The American journal *Archives of General Psychiatry* (December 1991) was cited.
19. Ruse, ch. 6.
20. ibid., pp. 15–16, commenting on Foucault.
21. Elizabeth Moberley, 'First Aid in Pastoral Care, 15: Counselling the Homosexual', *The Expository Times*, 96 (June 1985), pp. 262–6. See her *Psychogenesis* (London: Routledge & Kegan Paul, 1983) and *Homosexual-*

ity: A New Christian Ethic (Cambridge: James Clarke, 1983), for the research and theological support for this view.

22. ibid., (author's emphasis).

23. Rosemary Radford Ruether, 'Homophobia, Heterosexism, and Pastoral Practice' in Jeannine Gramick (ed.), *Homosexuality in the Priesthood and the Religious Life* (New York: Crossroad, 1989) p. 30.

24. General Assembly Special Committee on Human Sexuality, *Keeping Body and Soul Together: Sexuality, Spirituality, and Social Justice* (General Assembly Special Committee on Human Sexuality, Presbyterian Church, USA, 1991), p. 19.

25. James B. Nelson, *The Intimate Connection: Male Sexuality, Masculine Spirituality* (London: SPCK, 1992), pp. 61–2.

26. ibid., p. 62.

27. Peter Coleman, *Gay Christians: A Moral Dilemma* (London: SCM Press, 1989), Part 3, 'Searching the Scriptures'; Robin Scroggs, *The New Testament and Homosexuality* (Fortress Press, 1983); William Countryman, *Dirt, Greed and Sex* (London: SCM Press, 1989) *passim*; Homosexuality Working Party of the United Reformed Church, *Homosexuality* (London: United Reformed Church, 1991); *Issues in Human Sexuality: A Statement by the House of Bishops* (London: Church House Publishing, 1991), ch. 2; etc.

28. Coleman, p. 88.

29. Chris Glaser, *Come Home! Reclaiming Spirituality and Community as Gay Men and Lesbians* (San Francisco: Harper & Row, 1990), p. 31.

30. Boswell, p. 105.

31. Ruse, p. 189.

32. ibid., ch. 9.

33. The vast question of what mental illness is, or even whether it exists, is suspended here.

34. *Keeping Body and Soul Together*, p. 95.

35. Ruse, pp. 199–200.

36. ibid, p. 201.

37. John J. McNeil, *Taking a Chance on God: Liberating Theology for Gays, Lesbians and their Lovers, Families, and Friends* (Boston: Beacon Press, 1988), p. 58.

38. Ruse, p. 10.

39. For appropriate theological responses to AIDS see James Woodward (ed.), *Embracing the Chaos: Theological Responses to AIDS* (London: SPCK, 1990).

40. Paul Tillich, *The Shaking of the Foundations* (Harmondsworth: Pelican Books, 1962), p. 163 (author's emphasis).

41. McNeil, p. 125.

42. John J. McNeil, *The Church and the Homosexual* (Boston: Beacon Press, 1988), and 'Homosexuality, Lesbianism and the Future: The Creative Role of the Gay Community in Building a More Humane Society' in Robert Nugent (ed.), *A Challenge to Love: Gay and Lesbian Catholics in the Church* (New York: Crossroad, 1984).

43. McNeil, *Taking a Chance*, p. 156.

44. ibid., p. 201.

45. ibid., pp. 191–2.

46. Sacred Congregation for the Doctrine of the Faith, 'Declaration on Certain Problems of Sexual Ethics', §8. see Austin Flannery OP, *Vatican Council II: More Post Conciliar Documents* (Leominster, Hereford: Fowler Wright, 1982), p. 491.

47. Texts in Coleman, p. 146.

48. McNeil, p.36.

CHAPTER 10

Lifelong Unions for Gay and Lesbian People

The demands of neighbourly love and sexual justice lead to the conclusion that the blessing of lesbian and gay unions by the churches is overdue. This chapter proposes that marriage become inclusive of sexual minorities. The term 'union' is preferred to 'marriage'. The theological arguments of the Anglican bishops, that homosexuality is an inferior orientation, are criticized, and the insistence upon compulsory celibacy for clergy is rejected. Some negative pastoral consequences of the failure to recognize gay unions are described. Lesbian sexuality is discussed and lifelong unions advocated as a strong option for lesbian Christian women. Finally a plea is made for greater understanding of bisexual people.

Inclusive marriages

The Second Vatican Council expressed a positive view of married love: '[It is] an affection between two persons rooted in the will and it embraces the good of the whole person; it can enrich the sentiments of the spirit and their physical expression with a unique dignity and ennoble them as the special elements and signs of the friendship proper to marriage.' It is a sharing in the divine love. It 'leads the partners to a free and mutual giving of self, experienced in tenderness and action, and permeates their whole lives.' 'The acts in marriage by which the intimate and chaste union of the spouses take place are noble and honourable.' Married love is 'consecrated by Christ's sacrament'.[1]

The time has come for marriage to be extended to lesbian and gay partners. It should be inclusive of all who desire it and no longer exclusive to heterosexual people only. The Vatican statement is shot through with the assumption that 'marriage and married love are by nature ordered to the procreation and education of children'.[2] Without this assumption the description of married love, including its sacramental dimension, could equally apply to committed lesbian and gay couples. There are signposts, even in this text, towards a more inclusive view of marriage. That married love is 'an eminently human love' might suggest to some that 'human love' is broader than heterosexual love,[3] that is, it could include all human beings within the spectrum of orientations observed in chapter 9. For married but childless heterosexual couples 'marriage still retains its character of being a whole manner and communion of life and preserves its value and indissolubility'.[4] A homosexual couple might be fairly compared with a heterosexual childless couple. That would not be a demeaning reference to a common lack. It would be only a reminder that the fruitfulness and creativity of marriages is neither defined by, nor exhausted by, having children. Procreation is unnecessary to the success of marriage.

Once the purposes of marriage are widened from a purely procreative basis, those purposes are clearly able to be fulfilled by lesbian women and gay men. The second of the three purposes of marriage in the Book of Common Prayer is 'a remedy against sin, and to avoid fornication'. Since homosexual people are just as randy as heterosexual people, this blunt concession is clearly applicable to them if it is applicable to anyone (it is dropped from the 1980 Alternative Service Book). If marriage really is given to avoid fornication then the refusal of it to gay people is indefensible, since they are being denied the principal means for the avoidance of it. So much for the charge of promiscuity!

The Alternative Service Book declares instead that:

> Marriage is given . . . that husband and wife may comfort and help each other, living faithfully together in need and in plenty, in sorrow and in joy. It is given, that with delight and tenderness they may know each other in love, and, through the joy of their bodily union, may strengthen the union of their hearts and lives.[4]

The third purpose is having and caring for children. The first two purposes would clearly apply to same-sex marriages. The third one does not. But this purpose cannot apply either to couples requesting marriage who are unable or too old to have children. The inapplicability of the procreative purpose to such marriages is no reason for the church not performing the marriage: neither should it be so when lesbian women and gay men seek the blessing of God on their lifelong unions.

We have already noted that, according to a thirteenth-century interpretation, marriage was established by consent between the parties, with the corollary that 'coitus (though a normal feature of marital life) is merely an accessory, and not an intrinsic element in matrimony itself'.[5] This account of marriage is unsatisfactory (and far from the teaching of Jesus about one flesh). Nonetheless, the implication is clear. In the thirteenth century (though not now in our own), coitus must precede procreation. Yet coitus is severely discouraged and never praised more than when it doesn't happen. If marriage is essentially 'a purely consensual union' there is simply no point in confining it to heterosexual couples.

Those same-sex couples who have committed themselves to a faithful lifelong union before God, *are* married before God. That is because, as Aquinas says, 'the ministers of the sacrament of marriage are the bride and bridegroom themselves, and the form of the sacrament is their consent'.[6] They are denied recognition, and so solemnization and blessing from the church, but God and the church are often on different sides. And since the church does not recognize their union, nation states have not yet legislated to provide secular recognition either. But lesbian and gay couples will testify to the sacramental character of their unions: they may be even more conscious of it than their heterosexual counterparts since the discernment of God's grace has to be made out of much religious and social disapproval. That moving description in the Alternative Service Book of the married relationship fits the actual, lived experience of same-sex couples in the same way as the conventionally married.

The grounds for continuing to refuse the blessing of the church on lesbian and gay unions have crumbled away. The greater visibility of same-sex unions surely provides sufficient evidence for sceptics that God does not withhold sacramentality from them even if the church does. That there exists committed love between both homosexual and heterosexual persons is perhaps a state of affairs at which Trinitarian theology might have already hinted. In God each of the Persons transcends gender difference. The love between them is clearly not heterosexual. There is a blessing to be derived from a liturgy performed in the name of Jesus by the people of God which links the experience of the couple to the Christian tradition they both affirm, and this blessing is officially withheld. The withholding of a good cannot arguably be justified unless there is a greater good which it brings about. But the confinement of marriage to heterosexual couples is no such greater good. Indeed it is quite obviously a harm. The denial of blessing to lesbian and gay people is a major cause of uncertainty in their communities about whether monogamous unions are goods at all.

Why 'marriage'?

Is 'marriage' a suitable term for the blessing of same-sex unions? There are arguments here on both sides. Some would argue that heterosexual marriage is fundamentally unequal and the partners bound by conventional and patriarchal roles. 'Marriage' would misname the type of permanent relationship sought by lesbians and gays. Again, marriage is so strongly associated in the popular mind with heterosexuals and children that the extension of the term to homosexual relationships would invite confusion (and misdescription). On the other side it may be stressed that if same-sex unions are not marriages, then they are something else, and that something else is certain to be regarded as inferior, 'substandard' or 'abnormal'.[7] The understanding and practice of marriage has changed historically, and a further change, which includes same-sex unions but without a change of name, is now appropriate.

Robert Williams has recently proposed an inclusive working definition of marriage (based on the canons of the Episcopal Church of the USA). It is:

> A lifelong union of two persons in heart, body, and mind, as set forth in liturgical forms authorized by this Church, for the purpose of mutual joy, for the help and comfort given one another in prosperity and adversity; sometimes also for the procreation and/or rearing of children, and their physical and spiritual nurture.[8]

'Lifelong union' preserves one of marriage's essential elements. It is what makes a marriage a marriage. As long as any ceremony honours and blesses an intended lifelong union, I cannot see that the failure to call it 'marriage' in any sense implies its inferiority. 'Holy union' or 'lifelong union' are also available.

More important is whether marriage is appropriate among lesbians and gays at all. Marriages are sometimes violent and frequently end in divorce. Is it not more appropriate to abandon lifelong monogamy in favour of other patterns of relationship, say serial monogamy, or friendships, some of which may be sexual? The issue is a legitimate one among gay Christians. All the benefits of marriage described in chapter 6 are available to lifelong faithful partners, including its sacramentality, children excepted. Even as an option it is still an attractive one. John McNeil, a noted spokesperson for the lesbian and gay Christian community, agrees. He argues that:

> A committed, faithful, loving relationship as the ideal context for all human sexual expression is based on the nature of being human . . . We are dealing with a fundamental need built into human nature that has to do with the development of trust and love and the greatest possible development of psychic maturity and health.[9]

Inferior orientations?

The statement by the Church of England House of Bishops, *Issues in Human Sexuality*, is in many respects a progressive document. Elizabeth Stuart has drawn attention to the 'marked difference in tone and style' between this statement and the 1986 Vatican letter on homosexuality.[10] However it stops far short of the proposal for recognizing and blessing the lifelong unions of lesbian women and gay men, limply noting that 'the mind of the church' is not ready for such matters.[11] It is necessary to comment on this element of the statement, and thereby to contribute to the bishops' intention 'to help forward a general process, marked by greater trust and openness, of Christian reflection on the subject of human sexuality'.[12]

The bishops state:

> Homophile[13] orientation and its expression in sexual activity do not constitute a parallel and alternative form of human sexuality as complete within the terms of the created order as the heterosexual . . . Heterosexuality and homosexuality are not equally congruous with the observed order of creation or with the insights of revelation. . .'.[14]

They firmly deny that their position denigrates homophile people or their sexuality. Sexuality is

> . . . a very important and influential element in our human make-up, but it is only one aspect of it. Our sexuality may vary from the norm in many ways, of which a homophile orientation is but one, without affecting our equal worth and dignity as human beings, which rests on the fact that all of us alike are made in the image of God.[15]

Nonetheless 'a loving and faithful homophile partnership, in intention lifelong' is not rejected, and 'homophile' Christians may appeal to the authority of conscience in arriving at such partnerships.[16]

Compulsory celibacy and Anglican clergy

With clergy, however, matters are different. The lives of clergy 'must be free of anything which will make it difficult for others to have confidence in them as messengers, watchmen and stewards of the Lord'.[17] Since the church cannot commend 'homophile relationships', gay clergy must be celibate. They cannot be allowed to help to overcome the dire shortage of 'role models' for gay marriages: 'It is unrealistic to suppose that these clergy could in most parishes be accepted as examples to the whole flock as distinct from the homophiles within it.'[18] If the church were to permit the clergy 'to enter into sexually active homophile relationships', that would invite the charge from outside the church that such relationships were 'on a par with heterosexual marriage as a reflection of God's purposes in creation'. Such 'parity' would have no warrant from Scripture, tradition or experience.[19]

All British churches expect celibacy of gay clergy. The ministerial recognition rules of the Baptist Union state, 'homosexual genital practice is to be regarded as unacceptable in the pastoral office', and even the advocacy of 'homosexual or lesbian genital relationships as acceptable alternatives to male/female partnership in marriage' is regarded as 'conduct unbecoming to the ministry'.[20] The bishops are clearly worried about parity of esteem or status between homosexuals and heterosexuals and their unions. That is why they are said not to be 'equally congruous with the observed order of creation', and their unions are not 'on a par with' each other. In a further comment the Archbishop of York adds that homophile relationships 'must not be regarded as on a par with marriage'.[21] But the deeper issue that needs attention is not parity at all, but the acceptance of diversity. Heterosexual marriage is set up as the norm by which homosexual unions are to be judged, and found wanting. Even this might be accepted by lesbian and gay people if 'norm' meant what most people's sexual preferences are, and those with different preferences received equal treatment. But it does not mean that. Talk of norms implies deviations, and there are no deviations without deviants.

The claim that homosexual unions are not congruous with 'the observed order of creation' refers back to 'the purposes of procreation' in the creation narratives and the 'complementarity' between men and women which is said to be found there.[22] We have already noted (see chapter 8) that within creation narratives we are likely to find an explanation for the creation and transmission of life, not pastoral guidance about something else. But the Archbishop of York's worry about parity is based on a different argument. He is against parity of esteem because, as he says, while the essence of heterosexual marriage is 'grounded in a publicly acknowledged social institution', permanent homosexual relationships are 'just a personal relationship between two individuals', and public and private arrangements should not be confused. The hidden premise of this argument is that the *status quo* can't change, rather like saying (as some doubtless did say, at the beginning of this century) that women's votes, unlike men's votes, would not be real votes, because historically and institutionally voting has been confined to men. If gay marriages lack public acknowledgement as a social institution, no one is in a stronger position than an Archbishop to do something about it.

There is a more serious problem with the bishops' estimate of homosexual orientation. The bishops have said that sexuality can differ from the norm; that any difference from the norm makes no difference to the equal worth and status of human beings; and that this status is guaranteed by all of us having been made in the image of God. This looks innocent theological comment, but it is no such thing. By separating out sexuality, equality and the image of God, sexuality and the image of God have also become separated from each other. The image of God functions (rightly) to guarantee the equal dignity and worth of each human being. But that is its only function. The sexuality of the human being has become tacitly removed from what the human being is allowed to image of God. And this cannot be right. It may be true that sexuality is only part of a person's nature, but that is no reason for excluding it from imaging God. It was argued in earlier chapters that sexuality, and the accompanying desire, image God as fully as any other part of a person's nature. What the bishops have done is to separate lesbian and gay orientation from any discussion of their orientation reflecting God's image. And that is exactly what needs discussion, not evasion.

Other powerful arguments are not allowed expression in the statement. Gay partnerships are not rejected in the Christian community on grounds of conscience. The danger here is that the appeal to conscience is the appeal of last resort, an appeal to private judgement when public action-guiding principles point the other way. But the tradition is not uniformly anti-gay or without signposts that point towards the acceptance of same-sex marriages. The remarkable work of John Boswell itself suggests a different story. 'The early Christian church does not appear to have opposed homosexual behavior per se . . . no prominent writers seem to have considered homosexual attraction "unnatural"'.[23] Elsewhere he writes of a strand of spirituality in religious communities (of the sixth century) which 'not only accepted but idealized love between persons of the same sex, both in and out of religious life'. Religious ceremonies for same-sex unions exist as evidence of their practice.[24] The case for same-sex unions has arguments and precedents to support it, as well as the authority of conscience.

One precedent may be found in the Old Testament. There is 'significant biblical precedent for celebrating a covenant between individuals of the same sex . . . "Jonathan and David made a solemn compact because each loved the other as dearly as himself." (1 Samuel 18.3–4) . . . This sealed a relationship that at least one parent saw as sexually perverse.'[25] A male ordination candidate today who declared he had made a compact with someone he loved as dearly as himself would not get as far as the selection conference.

What the punters can stand

The difficulty the bishops face is that the arguments take them further than the laity is prepared to go. There can be no actively gay clergy in lifelong unions because clergy have to lead exemplary lives beyond the standards expected of the laity, and since heterosexual standards are higher than homosexual ones, 'sexually active homophile relationships' are open to the laity only. Well, this clearly is no more than a temporary position since its difficulties are embarrassingly obvious. There are assumptions about the inferior ministry of the laity which must not detain us. Either lifelong unions are blessed by God or they are not. The statement promotes a further unwelcome dualism, that of orientation and practice. It is OK to be gay (although gayness may not image God), but if you are a minister you may not give expression to being gay. In other words, the Church of England demands of homosexual clergy what the Roman Catholic Church demands of all clergy: compulsory celibacy. And now the report is contradictory, for the bishops have already granted, 'It is . . . increasingly recognised in the Churches today that celibacy is a special gift and calling of the Holy Spirit . . . Celibacy cannot be prescribed for anyone.'[26] Yet they go on to prescribe it for all gay clergy.

The position that homosexual orientation is good but practice is not, was parodied in 1986, before the bishops wrote, as the 'be-but-don't-do' position.[27] All British churches require celibacy of their homosexual ministers. Compulsory celibacy is the product of patriarchy, the suppression of sex and the oppression of the sexual subject. Protestant churches have rejected compulsory celibacy. The Reformation tradition redefined the purposes of marriage to include mutual love. The Protestant churches should not now impose celibacy on gay clergy but instead complete the unfinished business of the Reformation and permit lifelong unions to all those gay ministers whom God continues to call. Gay clergy are now being required to bear the weight of homophobic discrimination, and the official reason is that the mind of the church is not ready for change. As one priest wrote, irreverently but accurately, 'If the punters would accept it, the clergy could do it!' [28] Fortunately the bishops acknowledge that the church has only just 'begun to listen to its homophile brothers and sisters, and must deepen and extend that listening, finding through joint prayer and reflection a truer understanding and the love that casts out fear'.[29] Matters cannot rest where they are.

Pastoral consequences

Much unhappiness among homosexuals is directly attributable to heterosexist intolerance of sexual diversity. The churches have contributed to this, and some are beginning to recognize the need for repentance and restitution. The pastoral consequences of heterosexism are apparent to all clergy. What advice is to be given to adolescents who present themselves as homosexual, or who do not identify comfortably with either classificatory term? How many could, or would, confide in their minister? How many ministers are informed about research on sexual orientation? The blanket of silence, shattered occasionally by pulpit condemnation, powerfully contributes to religious alienation and the internalization of guilt, whereas an uncompromising Christian sexual theology sees sexuality, regardless of orientation, as a gift from God, which bestows the power of self-acceptance and confers the grace of responsible, joyful loving.

Pastoral advice commonly leads to an ultimatum. Remain celibate or look for an opposite-sex partner. Since orientation is sometimes not as fixed as the labels 'homosexual' and 'lesbian' imply, the expectation of definiteness is sometimes unrealized, leading to unhappiness and confusion. But celibacy is a 'gift' (1 Corinthians 7.7), and that term implies most of us do not have it.   A quarter of gay men are married (to women). Why? Possible reasons why gay men *and* women marry include 'insufficient awareness of one's gayness at the time of marriage', 'a conscious desire to escape from the knowledge of one's gayness', 'rational choice', and 'social and familial pressures'.[30]

In most cases 'the heterosexual spouse *is not aware of his or her partner's homosexuality*'.[31] Simple social acceptance of sexual diversity and a mature sexual theology which celebrates sexuality without regard to fixed orientations would help immeasurably. Perhaps one of the saddest pastoral situations is the Christian lesbian or gay person who, lacking the gift of celibacy and aching for love, confuses the influence of bad procreative theology and insistent heterosexism with the call of God to live a celibate life. Celibacy is indeed a gift; compulsory celibacy never.

Lesbian unions

Lesbian women and gay men lead different and separate lives. They sometimes come together because of common interests. But even the phrase 'lesbian and gay' can be an invitation to heterosexuals to lump together all homosexuals as if there were no significant differences between their lifestyles. This is a mistake.

When women love women they begin to free themselves from male assumptions about love and love-making. This freedom extends more broadly into freedom from male definitions and expectations. Men become unnecessary for women's sexual fulfilment. Procreative sex is not on the agenda. Neither is the penetrative sex that accomplishes it nor the contraceptive measures necessary to prevent it. Discharged semen does not have to be taken care of. As one of Hite's interviewees remarked when explaining why she preferred sex with a woman, 'We had no need of the vagina except for what felt good to the possessor of it.'[32] Another difference is that lesbian women are less promiscuous than gay men.[33]

There is growing evidence that more women choose to become lesbian than men choose to become gay, as a conscious political option. This finding introduces a further bundle of complications for a theology which works with heterosexism and procreation as approved sexual norms. It may be too hasty (and convenient) to assert that homosexuality is inevitably 'not something one chooses, it is something one is'.[34] The Hite Report declared, 'Amazingly, 24% of the gay women in this study were having a lesbian relationship for the first time after age 40; this represents a definite departure from past statistics.'[35] 32 per cent of gay women in the same study were heterosexually married before embarking on lesbian relationships, and 92 per cent over 35 in gay relationships say 'this is providing them with an excellent base for their lives'.[36] Lesbians and gays are at last becoming more visible, and the possibility of meeting other lesbian women is greater than it has probably ever been. The Hite Report also catalogues the discontent that women report with their marriages, based on continued inequality and the persistence of patriarchal attitudes. They do not expect to encounter these in relationships with women, and are more confident and autonomous to undertake them.

Rosemary Ruether's reaffirmation of the original bisexuality of all women and men *may* help to explain the choices of heterosexual women who enter into lesbian relationships. She writes:

> There is some evidence that notions of rigid sex orientation are less prevalent among women than men. Lesbians are more likely to say that their homosexuality is an expression of their general capacity to be sexual, and that this reflects their general capacity to love, to be attracted to and affectionate toward other people, female or male. These women see their lesbianism less as a fixed biological necessity than as a social choice. They would say that they have chosen to love women rather than men because, in a patriarchal society, lesbian relations are less violent and coercive and more conducive to loving mutuality than are relations with males. Since patriarchal society sets up heterosexual marriage as a relationship of domination and subordination, fully moral – that is, loving and mutual – relations are possible only between women. Lesbianism is an expression of this social morality.[37]

Lesbian relationships are thus a political response to patriarchy, either to the cramping experience of it in heterosexual marriages, or to the heterosexual conditioning which channels our original 'polymorphous bisexuality' towards heterosexual marriage 'for the purpose of procreation and child-raising'.[38] This conditioning includes availability only to people who are of the right gender, race and class, that is, 'people who are "marriageable", according to racial and ethnic endogamy and hierarchy'. The causes of our actual sexual preferences are as much a mystery as they ever were. 'As in all human development, the biological and the social are so deeply intertwined as to be inextricable.'[39] Orientation is complicated, and bisexual orientation will shortly complicate it further.

This is a disturbing analysis for conventional theology. Its bisexual premise must be treated cautiously. We must note that the turning away of some 'heterosexual' women from marriage, together with the refusal of some lesbian women to adopt arrangements which resemble it, may in large part be due to its patriarchal form, not to its inherent defects or structural inequalities. Faithful unions of Christian lesbian women are able to contribute greatly to that working out of a non-patriarchal form of marriage which is not yet secured. While there are strong arguments for the recognition and blessing of lesbian unions as a plain matter of justice, the question is whether lesbians actually want this for themselves. Romantic marriage needs to be supplemented by a deep-rooted mimesis and non-possessive devotion which has sacramental roots and is grounded in holy trinitarian love. Some lesbian and gay Christians already claim this sacramental grace for their unions. All that is described in the Christian vision for marriage in chapter 6 except for having children is open to lesbian women who commit themselves to each other in the name of God and the pledge of lifelong love.

Lesbian women cannot yet trust the churches. Elaine Willis writes of the unbearable tension between training as an Anglican deaconess and her lesbian identity, and her rage against traditional Christian worship, not least because 'lesbian women's lives are rendered invisible always by it'.[40] Jeannine Gramick writes of the countless letters from nuns 'desperately seeking information and counsel to grapple with the question "How do I know if I am gay?"'[41] There are countless testimonies from Christian lesbian women who speak honestly of their orientation and its clash with an uncomprehending and judgemental church.[42] Until lesbian sexuality is also accepted, honoured and celebrated by the whole people of God as a gift which images the divine love as heterosexuality does, churches will continue to be unsafe places for lesbian women to be themselves and offer themselves in worship to God.

The predicament of bisexual people

Bisexual people are almost always overlooked in discussions of sexuality. Bisexual people experience erotic attraction towards members of both sexes. They are likely to be more hidden even than gays and lesbians, and to be misunderstood by both groups as failing fully to 'come out' or as attempting to have the best of both worlds.[43] The over-used and over-tidy categories of 'heterosexual' and 'homosexual' leave little room for further orientations, yet according to the orientation scale (see p.128), everyone from points 1 to 5 has at least incidental sexual experience with people of both sexes while only those on point 3 are classified as primarily bisexual. Classification almost breaks down at this point. A bisexual person might be one equally attracted to women or to men, yet if the balance is slightly altered he or she might be classified 'basically heterosexual' or 'basically homosexual'. Such a person may in any case be unable or unwilling to engage in such precise self-definitions. It is suggested that, according to one reading of orientation, 'There are enormous numbers of bisexuals in the world - probably over one third of the population – but most do not call themselves bisexual yet.'[44] The very existence of bisexual people 'in significant numbers', let us say, provides further support for the assumption that there is a basic bisexuality in all of us which biological and social influences help to channel towards our eventual sexual orientation.

It may be many years before theology catches up with bisexual, in addition to homosexual, orientation. The single paragraph in the bishops' statement about bisexuals is oppressive towards them. Their orientation is 'ambiguous', and 'bisexual activity must always be wrong' because 'it inevitably involves being unfaithful'. They should 'follow the way of holiness in either celibacy or abstinence or heterosexual marriage'. Counselling might also help bisexuals 'to discover the truth of their personality and to achieve a degree of inner healing.'[45]

The paragraph has been called 'insensitive, ignorant, simplistic and inconsistent',[46] and it is difficult not to agree with this harsh but accurate judgement. Bisexual orientation is ambiguous only in relation to fixed alternatives. Might it be these that are ambiguous, rather than bisexual people? No reference is made to the research on orientation. Is it too disturbing (another version of what the punters cannot stand)? The stark choice between celibacy or heterosexual marriage places it within a framework that knows nothing of bisexuality and cannot cope with it. Even homosexuals were allowed the right of conscience. Bisexuals have only compulsory celibacy or heterosexual marriage to choose from. But, as we have observed, celibacy is a gift not a requirement, and heterosexual marriage, while it is an option, may lead to serious complications later. The reference to healing makes sense only if one is sick.

Once again testimony is the key to an adequate theology of sex. Whatever heterosexual filter is placed over the lens that scrutinizes bisexual people, they will continue to report, honestly, that attraction to both sexes is powerful and integral to their lives. Much attention needs to be given to them which is not based solely on past solutions involving procreation and abstinence. The bishops are right to identify fidelity as a central issue. Is a bisexual person someone who is *attracted* to people of either sex or someone who *needs* sexual contact with people of both sexes? Do we know? Can we know? A 'need' can be confused with a 'want' yet the two are very different. Is there a married person alive who has never at some time wanted someone sexually other than his or her spouse? Is there a case for bisexuals behaving differently?

Perhaps marriage is unsuitable for bisexual people? It is difficult to see how marriages can withstand the strain of one partner also in a homosexual relationship outside the marriage, but such marriages exist, inside and outside the Church, and some of them appear strong, fortresses of acceptance and love. If it were possible, it would certainly be valuable to listen to further testimony from married bisexuals in the churches, and to learn of their experiences of pain, as well as grace. The question 'How do I love my wife and my male partner with integrity?' was posed at a recent conference on pastoral care for lesbian and gay people.[47] Does that question not assume even trickier prior questions have been resolved in a certain way? Given the invisibility of bisexual people in Christian theology, it is no surprise that at present we can only table questions.

The framework of this chapter has been marriage and its extension to encompass sexual minorities. But marriage and celibacy are not the only options. Sexual friendships may provide some new answers and raise new questions. They are considered next.

Notes

1. *Gaudium et Spes*, §49, see Austin Flannery OP (ed.), *Vatican Council II: The Conciliar and Post Conciliar Documents* (Leominster, Hereford: Fowler Wright, rev. edn 1988), p. 952.
2. ibid., §50.
3. Daniel Maguire, *The Moral Revolution: A Christian Humanist Vision* (San Francisco: Harper & Row, 1986), p. 94.
4. *The Alternative Service Book 1980* (London: Clowes, et al.), p. 288.
5. D. Sherwin Bailey, *The Man–Woman Relation in Christian Thought* (London: Longman, 1959), p. 131.
6. *Sent.* IV, xxvi 2, art. 1, ad. 1; see Bailey, p.141.
7. Robert Williams, 'Towards a Theology for Lesbian and Gay Marriage', *Anglican Theological Review*, 72 (1990), p. 137.
8. ibid., p. 138.
9. John J. McNeil, *Taking a Chance on God: Liberating Theology for Gays, Lesbians and their Lovers, Families and Friends* (Boston: Beacon Press, 1988), pp. 134–5; and see *The Church and the Homosexual* (Boston: Beacon Press, 1988), p. 205.
10. Elizabeth Stuart, *Quest Journal*, 18, Supplement B (June 1992), p. 31.
11. *Issues in Human Sexuality: A Statement by the House of Bishops* (London: Church House Publishing, 1991), §5.15.
12. ibid., §1.9.
13. The term is used 'to refer to those who feel erotic love for someone of the same sex' (ibid., §4.1), to avoid negative overtones in 'homosexual' and 'to avoid clumsy circumlocutions'. But the word has a 'technical ring' as the statement acknowledges, and so risks stigmatization, as well as confusion.
14. ibid., §5.2.

15. ibid., §5.3.
16. ibid., §5.6.
17. ibid., §5.14.
18. ibid., §5.16.
19. ibid., §5.17.
20. Supplement to *Ministerial Recognition Rules* (Baptist Union of Great Britain, 1991).
21. John Habgood, *Church Times*, 10 January 1992.
22. *Issues in Human Sexuality*, §4.
23. John Boswell, *Christianity, Social Tolerance, and Homosexuality: Gay People in Western Europe from the Beginning of the Christian Era to the Fourteenth Century* (Chicago: University of Chicago Press, 1980), p. 333.
24. John Boswell, 'Homosexuality and Religious Life: A Historical Approach' in Jeannine Gramick (ed.), *Homosexuality in the Priesthood and the Religious Life* (New York: Crossroad, 1989), pp. 12–13.
25. Michael Vasey, in a letter to the *Church Times*, 23 April 1992.
26. *Issues in Human Sexuality*, §3.15.
27. Maguire, p. 89.
28. Fr Brian Smith, in a letter to *The Guardian*, 5 December 1991.
29. *Issues in Human Sexuality*, §5.24.
30. Jack Babuscio, *We Speak For Ourselves: The Experiences of Gay Men and Lesbians* (London: SPCK, 1988), p. 72.
31. ibid. (emphasis added). But note the casework on which this statement was based, was done before 1976. New sets of pastoral problems then develop. Some of these are identified, and possible solutions suggested, by Robert Nugent, 'Married Homosexuals', *Journal of Pastoral Care*, 37 (December 1983), pp. 243–51.
32. Shere Hite, *The Hite Report: Women and Love* (London: Penguin/Viking, 1988), p. 581.
33. E.g. Michael Ruse, *Homosexuality: A Philosophical Inquiry* (Oxford: Blackwell, 1988), pp. 9–11.
34. John Shelby Spong, *Living in Sin? A Bishop Rethinks Human Sexuality* (San Francisco: Harper & Row, 1988), p. 198.
35. Hite, *Women and Love*, p. 622.
36. ibid., p. 643.
37. Rosemary Radford Ruether, 'Homophobia, Heterosexism and Pastoral Practice' in Gramick, p. 28.
38. ibid., p. 31.
39. ibid., p. 30.
40. Elaine Willis, 'Nothing is Sacred, All is Profane: Lesbian Identity and Religious Purpose' in Linda Hurcombe, *Sex and God: Some Varieties of Women's Religious Experience* (New York and London: Routledge & Kegan Paul, 1987), p. 108.
41. Jeannine Gramick, 'Lesbian Nuns: Identity, Affirmation, and Gender Differences' in Gramick, pp. 219–20.
42. E.g. Babuscio, ch. 5.
43. A recurring theme of the testimonies in *Bisexual Lives* (London: Off Pink Publishing, 1988).
44. *Bisexual Lives*, p. 114.
45. *Issues in Human Sexuality*, §5.8.

46. Press statement, issued by the Lesbian and Gay Christian Movement on 4 December 1991, about *Issues in Human Sexuality*; see also Stuart, p. 38.
47. Mary Hunt, in Elaine Willis and Ian Dunn (eds), *The Dunblane Papers: Report of the Second Pastoral Approaches to Lesbian and Gay People Conference* (London: Institute for the Study of Christianity and Sexuality, 1990), p. 23.

CHAPTER 11

Sexual Friendships

This chapter attempts to contribute to the acceptance among Christians of sexual friendships. Compulsory celibacy for the unmarried is rejected. The teaching of Jesus about friendship is examined, and the patriarchal influence on the understanding and neglect of friendship in Christian theology is noted. The grounds for maintaining friendship as a relationship which must lack sexual sexual expression are considered in detail, and found to be insubstantial. A different understanding of friendship is sought which develops the idea of 'appropriate vulnerability', and draws from the writings of some Christian lesbian feminists. Some suggestions for a theology of sexual friendship are made, which rest in the friendship and vulnerability of Christ.

Singleness and sex

Single people are half the adult population of some countries. In the USA 53 per cent of women are single, 20 per cent never marry, and 33 per cent are divorced or widowed. The minority which at any one time are married, are married for 'less than half the total number of years they may expect to live as an adult'.[1] A recent report from the Evangelical Alliance in Britain indicated that 44 per cent of men under 30 who attend Evangelical churches are single, and that loneliness and anxiety about sex are commonly felt among them.[2] Between one third and one half of the composition of a church congregation is likely to be of single people.

The traditional teaching of the Christian churches is that chastity is a requirement for all such people, since marriage is the only context where sexual intercourse is authorized. In this book the case has been made for retaining marriage as the principle context for sexual intercourse and the sole context for procreative sex. At the same time a non-patriarchal understanding of marriage has been advocated together with the extension of the married state to include couples who are ceremonially pre-married but committed, and committed couples who are lesbian or gay. These revisionary proposals, however radical they will appear to some Christians, in fact leave marriage as the central reference point for sexual expression. It is time now to consider the possibility that full sexual experience may be honourable and holy without any legitimizing reference to lifelong union.

The context in which this experience may appear is friendship. Friendship, that is, *philia*, or love between friends, remains a largely unexplored possibility in Christian thought as a basis for sexual relationships. If *Issues in Human Sexuality* had started with friendship, instead of marriage, as its model for relationships, it might have reached very different conclusions.[3] Since friendship is broader than marriage, marriage may well be considered as a sub-species of friendship within which friends undertake particular obligations to each other. What then is friendship, and why have friendships been thought by Christians strictly to rule out sexual expression?

The teaching of Jesus about friendship

Friendship is central to the teaching of Jesus. John's Gospel has him say:

> This is my commandment: love one another, as I have loved you. There is no greater love than this, that someone should lay down his life for his friends. You are my friends, if you do what I command you. No longer do I call you servants, for a servant does not know what his master is about. I have called you friends, because I have disclosed to you everything that I heard from my Father. (John 15.12–15)

This passage anchors friendship firmly in the context of commitment, intimacy, equality and agape-love. Elsewhere Jesus speaks of the love of one's enemies (Matthew 5.44) and this is arguably a 'greater' love than the love of friends. But it would be wrong to force comparisons between love for friends and love for enemies since in the teaching of Jesus as a whole, no one is excluded from being a friend of Christ. The passage confirms first that friendships may come to involve deep self-giving commitments. Second, friends are contrasted with servants. Master–servant relationships are excluded from that renewed life which Jesus offers and inaugurates. Patterns of dominance and submission, inequality and ownership, so long a feature of patriarchal marriage, belong to 'the world' (John 15.18–20). They have no place among the friends of Jesus.

Third, the friendship between Christ and the disciples is based on intimate personal disclosure. They are the friends of Jesus on account of what they have come to know of him and of God the Father through him. The dynamics of human friendship rely on mutual personal disclosure. The greater the disclosure, the deeper the friendship. Jesus is the friend of the disciples precisely because this detail drawn from the dynamics of human friendship applies in an intensified sense to his relationship to them. Friends become friends by disclosing themselves. Jesus is friend because in disclosing himself he discloses God as well, indeed everything he heard from his Father. Fourth, we note that because friendship is a relationship of mutuality it is vulnerable to friends damaging or reversing their friendships. This further feature of human friendship lies behind the saying, 'You are my friends, if you do what I command you.' The surface meaning of the conditional statement 'if . . .' might lead to the mistaken conclusion that failure to obey the command of Christ leads to the forfeiture of his friendship. But Christ's friendship is not conditional on anything. Failure to keep the simple commandment, 'love one another' (John 15.12,17), inevitably means that friendship is damaged, since loving one another *is* the practice of friendship. Human friendships are one of the means of God's disclosure as Love.

The influence of Aristotle

The teaching of Jesus in John's Gospel about friends is the key source for a Christian theology of friendship. But we are still some distance from sexual friendships, and if we leave the sayings about friendship in their context in John's Gospel just prior to Good Friday, we must admit that all those who first heard them were men. Surprisingly, pagan sources have been more influential than John's Gospel in historical discussion of friendship, in particular Cicero's *On Friendship*, and Aristotle's *Nicomachean Ethics*, books eight and nine. Friendship, thought Aristotle, is 'the mutually acknowledged and reciprocal exchange of good will and affection that exists among individuals who share an interest in each other on the basis of virtue, pleasure, or utility'.[4] Friendships based on virtue have a higher value than the other kinds. They are founded on equality.[5] In choosing friends, 'We choose to arrange our lives around a loyalty to another, and around a willingness to choose ends and pursuits within the context of this loyalty . . . These are the choices that indicate two lives can be interwoven together into some coherent pattern of good living.'[6] In choosing a friend, 'One chooses to make that person a part of one's life and to arrange one's life with that person's flourishing (as well as one's own) in mind.'[7] For Aristotle the 'fundamental reason for including friendship within the happy life is that it enhances one's own awareness and understanding of one's agency and activities'.[8]

Aristotle was the first western thinker to have written extensively on friendship. It was an impressive achievement, and classical theologians who were aware of his text felt able to follow him. But perhaps inevitably Aristotle's account of friendship bristles with difficulties for the contemporary reader. Friendships between women, and between women and men, are impossible since Aristotle notoriously held that women were 'rationally defective', 'lacking control of their passions' and possessing little if any virtue.[9] He thought friendship with and between old people was difficult since they 'take small pleasure in society',[10] and the material conditions necessary for the full pursuit of friendship ensure that it 'will be within the reach of only those of a certain class'.[11] In short, Aristotle's account is sexist, ageist and classist. Worse, as feminists have pointed out, the human experiences which inform his account are all male. Women's experience of friendship is not even regarded as a possibility. What Aristotle has described is not friendship but 'male bonding' as practised by classical 'heterosexual patriarchy'.[12]

Sexless friendships

It is easy to see why, historically, friendships are without sexual expression. For a long time men thought that they alone were capable of them. Monastic communities became the principle places for the exercise of close, intimate friendship, while closeness between particular men was always in danger of subverting the harmony and unity of the community.[13] But now let us remove the patriarchal premises. Men have no monopoly on the virtue that makes friendship possible: it is no longer thinkable that friendship should be confined to well-off males. Friendships exist between men and women and between women and women and the dynamics of these relationships cannot be described in patriarchal terms or made to fit limited patriarchal experience where sexual expression is inevitably a threat to the social and moral order. It is an accomplished social fact that friendship is no longer restricted to the participants envisaged by Aristotle nor understood through his language. Why then retain a particular characteristic of male friendship, that is, celibacy, and insist that it must regulate all male–female and female–female friendships? There may of course be many reasons why it should be retained, but they should at least be stated, not simply assumed.

Aristotle was right to insist that there were different types of friendship. He understood there would be different degrees of commitment between different friends. Given the enlargement of friendship to include women, and men and women of all ages and classes, it is still likely to be true that most friendships will be non-sexual. But is it true that all of them will be? 'Full physical sexual relations', the bishops' statement assures us, '. . . have no place in friendship or, indeed, in the life of the single person in general'.[14] Their positive view of friendship provides clear guidance to unmarried people about the place of sex in their lives. There isn't any. Sexual intercourse belongs within the exclusive relationship of marriage and friendship is not exclusive. Again, the bishops describe sex within, and only within, marriage, as the 'ideal':

> The proper fulfilment of such relations [is within] unique lifelong commitment to one partner. Where such commitment is not possible, the effect of the physical relationship is not in the end to enhance life for those concerned but to impair it. It frustrates both parties because their love can never achieve the purpose at all levels for which God intends it.[15]

The friendship between David and Jonathan is mentioned approvingly, together with other well-known same-sex and opposite-sex friendships in the Christian tradition, but any suggestion that these friendships contained any 'hidden homosexual or heterosexual involvement' is said to be a characteristic reflection of our modern readiness to ascribe sexual motives and practices to innocent behaviour.

The argument that making love belongs only to the exclusive relationship of marriage is based, among other reasons, on the allegedly exclusive meanings of genital intercourse. When people make love, they 'say' something to each other about their relationship. This argument is also used by Pope John Paul II in the encyclical *Familiaris Consortio*. Sexuality, including the 'acts which are proper and exclusive to spouses', is

> . . . realized in a truly human way only if it is an integral part of the love by which a man and a woman commit themselves totally to one another until death. The total physical self-giving

would be a lie if it were not the sign and fruit of a total personal self-giving.[16]

These observations doubtless apply to all partners in fruitful and happy lifelong unions. But unfortunately the arguments in both works are flawed. They assume rightly that love-making is expressive, and that between two partners who are committed to each other for life sexual acts symbolize their mutual self-giving. But now the problems arise. While sex acts may express or symbolize married love, they may not. Unfortunately there is loveless sex within marriage and loving sex outside it. The argument appears to run from the premise 'Sex can sometimes express a lifelong commitment', to the conclusion 'Sex ought always to express a lifelong commitment'. Armed with this conclusion any sex outside marriage is then conveniently proscribed because only marriage is thought to provide the commitment that sexual relations express. But the conclusion does not follow. The argument moves from 'sometimes' to 'always' (a common fallacy). And it moves from saying something 'is' to something 'ought', a move that has vexed philosophers for over two hundred years. Eating out is sometimes a more pleasant alternative to eating in. Surely no one would argue from this that one ought to eat out always, or that eating out ought always to be more pleasant than eating in.

More bad arguments

A similar difficulty is raised by the choice of the word 'ideal' in relation to the restriction of sexual intercourse to marriage. Unfortunately 'ideal' and 'real' are notorious contrasts. Our ideal home is probably not the home we actually live in, nor is our ideal holiday the one we have just taken. Ideals do not exclude alternatives which are less ideal. Even if we were, impossibly, to compile a list of sexual relationships and list them top downwards beginning with that ideal relationship which was most pleasing to God, those which were below the number one position would not automatically be displeasing to God. They would only be *less* pleasing to God, an entirely different matter.

Neither is it at all obvious that sex between friends automatically has the pessimistic consequences of impairing and frustrating their lives. It is of course a possible consequence, but no more. Another possible consequence is that it may enrich and enhance. It may be an expressive celebration of the friendship. One wonders how the authors know in advance that sexual friendships are bad for us, or that they fall short of God's purpose for us. If God's purpose for our sexuality is understood to be that there should be sexual expression only within marriage and never between friends, clearly sexual friendships are contrary to God's will. But that is a circular argument, since God's purpose or will is what we are trying to establish, to argue *towards* and not to argue *from*.

We might also wonder whether the friendship between, say, David and Jonathan is quite as innocent as the bishops say. Since any suggestion that these friendships included sexual activity will be met by the charge of sexual obsession in the mind of the reader, it must be made diffidently. We do not know whether the friendship between David and Jonathan had a physical element or not. But the language used does not suggest that it did not have one. And neither of them would have been likely to have possessed a dualistic understanding of themselves which would inhibit physical love. This is of course pure (impure?) speculation. Perhaps neither of the two men was much exercised about 'how far' such expression was allowed to go, if indeed it existed at all. The point of such speculation is to envisage the possibility that a different but prior assumption is being brought to the story, namely that because a relationship was a friendship it must therefore have lacked sexual expression.

Some have argued that it is a 'necessary condition' of a relationship being a friendship that it be without sexual expression, that 'friendship is a non-sexual relationship'.[17] The procedure here is to define friendship so that sexual expression is excluded. Others have contrasted sexless friendships with sexual ones but reserved the term 'friendship' for the former category. 'Intentional friendship' is said to be 'a relationship between two persons who feel emotional affectivity for one another without sharing partial or complete sexual activity'.[18] Where partial or complete sexual activity is included in the relationship the resulting state is called 'coupling'. Once a relationship is sexual it becomes exclusive in that others cannot opt into it. Friendship, however, remains inclusive. Friendship and coupling alike are states of unity, yet in friendships, 'We have no memories held by the sharing of the particularities and certainties of sensual touching. Our unity dwells in the more elusive realm of sensing.'[19]

These discussions of friendship belong within a broader theme of celibacy, though they are thought to apply to everyone. However they are not convincing. 'Some' or 'most' has been confused with 'all' and definitions have been tidily imposed on realities so that friendship is stipulated to be void of sexual expression. It is misleading to say a sexual friendship is exclusive since a couple who are sexual friends may still share friends as a couple or singly. 'Coupling' too, seems to have been deliberately chosen for its derogatory connotation. Men and women who are merely friends nonetheless 'may crave at times for physical bonding'.[20] One may surmise that such craving may not always have to be seen as temptation which is to be resisted, but may on occasion be a holy prompt toward that 'sensual touching' that has been defined out of friendship in advance.

These stipulations of sexless friendships reveal a residual patriarchal understanding both of friendship and of marriage. If sex is licit only when it is procreative, then clearly friendship should be sexless. If friendship exists only between men of the same class, clear patriarchal rules will rule out homosexual sexual activity absolutely. But our understandings of both marriage and friendship have been amplified and extended, and the admission of sexual friendships is a further extension of processes which have already occurred. The possibility exists that in some friendships, perhaps only a very few, the regard which each has for the other may reach sexual expression. The symbolic meaning of the expression will express loyalty, affection and love, yet without the total and permanent commitment which is essential to a particular kind of friendship, mainly marriage. The foundations for such relationships need further excavation.

Appropriate vulnerability

Karen Lebacqz wants to construct a sexual ethic for single people on 'appropriate vulnerability'.[21] She is under no illusions about the adequacy of a sexual ethic which offers only the blanket of enforced celibacy to cover over the sexual feelings of the unmarried. The foundation for a different ethic lies in our vulnerability. In our sexual relationships we are vulnerable. In theory, 'The commitment of a stable and monogamous marriage provides a supportive context for vulnerable expressions of the self.' Singleness 'carries no such protections',[22] and where men have more power than women, women are more vulnerable than men. We need, she says, 'a theology of vulnerability'.[23] She is right, but she has not yet provided it.

A theology of vulnerability is strongly suggested by reflection on the cross of Christ and the accounts of incarnation and atonement used in this book. 'Vulnerable' means 'open to being wounded', and Christians have found direct reference to Christ in the words of the prophet, 'by his wounds we are healed' (Isaiah 53.5). God's love is known in the vulnerability of Jesus. Jesus' willingness to be vulnerable is the human expression of the divine nature.

Any theological insight deriving from the wounds of Christ has to avoid mawkishness on the one hand and revulsion on the other. A theology of vulnerability may avoid these extremes. The cross of Christ is God's self-identification with the vulnerable. Being vulnerable is an expression of love. It can also be very foolish. It can only happen when mutual trust is present, and this presupposes much prior personal knowledge. If I love another person sexually and fully, I must be vulnerable to him or her and my love must be healing, not wounding. I must honour that person's vulnerability. In our loving we participate in the love which God has for each of us and which is God's own inter-Personal nature. The Christian demand within sexual loving is to embody that love which is God for the beloved, representing and expressing it, incarnating it in whatever sexual communication takes place between lovers. This is a love which honours vulnerability and is itself an expression of it.

Women friends

Mary Hunt and Carter Heyward have both written about friendship recently. They are Christian, lesbian feminists whose work is refreshingly free from male, heterosexual and patriarchal presuppositions. Mary Hunt says that a consequence of the patriarchal conditioning of women has been to persuade them to see themselves as rivals for the attention of men. Historically this has made friendship between women difficult to sustain and, when it happened, 'Patriarchy eclipsed the meaning of such friendship by insisting, with the help of the Christian churches, that marriage and not friendship was the ideal for human interaction.'[24] Patriarchal men find women's friendships difficult to tolerate because they testify that men are inessential to women's happiness. For similar reasons, 'The presence of open lesbians becomes something that a patriarchal society must erase.'[25] When friendship becomes sexual, then loving women becomes a political activity, 'not the privatized activity of mysterious feelings'. Agonies of doubt about the bodily expression of love disappear in 'the delightful experience of finding that body and spirit need not be split, that friends can be lovers.' What women lovers look for in their love is intimacy, not genitality.[26] Genital experience, that substantive, fearsome problem area which looms large and serious in much heterosexual theology and ethics, is incidental to intimate relationships.

A model for women's friendships is developed in Hunt's *Fierce Tenderness*. A friendship is an interplay of four elements - love, power, embodiment and spirituality. Love is 'an orientation toward the world as if my friend and I were more united than separated, more at one among the many than separate and alone'. Power is 'the ability to make choices for ourselves, for our dependent children, and with our community'.[27] The power dynamics of relationships are played out where social or structural power and personal or individual power intersect. Human relationships themselves involve power struggles, whether recognized or not, and friendship 'is that relationship in which empowerment and relinquishment are most likely to take place. It is the setting in which the exchange of power and the transformation of power dynamics will be stimulated.'[28]

The place of embodiment in the model reminds us that '. . . *virtually everything we do and who we are is mediated by our bodies.'* It is necessary also in order to 'make up for the centuries of disembodied writings that have shaped the Christian ethical tradition'.[29] Absence of dualistic tensions leads to confidence in affirming the goodness of bodily pleasure. Embodiment enables us to celebrate the fact that we are 'incarnate beings'.

> Sex between friends, if/when both are consenting, careful, and committed to the well-being of themselves and one another, has everything to recommend it. . . . [Women friends] touch, cuddle, embrace, kiss, comfort, massage, make love, pat, prod, and otherwise show feelings in a physical way without the degree of homophobic embarrassment that limits most men to distance or athletic, buddy-like behavior . . . Spirituality in my model means *making choices about the quality of life for oneself and for one's community.*[30]

Any breakdown in friendship can be envisaged as a distorting movement brought about by an over-emphasis (or under-emphasis) of one of the components which then disrupts (and perhaps destroys) the whole.

Carter Heyward also has a model of friendship, indeed, a developed theology of erotic love in which 'undying erotic friendship' provides the 'foundations for sexual ethics'.[31] This theology combines a realistic description of the influence of 'alienated power'[32] in personal and social life with the conviction that erotic love, rightly ordered and unselfishly expressed, is a sharing in the Holy or God. Like Hunt, Heyward sees an analysis of power as a prerequisite for understanding personal sexual relations, because:

> The food we eat, the air we breathe, the energy we burn, the love we make, even the dreams we nurture, are controlled to a significant degree by the structural configurations of power that have been shaped by the interests of affluent white males who usually fail to see any more clearly than the rest of us the exploitative character of their own lives.[33]

'Our love-making reflects what we have assimilated from the wider configurations of power that impinge upon us. Our attitudes to our own bodies, and those of our lovers, are shaped for us before they are shaped by us. Unavoidably then, "Having sex", if it is erotic, is about power-sharing.'[34]

Right relation

God the Spirit is the power of right-relation, the transformer of alienated power relations in social, personal and sexual life. Patriarchal influences on Christian faith, which are themselves the residues of past alienated power relations, have first to be exposed. 'The traditional christian understanding of love fails to value adequately the embodied human experience of love among friends and sexual partners *because* it assumes the negative, dangerous, and nonspiritual character of sensual, erotic, and sexual feelings and expressions.'[35] Whereas patriarchal theology fears sexual experience, in Heyward's theology, 'The erotic is our most fully embodied experience of the love of God. As such, it is the source of our capacity for transcendence . . . The erotic is the divine Spirit's yearning, through our bodyselves, toward mutually empowering relation, which is our most fully embodied experience of God as love . . .'.

The identification of erotic experience with the experience of God is grounded neither in stipulation nor speculation, but in phenomenal elements of erotic relationships which lead to our fulfilment as persons. God uses friends to enrich mutually each other's lives. Through mutuality 'we are called forth more fully into becoming who we are . . .'. The erotic experience of the power of God is 'the root of our theological epistemology. It is the basis of our knowledge and love of God. It is a calling forth, an occasion to touch each other's lives, and an open invitation into the healing of common woundedness . . .'.[36] This is a starting point both for sexual theology and also for coming to

> . . . know ourselves as holy and to imagine ourselves sharing in the creation of one another and of our common well-being. As we recognize the faces of the Holy in the faces of our lovers and friends, as well as in our own, we begin to feel at ease in our bodyselves – sensual, connected, and empowered.[37]

The belief that erotic power is sacred is capable of leading Christians to different conclusions and lifestyles. We may conclude that the sacredness of sex obliges us to reserve expression of it 'in relation to one person'. For others, celibacy, equally but perhaps surprisingly may follow from the same belief, since 'we may believe ourselves obligated to reserve the full physical expression of this power in all of our relationships'.[38] But there is a third, non-monogamous, alternative, that of sexual friendship: 'We may believe that we are not obligated to withhold expression of this power in relation to those friends with whom we are most mutually involved . . . We may prefer to think of ourselves as open to sexual friendships.' Since these friendships are grounded in a sacred, mutually empowering love, the 'non-monogamous' character of this option stands very far from casual or promiscuous sex.

Sexual friendships are governed by values and obligations. We are obliged to 'respect our own and others' bodily integrity and to protect, especially, the bodily integrity of children, women, and sexually vulnerable men'. We must 'act sexually only in mutual relationships, in which the erotic moves between us to evoke that which is most fully human in each of us'.[39] A second basic value is faithfulness. Whichever option, monogamy, non-monogamy or celibacy, is chosen,

> We are obligated to approach each other's lives with a profound sense of tenderness, respect, and openness to learning *with* others how we might become more faithful friends – in relation not only to each other but to the larger world as well, to helping to make it a more just and peaceful resource of pleasure for all living creatures'.[40]

All three options can be lived out 'in alienation or in fidelity'.

Sexual friendships – an assessment

Heyward's model of friendship is less systematic than Hunt's. There is a 'character structure' of friendship which includes courage, compassion, anger, forgiveness, touching, healing and faith.[41] Different elements will predominate in different friendships and at different times. Taken together their analysis of friendship is remarkable. Writing about friendship is rare, and these analyses not only begin to fill a vacuum, they bring a Christian, lesbian, feminist perspective to Christian sexual ethics and theology which is still in the grip of heterosexist and patriarchal norms. This perspective is not only valuable in its own right. It is an obvious aid to heterosexual theology to think more critically about itself.

There is no disastrous split to be found in these writings between spirit and flesh, mind and body, reason and passion. The body is restored to its dignity where it is a source of pleasure and not of shame. The celebration of sexual pleasure without guilt is a religious achievement of lesbian Christians which can enrich the wider religious community. Lesbian sexual friendships provide space from the domination of women by men where the goal of male orgasm and the satisfaction of male desire is excluded. Lesbian love is free of the anxieties of procreative sex. It is not performance-oriented and it is clear from women's descriptions that playfulness and tenderness in love-making are cherished spiritual qualities of relationships. The sexual frankness of the writing must also be honoured. This is itself a refreshing change from the ominous silence about, and disowning of, sexual feeling which is a trademark of patriarchal orthodoxy.

Despite the merits of these writings, I still have some reservations about the account of friendship that emerges. The identification of eros with God may overlook the extent to which the realization of eros is alienated in life-situations. The epistemological basis of the human love for God may need to plot more carefully both the intermingling of eros and agape in human friendships and the mutual participation of these in Holy Spirit. A theology of friendship may be able to be more obviously rooted in the teaching of Jesus than Heyward or Hunt envisage. The passage analysed earlier in this chapter already provides the elements for this, not least in the suggestion that the love of God is made known through friends as it clearly was in the case of the disciples who were shown God through the friendship of Jesus. I think Hunt's friendship model sometimes runs into the difficulty of conceptual instability. In particular 'love' and 'spirituality' might contribute better to the model if their meanings were more congruent with extant theological uses.

Clearly this feminist perspective on friendship is more wholehearted in its endorsement of sexual friendships than the cautious steps towards recognition with which this chapter began. Lifelong unions, not friendship, provide the most appropriate context for having children. Procreative sex should, for the sake of any children that might result, happen within a long-term relationship of total commitment. The decision to have a child implies a commitment of a couple to each other which also extends to their children and continues until they all become independent adults. Procreative sex belongs where these commitments have been entered into. But there will be countless other contexts where sexual activity is an appropriate expression of love. That love will not have as its intended outcome children or be a commitment until death. These contexts are sexual friendships.

The great majority of friendships will not come to sexual expression. Sexual friendships between married and unmarried people would be adulterous; between close relatives they would be incestuous; and with minors they would be exploitative and illegal. The great majority of close friends would, one assumes, be alarmed at the possibility of expressing their fondness for each other in a sexual way. 'Sexual expression' could cover everything from a lingering grasp of the hand to sexual envelopment. Christians have clear grounds for locating procreative sex firmly within the marriage bond, but procreative sex is fairly rare. Touching, embracing, hugging and kissing are usually socially acceptable gestures. Most friends do these things at least in a ritual way. A few will do so in an overtly sexual way.

Friends anxious about the extent of intimacy they are prepared to allow themselves may want to use the 'principle of proportionality'. According to this principle 'the level of sexual expression should be commensurate with the level of commitment in the relationship'.[42] Sexual friendships must be rooted in that friendship which Christ himself taught and offered. Christ's friendship abolishes the master-servant relationship, and with it any vestige of unequal power-relations, whether of domination and submission, user and used, or exploiter and exploited. While the experience of friendship may be light-hearted and playful, there is also an offering of friends to each other which knows no bounds, perhaps not even the bounds of death. Christ, we surmised, was the friend of sinners because, in befriending them, he disclosed the very nature of God as healing, empowering love. Love between friends is also, for Christians, an expression of God's friendship. Each friend conveys to the other the friendship love of God. As Aelred of Rievaulx famously remarked, 'God is friendship.'

Sexual friendships require the honouring of vulnerability. Jesus identified himself with the naked, the hungry and the homeless, teaching that any act of kindness done to them was equivalent to an act of kindness done to him directly and personally (Matthew 25.31–46). We must not confuse the nakedness of people whose lives are so desperate that they are unclothed, with the nakedness of ourselves and our partners as we make love. There is, however, a common principle to be discerned in these different situations, although they are unequal in almost every other respect. The common principle is that we glimpse the face of Christ in our neighbour, and the body of Christ in the vulnerable bodies of his friends, whether they are also our lovers sexually, or awaiting our love in different but equally physical circumstances.

In thinking of sexual friendships in these ways we complement the feminist analyses of friendship just surveyed. Sexual friendships may be particularly apt among the elderly, although they will not be confined to them. We now understand that men and women may remain sexually active long after the intention or possibility of having a child has passed. Some will be post-married, or widows or widowers. There is another embarrassing silence in the churches about sexual activity in this age range. If the main purpose of sex is having children, sex after the age when conception is impossible lacks justification. Widows and widowers have long been expected to remain celibate or to remarry. Marriage is open to them. But they may just be friends. Anyone worried about the possible encouragement of promiscuity as a consequence of the encouragement of sexual friendships might reread the account of sexual sin in chapter 5. Christian friends and lovers are called to be holy in all their relationships and guidance will be found there about how our loving may participate in the love of God or be something less. These guidelines apply to sexual friends just as much as they apply to everyone else.

Notes

1. Shere Hite, *The Hite Report: Women and Love* (London: Penguin/Viking, 1988), p. 295.
2. Research undertaken by Steve Chilcraft and reviewed by Colin Moreton, in the *Church Times*, October 1992.
3. A point made by Canon Jeremy Davies in the *Church Times*, 20 December 1991.
4. See Nancy Sherman, *The Fabric of Character: Aristotle's Theory of Virtue* (Oxford: Clarendon Press, 1991), p. 124, summarizing Aristotle's description in *Nicomachean Ethics* 8.2.
5. Aristotle, 8.6.
6. Sherman, p. 132.
7. ibid., pp. 132–3.
8. ibid., p. 142.
9. ibid., p. 154.
10. Aristotle, 8.6.
11. Sherman, p. 156.
12. Mary E. Hunt, *Fierce Tenderness: A Feminist Theology of Friendship* (New York: Crossroad, 1991), p. 92.
13. Elizabeth Zarelli Turner, 'Love, Marriage and Friendship' in Philip Turner (ed.), *Men and Women: Sexual Ethics in Turbulent Times* (New York: Cowley), p. 162.
14. *Issues in Human Sexuality: A Statement by the House of Bishops* (London: Church House Publishing, 1991), §3.14.
15. ibid., §3.8.
16. Pope John Paul II, *Familiaris Consortio*, §11.
17. Turner, in Turner, p. 159.
18. Virginia Sullivan Finn, 'Two Ways of Loving' in Mary Anne Huddleston

(ed.), *Celibate Loving: Encounter in Three Dimensions* (New York: Paulist Press, 1984), p. 30.

19. ibid., p. 34.
20. ibid.
21. Karen Lebacqz, 'Appropriate Vulnerability: A Sexual Ethic for Singles', *Christian Century*, 104 (6 May 1988), pp. 435–8.
22. ibid., p. 437.
23. ibid., p. 438.
24. Mary E. Hunt, 'Friends in Deed' in Linda Hurcombe (ed.), *Sex and God: Some Varieties of Women's Religious Experience* (New York and London: Routledge & Kegan Paul, 1987), p. 48.
25. ibid., p. 49.
26. ibid., pp. 50–1.
27. Mary E. Hunt, *Fierce Tenderness*, pp. 100–1.
28. ibid., p. 102.
29. ibid., pp. 102, 104 (author's emphasis).
30. ibid., p. 105 (author's emphasis).
31. Carter Heyward, *Touching our Strength: The Erotic as Power and the Love of God* (San Francisco: Harper & Row, 1989), ch. 7.
32. ibid., p. 54.
33. ibid., p. 53.
34. ibid., p. 108.
35. ibid., pp. 98–9 (author's emphasis).
36. ibid., p. 99.
37. ibid., p. 102.
38. ibid., pp. 120, 121.
39. ibid., p. 128, 129.
40. ibid., p. 135.
41. ibid., p. 139.
42. Lebacqz, *op. cit.*, p. 437.

CHAPTER 12

Sex and Solitude

The theology of sex which has been developed in this book has emphasized that persons are constituted by relationships. Whereas all of us exist in and through relationships, some will never form sexual relationships, and others will refrain from them for indefinite periods. The themes of this chapter may apply particularly (but not at all exclusively) to people who are sexually 'in solitude'. Celibacy is honoured, whether among religious, Christian or non-Christian people, and an attempt is made to disentangle it from past dishonourable justifications for it. Chastity is emphasized as a Christian virtue. A positive assessment of masturbation is offered for singles and non-singles, men and women. A reserved welcome is given to some, but not all, sexual fantasies. But the liberality shown to masturbation and fantasy is not extended to pornography. This, it is argued, is sinful, and has no place in the new life offered by God in Christ.

Partnerless people

A book about sexual theology must not marginalize those women and men who, for whatever reason, are not sexually active. We have considered a wide spectrum of sexual orientation. We must not forget there is also a wide variation in what is usually called libido, or sex drive. It is easier for some to refrain from sexual activity than for others. This simple observation can be liberating. It assumes that insistent relentless desire has at least as much to do with the biochemistry of the brain as it has to do with weakness of will.

But this same observation can also stereotype celibate people.

Celibacy is abstinence from sexual activity and sexual relationships. It would be misleading to say that celibate people are those with lower sex drives. In other words, a celibate person lacks a property which the defining majority possesses. A new phrase might be coined for the device of defining minorities by what majorities perceive as a lack – 'the tactic of deficient description'. Homosexual people have had to endure the accusation that they lack proper child development; non-white people, women, children and slaves have all been treated in different ways as deficient. Celibate men and women must be spared the indignity of being stereotyped as lacking in anything. They are different. They are certainly not lacking in passion. They may instead redirect their sexual energies in other directions, towards a different realization of neighbourly love.

Celibacy and patriarchy

Unfortunately celibacy has been advocated for centuries by means of arguments which denigrate sexuality and the bodies of both men and women. That is why Polly Blue asks 'whether a life commitment with its roots in such a swamp is the only or the best way'.[1] Celibacy has become a highly focused expression of patriarchy. It is necessary to disentangle the one from the other, not least so that celibacy may re-emerge as a genuine non-patriarchal possibility for men and women, either for particular periods of their lives or, more rarely, as a particular form of lifelong commitment to the love of God and neighbour. Once this attempt at disentanglement gets going, the full horror of the patriarchal revulsion of sex stands exposed.

A recent study of the Desert Fathers shows that the sanctity for which they became renowned was obtained at the price of a disabling repression of the body and a disgraceful stereotyping of women as the cause of temptation and disorder in men.[2] There is little to pursue here in the quest for contemporary models of wholeness. Two physiological considerations are essential to understanding these ascetic-minded Christians: a set of false beliefs about how sexual desire arose, and the inescapable fact that men who do not discharge semen in normal sexual activity discharge it anyway during sleep, in 'wet dreams', or, as a previous generation coyly called them, 'nocturnal emissions'.

Sexual desire was thought to be stimulated by an excess of food. Based on the ancient theory of humours (the four chief fluids of the body – blood, phlegm, choler and melancholy) it was thought that 'Damp humors lurked in the lower parts, and were transformed, through the heat generated by excessive food, into sexual drives.'[3] Tears, too, were signs of excessive humour. It was once held that men who did not cry tears over their sins had had their humour dried up by the Devil and diverted to their 'lower parts'.[4] The bodies of Adam and Eve had been able, so it was thought, to run on their natural 'heat', requiring only that nourishment which was capable of keeping the heat alive.[5] There was therefore a strong sexual reason for frugality over food. Severe dietary restrictions would also cause amenorrhoea among women. That is why Jerome and others recommended it for them.

The persistence of involuntary ejaculations and their accompaniment by sexual fantasies seems to have been a kind of spiritual torture for celibate males. Wet dreams generated a theology of their own! They were thought to provide convincing concrete proof that the will, even the dedicated will of the consecrated monk, was not in control of the body, and so the fall of Adam was confirmed in every erection and emission (as Augustine and others also believed).[6] Only a few could enjoy that longed-for state of 'purity of heart'. Even this, it is clear, was not a cessation of wet dreams; only of the dream element associated with them.[7] Every sexual thought would, in this frenetic atmosphere, have been interpreted as caused by an evil demon and would have been taken to imply willing collaboration with it.[8] Ambrose, believing Christ to have been conceived without sexual desire and to have known no such desire in his earthly life, thought that the body of Christ, ' "unscarred" by the double taint of a sexual origin and of sexual impulses', represented 'human flesh as it should be'.[9]

Better reasons for celibacy

Unfortunately the tortuous experiences of celibate men of another age still retain an influence over Christian attitudes to sexuality and the body. They represent a spirituality which has no positive theology of flesh and which leads all too easily to the segmented consciousness described in chapter 3. They lie behind the modern insistence that homosexual persons must be celibate. Where celibacy is practised in the church as a condition of leadership,[10] it is unthinkable that concessions be granted to homosexuals, whether clerical or lay. Clerical celibacy is a statement that the power of sex itself can be overcome, so homosexuals too must overcome it. Sadly, this requirement is often insisted on by heterosexuals who are not celibate themselves and who have forgotten the origins of the demand they make on others. A better reason for celibacy is the biblical one, that it is a 'gift', which enables those who have it 'to be beyond criticism and be free from distraction in your devotion to the Lord' (1 Corinthians 7.7, 35).

Paul knew well that only a few have the gift of celibacy; that is probably why the term 'gift' is chosen. He is firmly against compulsion in the matter. Compulsoriness destroys its gift-like character by making it a requirement. It is hard to see, at least from our distant vantage point, how compulsory celibacy has been experienced as a gift at all. Is not the example and teaching of Jesus a stronger reason? Perhaps, though we cannot be certain, Jesus was unmarried.[11] His teaching on celibacy (Matthew 19.10–12) is introduced, as we have seen, as a response to his disciples' incredulity towards his teaching on the permanence of the marriage bond. It is better for a man not to marry at all than to marry and divorce his wife. Only later does remaining unmarried become 'renouncing marriage', and this 'for the sake of the kingdom of Heaven' (Matthew 19.12).

Other more social reasons for celibacy were advanced, particularly for and by women. Arranged marriages, especially among the rich, made women's bodies 'the joining point of . . . relentless families'[12] and a reproductive mechanism for approved heirs. Women who signalled their unavailability for these purposes, whose bodies were 'intact' in the additional sense of being untouched by the 'worldly cares and social roles'[13] into which sexual activity would plunge them, acquired a grudging admiration. Social advantage combined with theological justification in creating virginity as a sacred condition. Their bodies appeared to be visible confirmation now of that future state foretold by Jesus: 'When they rise from the dead, men and women do not marry; they are like angels in heaven' (Mark 12.25). Female virgins 'escaped the high risk of death in childbirth and avoided the unwanted child whom good Christians could no longer expose or abort'.[15]

Viewed from a contemporary perspective it is possible to see the virginity of women in the ancient church in heroic terms, as 'marriage-resisters'[15] who refused the reproductive and domestic roles assigned to them in the social order shared by pagans and Christians alike. On this view, single and celibate people stand in the tradition of sexual and social dissent. In practice, even the decision to remain virgin would probably have been taken by a girl's father, and her prospects would be unlikely to extend beyond residence in his house or the security of a convent. Nonetheless virginity would have been for some an attractive alternative to early, arranged marriage. In order to avoid 'the hideous sin of premarital sex' women were sometimes forcibly married while still children. This in turn led to early sexual experience, and, 'We can see ... from the ancients' medical books what physical problems the marriages of prepubescent girls were capable of causing.'[16]

Some celibates say celibacy is a demonstration to 'the world' that 'To become a loving, giving person is much more humanizing than the frantic search for intimacy and recognition.'[17] But is it not unhelpful to insist that celibate men and women need give *any* reason for their celibate state, not even that their celibacy frees them for the wider service of God? That way the very expectations giving rise to the question, that all people are sexually active unless there is something strange about, or wrong with, them, are subverted.

For some celibacy is an unchosen condition which suits them well. Others who have taken a vow of celibacy speak profoundly of the perspective on the social world which celibacy provides. Hannah Ward says being a celibate nun 'has to do with where I find I can see the clearest – the margins, the outskirts, the fringe. My lifestyle provides me with one way of living marginally to a society I feel is fundamentally sick.'[18] The celibate element of her lifestyle, she continues, 'challenges not only the notion that the nuclear family is the only viable social unit, but also the assumption that women are always sexually available for men whether as wife or lover'. These considerations can of course themselves be reasons for celibacy, but they are not justifications, since none need be given.

Chastity

The celibate life is shared not simply by full-time religious, but also by lay men and women and substantial numbers of people with no faith at all. The religions of the world have no monopoly on celibacy. Just as sexual intercourse can come to have religious and symbolic meanings attached to it, so too can the absence of sexual activity become religiously and symbolically charged. For some, neither sex nor the lack of it is symbolically charged at all. Perhaps celibacy would come to be valued more if it were seen as an open option to be chosen for particular times and periods of a person's life, defusing and refuting the assumption that 'to be' is 'to be sexually active'. When celibacy is understood in this way, it merges with *chastity*.

Chastity, or continence, used to be defined as 'the moral virtue that controls in the married and altogether excludes in the unmarried all voluntary expression of the sensitive appetite for venereal pleasure'.[19] This excessively negative view of chastity was rejected by the Second Vatican Council. According to a more contemporary definition it is 'that virtue which enables a person to transform the power of human sexuality into a creative and integrative force in his or her life'.[20]

A positive place for chastity is essential for a Christian sexual theology. Simply because sex is a divine gift and can be intensely pleasurable, we are likely, at least at times in our lives, to want it irrespective of consequences, commitment to others, and the relational contexts of ourselves and our partners. Having sex can become a 'genital imperative'. This imperative may be sufficiently strong for us to believe falsely that a strongly desired sexual relationship cannot but be 'a creative and integrative force'. A diagnosis of temptation which draws on structural sin, alienated desire and lust (see chapter 5) is likely to be necessary in the struggle against it. Chastity adds the power of discernment to the power of desire. Its exercise may be intensely difficult, yet its demands can strengthen primary relationships and actually improve sexual confidence.

Masturbation

Masturbation, the sexual arousal of oneself or another by manual stimulation of the genitals, is a positive, pleasurable activity which only a patriarchal understanding of sexuality condemns. Almost all men masturbate, whether married or single, and over half of women. Women generally masturbate less frequently than men, and start later. Women are masturbating more than their parents apparently did, and there is strong reason to think that the once powerful socialization against the practice has largely broken down. In a patriarchal order, the thought that women can obtain sexual pleasure without the presence or permission of men signals a threatening independence. The renewed emphasis on clitoral orgasm, as opposed to vaginal orgasm is an important reclamation of women's bodily experience. 'Generally being sexual with nobody but me' is how one female writer put it.[21] Masturbation, especially for men and women with no other sexual outlet, is a positive force in one's life. Yet most religious writing about masturbation condemns it. Why? In answering this question we will be disturbed once again by the androcentric and anti-body consciousness for which masturbation remains a grave sin.

Pollution and penitence

At one time, involuntary ejaculation (that is, 'unintended pollution') required a penance of the recitation of fifteen psalms. If ejaculation resulted from 'deliberately entertained provocative thoughts', a seven day penance of fasting on bread and water was prescribed. For the first 'offence' of masturbation, a penance of a hundred days was prescribed, to be extended to a year if the offence was repeated.[22] One wonders how often the offence was confessed! According to Jean Gerson (who devoted an entire book to the problem of 'daytime pollution'), at the end of the thirteenth century, young men and girls 'dared not confess the dissolute acts they had committed at the age of nine, ten, eleven, or twelve years of age with their brothers and sisters when as children they slept together'.[23] We have already seen how a range of dualisms were used to explain sexual desire, and so the desire to masturbate, and the guilt for having done so. It is clear that with the development of the doctrine of 'natural law' in the thirteenth century, a new battery of arguments was available to damn the guilty. Since a sexual act, in order to be classed as natural, was defined by the ejaculation of semen in a vagina, male masturbation was unnatural. It became associated with other 'unnatural acts' (e.g., anal intercourse and bestiality) and was regarded as worse than rape, which, although natural, was sinful for other reasons (see chapter 1). The idea of natural law has had small influence on Protestant Christians. Since 1710, when a Puritan physician called Bekkers wrote *Onania, or the Loathsome Sin of Self-Pollution*,[24] Protestants have generally used the story of Onan to discourage male masturbation. Whenever Onan 'lay with his brother's wife, he spilled his seed on the ground so as not to raise up offspring for his brother. What he did was wicked in the Lord's sight, and the LORD took away his life also' (Genesis 38.9–10). Onan's sin was not masturbation. It was his failure to practise Levirate marriage (Deuteronomy 25.5–10), that is, to provide a child for his dead brother's wife, and the means of preventing her conception may have been to withdraw his penis from her prior to ejaculation (*coitus interruptus*). This misreading of the text together with the implied conclusion that masturbation is a sin punishable by death is yet another distressingly destructive example of the literalism discussed in chapter 2.

Faulty physiology may also have been partly responsible for the taboo against masturbation. It was believed that the male body was capable of producing only a finite amount of semen. It should not therefore be wasted. Since semen was regarded (at least in the thirteenth century) as 'blood of an extremely pure sort that descends from the brain and turns white when it goes through the veins',[25] there seems to have been a genuine medical fear that loss of semen among boys and adolescents would lead to 'lassitude or idiocy'. Taboos against masturbation have survived well into this century.

Eighteenth-century writers, both theological and medical, seemed to think masturbation was the convenient cause of almost any medical condition, 'from pimples to suicide'.[26] The moral and medical panic which the practice caused in the eighteenth and nineteenth centuries requires some social explanation. One may assume that religious sanction against the practice was already too weak to keep it in check (if it ever did). In the eighteenth century the age at which young men and women married began to increase. The period after puberty and before marriage was therefore lengthened. If the fear of masturbation successfully inhibited the practice, it was thought that 'delayed gratification' in marriage would eventually occur, and the period of delay was thought to bring much moral and physical benefit.[27] Another social explanation is available. More male children were being sent to boarding school. Medical myths about the dangers of masturbation may have expressed parental anxiety about 'the moral development of their offspring'.[28]

We now know that moral, medical and theological objections to masturbation are groundless. The Roman doctor Galen was physiologically wrong but psychologically right in thinking that both men and women suffered from 'sperm retention'. 'If Galen had met a Christian monk or nun, he would have known exactly what to prescribe for them.'[29] Masturbation helps children to delight in their bodies. Play with their genitals, in that delightful blur of innocence, curiosity and self-affirmation should not be discouraged by parental intervention. For adults it is a way of relieving sexual tension. People who have particular difficulties in love-making may be able to overcome them by masturbating. Men who climax too quickly may be able to learn to hold back by masturbating almost to orgasm, then deliberately subsiding. Mutual masturbation is a form of safe sex (provided no oral contact is involved) and so finds a place in the list of alternative repertoires discussed in chapter 7. Since heterosexual intercourse is still likely to involve orgasm for the male partner only, there is a particular obligation on men to learn how to please their partners.

Since the Christian faith upholds the institution of monogamous marriage, it cannot but consistently uphold the practice of masturbation within it, at least at times, since partners may wish to have sex with different frequency, or be unavailable or parted from each other. Masturbation provides an innocent and innocuous outlet for sexual desire without recourse to promiscuous sex or partner-threatening liaisons. It is particularly unfortunate that the Vatican's Declaration on Sexual Ethics (1975) reaffirms that masturbation is 'gravely sinful' and 'an intrinsically and gravely disordered action'.[30] This is because 'the deliberate use of the sexual faculty, for whatever reason, outside of marriage is essentially contrary to its purpose', and 'all deliberate sexual activity must be referred to the married state'. All the old fears remain while the language is different. Marriage is the sole context for any and every sexual activity; masturbation is a breach of natural law; and sex must have procreative intent. Since we have had reason to disagree with all three suppositions, we will not be following the argument through to its conclusion.

Having disposed of most of the arguments against masturbation, it is important to recognize obvious dangers that may accompany it. It is an activity easily given to excess, like eating, drinking, gambling and shopping. Excess usually needs treatment. The 'culture of narcissism' may encourage certain people to settle for it as a substitute for starting relationships with other people which become sexual. People who find it difficult to mix socially may rely on it and so fail to address a deeper personal problem. The view of the person adopted in chapter 4 insists that we are made for relationships with others. Sexuality is for sharing. Masturbation may feature prominently in the lives of solitary men who fear or even hate women. In these circumstances it is likely to be associated with pornography and fantasy. It is essential that such people seek help, first for the sake of potential victims, and second for themselves, since fear and hate are contrary to the gospel and demeaning to God's children.

Fantasy

Sexual fantasies invite similar treatment. They are inevitably linked to masturbation. The weight of the tradition condemns them, yet there are powerful reasons for thinking that a different conclusion is available. Yet fantasy, like masturbation, cannot simply be accepted as benignly good. There are different kinds of fantasies, from the romantic to the bizarre. It is a fair assumption that they can contribute both positively and negatively to people's sex lives.

'Impure thoughts' have, of course, been posed and discussed from an androcentric perspective. It has become increasingly clear that women enjoy sexual fantasies as much as men, and are more prepared to admit and discuss them than formerly. The collection of women's fantasies, *My Secret Garden*, has been reprinted sixteen times since 1976.[31] There has been endless discussion of the subject in women's magazines over the last twenty years, which shows no sign of abating. Can a faith perspective not bring something positive to the very common fantasy experiences of women and men, other than a denunciation of 'impure thoughts' and an unwillingness to admit that fantasies exist?

Once again a very important biblical text has been misread, adding considerably to the guilt associated with sexual fantasies. Jesus himself said:

> 'You have heard that they were told, "Do not commit adultery." But what I tell you is this: If a man looks at a woman with a lustful eye, he has already committed adultery with her in his heart. If your right eye causes your downfall, tear it out and fling it away; it is better for you to lose one part of your body than for the whole of it to be thrown into hell.' (Matthew 5.27–9)

This appears to be a plain denunciation of lustful thoughts, together with a dire warning of the consequences, from the lips of the Lord himself. If the plain meaning of the text is diluted in any way, are we not guilty also of reducing the difficult demands of Jesus to something more manageable and less challenging?

The answer is an emphatic No. Attention to the text reveals that Matthew 5.21–48 contains a set of six illustrations which have been assembled by the Gospel writer to show how Jesus revised and deepened the teaching of the Old Testament Law as it was then understood and practised. Each of them is introduced by a formula which repeats the words 'They were told', and the topics covered, along with adultery, are murder, divorce, performing oaths, taking revenge, and hating enemies. The key to interpreting the illustrations is an obvious one. They have a *target* – the hypocrisy of particular scribes and Pharisees. They qualify the earlier saying of Jesus, 'I tell you, unless you show yourselves far better than the scribes and Pharisees, you can never enter the kingdom of Heaven' (Matthew 5.20).

The saying is not addressed to a general male audience wrestling with the common problem of the power of their sexual feelings towards women. It is addressed to male religious leaders who believed that, just because they refrained from adultery and so honoured the commandment, they had become morally and religiously righteous and their lifestyles were approved by God. The lustful eye exposes the moral gap between the legal purity which the religious congratulated themselves on having achieved, and their desires which they were unable to accomplish. The saying is not a condemnation of fantasy. It is rather a condemnation of a smug religiousness which congratulates itself on having kept the Law. Jesus reminds them that they have the same feelings as everyone else and are no better than anyone else. In fact, because they believe themselves to be better than real adulterers, they are guilty of conceit.

Matthew has edited these materials. The dreadful saying about the tearing out of the right eye was almost certainly not said at the same time as the saying about adultery of the heart. The saying about the right eye (in a lurid and exaggerated way that the hearers of Jesus would have understood) teaches that occasions of sin may come from any quarter, and must be resisted. Confirmation that this passage is not a blanket condemnation of lustful thoughts has recently come from Gareth Moore. He reminds us that the Greek word for 'woman' and 'wife' are the same, and he shows why 'wife' is the intended meaning here.[32] The action Jesus described is wrong precisely because it 'means breaking in on a marriage; it belongs to a spectrum of activities which ends in adultery'.[33] It is wrong not because it is an impure thought but because it involves a series of actions which we have just described as lacking the virtue of chastity. It may also, of course, be a form of sexual harassment. Adultery of the heart is not some supposed inner act as bad as the outward act of adultery. It is not an inner act at all. Moore disposes of a lingering dualism between 'inner' and 'outer' which accords well with our disposal of other dualisms in chapter 3. But he does not leave references to inner thoughts or acts without sense. Adultery of the heart is not some inner chain of events equally forbidden by the commandment. Rather the 'heart' is the totality of the human being: what he or she is on every occasion.

Jesus condemns hypocrisy, the pretence that conformity to the Law is itself sufficient for total integrity. The denial of sexual fantasies then, or the maintenance of an awkward silence about them, is hardly consistent with the way of Jesus, for that would be to maintain the sort of hypocrisy which is condemned in this passage. The warning against adultery of the heart is still a very serious warning. It is to be avoided by the owning of desire, the practice of continence, and the attempt to live with an honest and consistent character. Within such a framework, fantasies need not be denied. They need instead to be integrated.

It is therefore unsurprising that the conclusion about fantasy is similar to the conclusion about masturbation. It is positive, while combined with a warning. Jack Dominian has raised the problem of the occurrence of fantasies during the love-making of Christian partners which obviously involve participation in sexual scenes with others. His vast experience as a marriage counsellor leads him wisely to question 'whether morality should have any say at such intensely private moments', and to conclude, if such fantasies are a moral issue at all, 'It has to be accepted that the range of arousal, whatever its nature, is moral, provided it leads to mutually pleasurable experiences.'[34] The moral criterion, then, is whether fantasy, private or shared, contributes to the mutuality of the couple. Sexual fantasies can 'reawaken our capacities for playfulness'.[35] They can also be a substitute for relationships with real people, and perhaps an escape from them. As with masturbation, what counts is the place it has in a person's life. Fantasies however can dwell on the forbidden, the exploitative and the bizarre. The sense of sin described in chapter 5 should not lead us easily to acquiesce in any and every fantasy. If we are regularly turned on by the humiliation or exploitation of other people, usually of women by heterosexual men, God has something better for us.

Pornography – the unacceptable face of lust

The theology of relationships suggested in this book pronounces a negative judgement on pornography. That is because the use of pornography can be a harmful influence on sexual relationships, or even a substitute for them. There is no room here to survey the range of writings defining it and assessing its potentiality for harm. Distinctions are necessary between erotic and pornographic materials. So-called 'soft' pornography raises different (though not necessarily less serious) issues from the 'hard' variety. I shall concentrate instead on the probability that pornography encourages distorted thinking about women among some of its (predominantly male) users, and men's relationships with them, and claim that that probability is sufficient to earn the judgement that its use is likely to be morally wrong.[36] This judgement should be distinguished from a general condemnation of all users of pornography. What place does pornography come to have in a person's life? Is it a peripheral and temporary interest, brought about by loneliness or temporary absence from a partner, or simple curiosity? Users of pornography can hardly be condemned for expressing God-given sexual desire in ways which the commercialization and commodification of sex makes readily available. On the other hand, pornography may be contributing more generally to distorted or misogynistic attitudes, and preserving patriarchy in the name of harmless erotic entertainment. This criticism of pornography is much weightier than criticisms which appear merely to transfer to pornography guilt about the enjoyment of sexual arousal and so-called impure thoughts.

Pornography encourages the view that women are sex objects

whose function is to be available for male gratification. It can allow women's sexual enjoyment to be misrepresented, and it can harmfully widen the range of sexual activities that can be 'done' to women and that they supposedly enjoy. Men's orgasms may become linked by pornography to this distorted thinking about women, and this development may itself become a lasting barrier to uninhibited mutuality in love-making. Pornography generally depicts women as subordinate to men and often as willing objects of violence. Even when roles are reversed and men are dominated or humiliated, the themes of power and dominance are perversely affirmed by acting out their controlled and temporary denial. The devaluation and subordination of women in pornography is the reason why it is a potent symbol for their status in a patriarchal society. Anyone who takes such attitudes to a sexual relationship cannot also hope for mutuality or fulfilment.

Over half of boys under fourteen recently surveyed about the sources of their sexual knowledge, said pornography was their principle source.[37] Sex offenders admit to using it to excuse, justify and validate their perverse intentions. A distinction must be made between the harm done to the users of pornography and the harm done to women generally by some women being pornographically depicted. Let us grant that, for the sake of argument alone, some users of pornography are unharmed by it. Well, the price of their apparently harmless indulgence is that it is also available to those whose sexual identity is being formed, and the influence it has on them may have to be painfully recognized and discarded later in life. Exposure to violent pornography is also likely to desensitize users to the appalling crime of rape and in some cases even to encourage it. There is a sad complacency about studies which conclude the link between violent pornography and violence against women is unproven. This is because impossibly strict notions of causality are built into the arguments. For many years after lung cancer was linked to smoking, the case was regarded by tobacco companies and sceptics as unproven. However, in some matters, probability, not certainty, is a rational guide in our decision-taking.

The harm done to women by pornography may not be able to be satisfactorily measured. But human beings are poor at measuring both good and evil, and lack of ability to measure harm provides no evidence for the view that no harm is done. Feminist writers have provided a formidable indictment of the harm done by pornography to women.[38] What is to be made of the view that women too enjoy the pornography that their boyfriends and lovers buy and share with them? So they might, but their enjoyment might also be explicable by a failure to comprehend the lasting harm that pornography has already done. We have seen that greater equality for women can lead not to women exercising their choices in an equal but different way, but simply copying the behaviour of men. The pervasiveness of structural sin may lead to anyone being in a state of 'false consciousness' about where their interests lie, and women here may be as culpable as men.

The look

Rosalind Coward thinks that men eyeing up women is itself a ubiquitous expression of domination and distancing. Women may, of course, expect and encourage this behaviour. 'Looking has become a crucial aspect of sexual relations . . . because it is one of the ways in which domination and subordination are expressed.' Men's 'scrutiny of women', she says, is 'nothing less than a decided preference for a "distanced" view of the female body' which 'disguises a preference for *looking* at women's bodies, for keeping women separate'. She suggests that this 'sex-at-a-distance' may be 'the only complete secure relation which men can have with women'.[39]

Pornography on this view is a continuation of the segmented male consciousness that has so impoverished the churches down the ages. Women are confirmed as temptresses, while their subordination is confirmed by their instant availability. Pornography perpetuates by other means the obsessive preoccupation with genitalia that used to be a feature of Catholic moral and penitential writing.[40] It makes women present to men while demanding no relational response to them. As John Stoltenberg warns, 'The sexuality that the pornography industry needs you to have is not about communicating and caring; it's about "pornographizing" people – objectifying and conquering them, not being with them as a person. You do not have to buy into it.'[41]

Men who fear sexual rejection may prefer pornographic images of women to real women. They can control pornography, whereas the response of women to them in sexual situations is unpredictable and so beyond their control.[42] But this maintenance of 'power over' others and the unwillingness to be vulnerable has been ably described as itself a sin.[43]

No objection is made to pornography on the grounds that we ought not to desire beautiful bodies. Because human bodies are made by God they are potentially beautiful and holy. Everyone will admire and desire particular bodies during their lives, according to their different sexual orientations and libidos. This surging desire is itself a further means of our knowledge of God's love.⁴⁴ While the power of desire is to be owned and celebrated, realism about structural sin alerts us to the near certainty that our good desires will be endlessly stimulated by sexual images, some of which will demean our common humanity as women or men. Our relative affluence can usually purchase short-term gratification but at an uncertain longer-term price. Full equality of relationship between men and women cannot happen in pornographic depictions of them. Christian faith finds God incarnate in committed fleshly union. It discerns in reciprocal sexuality a mysterious participation in relationship which mirrors the Personal relationships in the triune God. In pornography such experiences are impossible to find.

Notes

1. Polly Blue, 'A Time to Refrain from Embracing' in Linda Hurcombe, *Sex and God: Some Varieties of Women's Religious Experience* (New York and London: Routledge & Kegan Paul, 1987), p. 59.
2. Peter Brown, *The Body and Society: Men, Women and Sexual Renunciation in Early Christianity* (London and Boston: Faber & Faber, 1990), part 2.
3. ibid., p. 238.
4. ibid., n. 121.
5. ibid., p. 223.
6. ibid, p. 406.
7. ibid, p. 231.
8. ibid, p. 166.
9. ibid, p. 351.
10. Eric Fuchs, 'Sex and Power in the Church' in J. Provost and K. Walf (eds), *Concilium* (1988), p. 23.
11. The possibility that he was married to Mary Magdalene is discussed in John Shelby Spong, *Born of a Woman* (San Francisco: HarperCollins, 1992).
12. Brown, p. 435.
13. Joyce E. Salisbury, *Church Fathers, Independent Virgins* (London and New York: Verso, 1991), p. 2, and especially ch. 8.
14. Robin Lane Fox, *Pagans and Christians* (Harmondsworth: Penguin Books, 1988), pp. 365–6.
15. Mary Daly, *Websters' First New Intergalactic Wickedary of the English Language* (Boston: Beacon Press, 1987), p. 176.
16. Fox, p. 367.
17. Martin W. Pable, 'Psychology and Asceticism of Celibacy' in Mary Anne Huddleston (ed.), *Celibate Loving: Encounter in Three Dimensions* (New York: Paulist Press, 1984), p. 17.
18. Hannah Ward, 'The Lion in the Marble: Choosing Celibacy as a Nun' in Hurcombe, p. 83.
19. A. Kosnik, et al. (eds), *Human Sexuality: New Directions in Catholic Thought* (London: Search Press, 1977), p. 100.

20. ibid., p. 101.
21. Blue, p. 69.
22. Kosnik, p. 40.
23. See his *Confessional*, cited in Jacques Rossiaud, *Medieval Prostitution* (Oxford: Blackwell, 1988), p. 90.
24. Uta Ranke-Heinemann, *Eunuchs for the Kingdom of Heaven: The Catholic Church and Sexuality* (London: Deutsch, 1990) p. 313.
25. Rossiaud, p. 91.
26. James B. Nelson, *Embodiment: An Approach to Sexuality and Christian Theology* (Minneapolis, MN: Augsburg, 1978), p. 169, where some of this literature is discussed.
27. B. S. Turner, *The Body and Society* (Oxford: Blackwell, 1984), p. 96.
28. ibid., p. 97.
29. Fox, p. 350.
30. §9, Austin Flannery, OP (ed.) *Vatican Council II: More Post Conciliar Documents* (Leominster, Hereford: Fowler Wright, 1982), p. 491.
31. Nancy Friday, *My Secret Garden: Women's Sexual Fantasies* (London and New York: Quartet Books, 1976). See also the sequel, *Women on Top* (London: Hutchinson, 1991).
32. Gareth Moore, *The Body in Context: Sex and Catholicism* (London: SCM Press, 1992), p. 14.
33. ibid p. 16.
34. Jack Dominian, *Passionate and Compassionate Love* (London: Darton, Longman & Todd, 1991), p. 92.
35. Nelson, p. 161.
36. See the new study by Kathy Itzin, *Pornography, Women, Violence and Civil Liberties: A Radical New View* (Oxford: Oxford University Press, 1992), and its powerful challenge to the complacent liberal view that pornography is harmless.
37. Quoted on the Channel 4 Television programme *Dispatches*, 5 November 1992.
38. E.g. Andrea Dworkin, *Pornography: Men Possessing Women* (London: The Women's Press, 1981); Susan Griffin, *Pornography and Silence* (London: The Women's Press, 1981).
39. Rosalind Coward, *Female Desire: Women's Sexuality Today* (London: Paladin, 1984), p. 76 (author's emphasis).
40. See John Marshall's amusing parallel between 'yesterday's manual of moral theology and pornography' in 'Sex and Christian Loving' in John Marshall (ed.), *The Future of Christian Marriage* (London: Geoffrey Chapman, 1989), p. 54.
41. John Stoltenberg, 'How Men Have (a) Sex', in Susan E. Davies and Eleanor H. Haney (eds), *Redefining Sexual Ethics* (Cleveland, OH: Pilgrim Press, 1991), p. 155.
42. See Michael Bywater, 'Porn again – why men can't resist it', *Cosmopolitan* July, 1991.
43. Lebacqz, p. 437.
44. This was the argument of Carter Heyward, discussed in ch. 11.

Epilogue

I sometimes ask theological students to keep a journal of critical reflection. They write down at regular intervals how they are responding to the themes of a course, what they are learning, how their outlooks are changing, and so on. I have not kept such a journal while writing this book, but I have learned much. I would like to describe very briefly three conclusions from the experience of writing *Liberating Sex*, of the kind students might write in their journals when their course has come to an end.

From ethics to theology

When I began to write the book I envisaged it as a book about sexual ethics. Aided by philosophy, rules and principles based on prior theories (like 'situation ethics') might have been devised and justified. The Bible and the Christian tradition would doubtless have helped to shape and illustrate the rules. Two big discoveries have spared my readers from such a book. First I have come to see that questions about what we ought to do and how we ought to behave have become distorted by a philosophical tradition which turns these matters into cerebral problems for experts to argue about. This is a continuation of philosophical dualism into the heart of intellectual life, and I think feminist criticisms of it are decisive.

But the main reason why this book quickly became a book of sexual *theology* is simpler. As I began to think about the great truths of Christian faith, it became obvious to me that they addressed sexual questions with an intensity, immediacy and directness that I had not realized before. Perhaps even those readers who disagree with my suggestions about sexual relationships will admit to excitement and surprise about the prolonged extent to which Christian doctrines 'come alive' in the contexts of thinking about and having sex.

The great dramas of the faith seemed to invite themselves into the questions that a book about sex should raise. I came to see that the incarnation of God in Christ said more about encountering God in the human body than any theory could express. The very revelation of God as a communion of Persons, a Being of inclusive, loving relationships, impressed itself as a judgement on excessive individualism in western societies, and as a model for human, sexual (and nonsexual) relationships. One by one the experience of Christian faith as reflected in the Church's doctrine illuminated sexual questions: redemption and atonement as the making possible of right relationships; the Eucharist as the sharing of a body in the celebration of love; lifelong union as a sacrament; faith as embodied knowledge; faithfulness as the experience of God's covenanted love, and so on.

Neither were these connections between Christian doctrine and Christian life merely intellectual. Relationships with each other and with God are personal and self-involving; indeed, human relationships are caught up in the mystery of that Personal threefold life which is divine. Christian life has always been 'in Christ' and 'in the Spirit', and 'in' means a participation in the transforming relationships of the triune God. Christ's resurrection, the inauguration of a new kind of life which overcomes the power of sin by the greater power of God, is itself a further proclamation about human bodiliness. Whatever we believe about life after death, it is as a living transformed *body* that Jesus returns to eternity. Even eternal life is embodied life.

From liberal theology to radical theology

The sexual theology of this book has assumed there is a 'realism' about God, that is, that God 'really does' exist independently of the human mind, and is not, say, a human construct, or human subjectivity or spirituality writ large. Again, I have assumed that there was a real incarnation of God in Christ, and that, in a manner uniquely appropriate to the ineffable mystery of God, God really is a holy communion of Persons. Christ really does become present in the Eucharist, and our knowledge of God, while fragmentary, is real knowledge. It seems to me that any 'non-realist' alternative does not deliver the spiritual goods. Incarnation is not just one optional way of speaking about the significance of Jesus; the Trinity is not just an historically conditioned (and barely intelligible) speculation; and the real presence at the Eucharist is not just another way of saying how important table fellowship became in the life of the Church. Inasmuch as 'liberal' theology represents a dilution, or an equivocation or an abandonment of these essential emphases of Christian faith, it becomes unserviceable in an ethical context.

Yet if liberal theology will not suffice, what is to replace it? This volume has been in some respects both conservative and catholic. It rests gratefully in the faith and creeds of the Church. Yet it has distanced itself from a conservatism which mistakenly identifies God's Word with the text of Scripture and a catholicism which in its preservation of tradition too often repeats the solutions to yesterday's questions. At its poorest it fails to distinguish itself from patriarchal and even misogynistic elements of itself which are an invitation to unbelief.

'Radical theology' may seem even less attractive than the systems of certainty it opposes. Radical theology perhaps even *deserves* its tarnished reputation after the excesses of the sixties. But we have also had excesses in conservatism, both evangelical and conservative, since the sixties, and the Church and the world desperately need a theology which they can believe in *and* question, and one which is recognizably the traditional faith, not some pale version of it that merely baptizes the folk religion of late-capitalist societies. 'Radical' theology is based on the *roots* of the faith (Latin *radix*, root). A genuine radical theology is not one which merely reflects leftish secular political trends (when they exist!) but which puts people who no longer inhabit the thought-world of classical Christianity (including many Christians) in touch with the roots of faith. Radical theology is suspicious enough of history to recognize patriarchy as an impediment to faith. It recognizes the breath of God's Spirit outside the institutions of Christianity. It is prepared to take risks with tradition while seeking to develop and commend it. It is closest to feminist and liberation theologies while it cannot claim to arise out of the oppression which lies at their source.

From applied theology to integrated theology

I do not have a sophisticated method for commending the Christian faith to a modern (or post-modern) world in the hope that it will graft itself back onto the roots from which it has become partially severed. 'Applied theology' seemed an attractive label for the neglected enterprise of putting the intellectual labours of academic theology to work in the service of the Church and all its members. But I have come to see that this label too is unhelpful. It assumes the real business of theology is done away from the world, in seminaries, by professionals. Then another branch of professionals is needed to 'apply' the shaky provisional conclusions of pure theological knowledge to practical situations like having sex or the inequities of global economics.

Integrated theology represents the needed advance.[1] Theology exists to serve the church in her proclamation of the great riches of Christian faith, in whatever circumstances her members find themselves. Integrated theology necessarily blends an academic tradition with the equally rigorous demands of Christian life. Sex is of course a prime candidate for integrated theology, for we are unavoidably sexual, and our sexuality is essential to our relationships, whether those relationships are sexual or not. I have discovered, during the writing of *Liberating Sex*, a new use for the phrase 'integrated theology'. Integrated theology assumes an encounter with God in shared experience and the joys, dilemmas and reflections that arise from it. I hope there will be more integrated theology, that there will be more educators, politicians, doctors, and so on, writing the theology of education, politics and medicine, where their lives become points of intersection between the gospel of Christ and contemporary unbelief.

Notes

1. I am grateful to John Matthews for reinforcing this point.

Index of Scripture References

Index of Names

Index of Names

Index of Subjects